INTERNATIONAL LAW

AUSTRALIA AND NEW ZEALAND
The Law Book Company Ltd.
Sydney : Melbourne : Perth

CANADA AND U.S.A.
The Carswell Company Ltd.
Agincourt, Ontario

INDIA
N.M. Tripathi Private Ltd
Bombay
and
Eastern Law House Private Ltd.
Calcutta and Delhi
M.P.P. House
Bangalore

ISRAEL
Steimatzky's Agency Ltd.
Jerusalem : Tel Aviv : Haifa

MALAYSIA : SINGAPORE : BRUNEI
Malayan Law Journal (Pte.) Ltd.
Singapore and Kuala Lumpar

PAKISTAN
Pakistan Law House
Karachi

INTERNATIONAL LAW
A Student Introduction

by

Rebecca M.M. Wallace, M.A., LL.B., Ph.D.
Lecturer in Law at the University of Strathclyde

LONDON
SWEET & MAXWELL
1986

Published in 1986 by
Sweet & Maxwell Limited
11, New Fetter Lane, London
Computerset by Burgess & Son (Abingdon) Ltd.
Printed in Great Britain by
The Garden City Press Limited, Letchworth, Hertfordshire

British Library Cataloguing in Publication Data

Wallace, Rebecca M.M.
    International law.
    1. International law
    I. Title
    341   JX3091
    ISBN 0–421–33500–9
    ISBN 0–421–33510–6 Pbk

To my parents

ACKNOWLEDGMENTS

I wish to express particular thanks to Mrs Helen Philos, Librarian at the American Society of International Law, Washington D.C. who, when I was researching this text, cheerfully allowed me to ransack the Library shelves daily for some twelve weeks; Mr Roger Holt for doing the diagrams in Chapters Five and Seven; and Mrs Elaine Smith for her efficient typing of the manuscript and for her invaluable assistance in checking the final text and compiling the table of cases and index.

PREFACE

The aim of this students' introductory text on international law is modest. Its *raison d'être* is to fill that slot in the market which currently exists on both sides of the Atlantic. There is an absence of a basic text, a "horn book" in American terminology, dovetailed to meet the needs of those students following a one year undergraduate course of some 50 to 70 hours and which can be used to accompany the existing recognised case books on the subject.

The book is not meant, therefore, to be a full blown textbook and should not be regarded as one. The market is already adequately supplied with treatises on international law. This text is intended rather as a primer. The basic principles of the international legal system are painted with a broad brush so that the student is presented succinctly with (i) a lucid and comprehensive exposition of the basic concepts necessary as a basis for the understanding of the international legal process; and (ii) a general and integrated overview of contemporary international law. Hopefully, it will promote a greater understanding of topical international issues for those who take the subject no further and, for those who do, it will provide the foundation for the now inevitable (owing to the increasing fragmentation of international law) specialisation.

So as not to overwhelm the student, who consider footnotes "as only more facts to learn" footnotes are limited to those strictly necessary. No particular issue is explored in depth, although some of the problems currently confronting contemporary international law, for example, the law-making character, if any, to be attributed to General Assembly Resolutions, are identified and reference is made for illustrative purposes to certain relatively recent events, such as the United States' withdrawal of its acceptance of the jurisdiction of the International Court of Justice.

As well as standing independently in its own right, this text is designed to be a narrative companion to Professor D.J. Harris' *Cases and Materials on International Law* (3rd ed., 1983) and accordingly the overall balance and emphasis of Harris is largely reflected in the text. The sources of international law receive, however, more detailed treatment while sovereign immunity, which is now governed by the 1978 State Immunity Act and therefore relatively uncontroversial, receives somewhat less emphasis. It could also be used equally well as a reader to any of the various American Casebooks, such as L. Henkin, R. Pugh, O. Schachter and H. Smit's *International Law: Cases and Materials* (1980) and J. Sweeny, C. Oliver and N. Leech's *The International Legal System: Cases and Materials* (1981).

Throughout the writing of this text two objectives have been paramount, namely to present the material clearly and simply.

International law is never static, however, and so books require a cut off date. Consequently the law presented within these covers is the position as of December 31, 1985.

Rebecca M.M. Wallace   December 31, 1985
The Law School
University of Strathclyde
Glasgow

CONTENTS

Acknowledgments	vii
Preface	ix
Table of Cases	xv
Table of Abbreviations	xxi

1. Introduction | 1
   Definition | 1
   Nature and Characteristics of International Law | 2
   The Development of International Law | 4
   Further Reading | 6

2. Sources | 7
   Custom | 8
   Treaties | 17
   General Principles of Law as Recognised by Civilised Nations | 19
   Equity | 21
   Judicial Decisions | 22
   Writers | 25
   Other Possible Sources of International Law | 26
   Further Reading | 30

3. International Law and Municipal Law | 31
   Monistic School | 32
   Dualistic School | 32
   Municipal Law in International Law | 33
   International Law Before Municipal Courts | 34
   Further Reading | 51

4. International Personality | 52
   States | 53
   International Organisations | 60
   Individuals | 65
   Other Entities—Anomalies | 67
   Conclusion | 68
   Recognition of States and Governments | 68

The Effect of Recognition in Municipal Law 73
Effect of Non-Recognition 76
Modes of According Recognition 79
Further Reading 80

5. Territory 81
Occupation 81
Prescription 85
Conquest 85
Cession 87
Accretion and Avulsion 87
New States 87
Polar Regions 88
Airspace 91
Outer Space 94
Conclusion 96
International Protection of the Environment 97
Further Reading 100

6. Jurisdiction 101
Exercise of Jurisdiction 101
Extradition 106
Illegal Arrest 107
Double Jeopardy 107
Immunity from Jurisdiction 108
Further Reading 118

7. The Law of the Sea 119
Territorial Sea 120
High Seas 131
Exclusive Economic Zone 138
Continental Shelf 143
Deep Sea Bed 149
Further Reading 154

8. State Responsibility 155
Nature of Liability 156
Treatment of Aliens—The Treatment of Nationals
of Other States 160
Further Reading 174

9. Human Rights 175
What are Human Rights? 175
Regional Level 176

International Regulation 186
Human Rights and International Criminal Law 193
Further Reading 195

10. The Law of Treaties 196
Definition of a Treaty 197
Treaty-Making Competence 198
Observance and Application of Treaties 203
Treaty Interpretation 204
Third States 206
Amendment and Modification 207
Validity of Treaties 207
Termination of a Treaty 209
Consequences of Invalidity, Termination or
Suspension 213
State Succession 214
Further Reading 216

11. The Use of Force 217
The Law Before 1945 217
The Law as of 1945 218
Nuclear Weapons 233
Further Reading 236

12. Arbitration and the Judicial Settlement of Disputes 237
Arbitration 238
The International Court of Justice 241
Further Reading 255

13. Conclusion 255

Index 259

TABLE OF CASES

Aaland Island Case, L.N.O.J., Spec.Supp., No. 3 (1920) 19
Adams v. Adams [1971] P. 188 76
Administrative Decision No. V (U.S. v. Germany), 7 R.I.A.A. 119 (1924) ..... 161n.
Aerial Incident of July 27, 1955 Case, I.C.J. Rep. 1960, p. 146 .... 247n.
Alabama Claims Arbitration, Moore Int. Arb. 495 (1872) 23, 33, 239
Ambatielos Arbitration (Greece v. U.K.), 12 R.I.A.A. 83 (1956); 23 I.L.R.
    306 (1956) .... 173n.
Anglo-Iranian Oil Co. Case, I.C.J. Rep. (Pleadings) 1951, p. 81 .... 165n., 166n.,
    205
Anglo-Norwegian Fisheries Case, I.C.J. Rep. 1951, p. 116 .... 12, 23, 84n., 120n.,
    122, 124n., 140
Antarctica Cases, I.C.J. Rep. 1956, pp. 12, 15 .... 245n.
Arantzazu Mendi Case [1939] A.C. 256 (H.L.) 73, 74
Asakura v. City of Seattle, 265 U.S. 332 (1924) .... 42n.
Asylum Case, I.C.J. Rep. 1950, p. 266 .... 10, 12, 244, 252n.
Attorney-General for Canada v. Attorney-General for Ontario [1937] A.C.
    326, P.C. 47
Attorney-General of the Government of Israel v. Eichmann (1961) 36 I.L.R.
    5, p. 105 .... 104, 105, 107

Baccus SRL v. Servico Nacional del Trigo [1957] 1 Q.B. 438 109
Baker v. Carr, 369 U.S. 186 (1962) .... 50n.
Banco Nacional de Cuba v. First National City Bank U.S. Supreme Ct. 406
    U.S. 759 (1972); 912 S.L.T. 1808 .... 49n.
—— v. Sabbatino, 376 U.S. 398 (1964) 48n., 49, 50
Barcelona Traction, Light & Power Co. Case, I.C.J. Rep. 1970, p. 3 ..... 20, 171,
    172
Beagle Channel Arbitration, 17 I.L.M. 623 (1978) 196
Belgian Linguistic (Merits) Case, Eur.Ct. H.R., ser. A, Vol. 16, Judgment of
    July 23, 1968; 1 E.H. R.R. 252 .... 184n.
Birdi v. Secretary of State for Home Affairs (1975) (unreported) .... 39n.
Bloxem v. Favre, 8 P.C. 101 (1883) .... 33n.
B.P. Case, 53 I.L.R. 297 165
Brazilian Loans Case, P.C.I.J. Rep., ser. A, No. 21 (1929) .... 34n.
Buvot v. Barbuit (1737) Cases t Talbot 281 34

Caire Claim, 5 R.I.A.A. 516 (1929) .... 157, 158n.
Callco Dealings Ltd. v. Inland Revenue Commrs. [1962] A.C. 1 (H.L.) .... 39n.
Campbell & Cosans Case, Eur.Ct. H.R., ser. A, Vol. 48, Judgment of Feb.
    25, 1982; 4 E.H.R.R. 293 .... 184n.
Campbell & Fell Case, Eur.Ct. H.R., ser. A, Vol. 80, Judgment of June 28,
    1984 .... 184n.
Canevaro Case (Italy v. Peru) 11 R.I.A.A. 397; 6 A.J.I.L. 746 (1912)
    Translation .... 170n.
Carl Zeiss Stiftung v. Rayner & Keeler Ltd. (No. 2) [1967] A.C. 855 76

Caroline Incident, The, 29 B.F.S.P. 1137–1138; 30 B.F.S.P. 195–196 222
Case Concerning U.S. Diplomatic & Consular Staff in Tehran (Provisional
    Measures) I.C.J. Rep. 1979, p. 7 .... 111n.
—— (Judgment) I.C.J. Rep. 1980, p. 3 .... 111n., 113n., 250, 252, 253n.
Certain Expenses of the United Nations Case, I.C.J. Rep. 1962, p. 151 229,
    231, 253
Certain German Interests in Polish Upper Silesia Case, P.C.I.J. Rep., ser. A,
    No. 7, p. 22 (1929) 165
Certain Norwegian Loans Case. *See* Norwegian Loans Case.
Chamizal Arbitration, 5 A.J.I.L. 782 (1911) .... 85n.
Chorzów Factory Case (Indemnity) (Merits) Case, P.C.I.J. Rep., ser. A, No.
    17, p. 29 (1927) 20n., 157, 159
Chung Chi Cheung v. The King [1939] A.C. 160 35
City of Berne, The v. Bank of England, (1804) 9 Ves. 347; 32 E.R. 636 (Ch.) .. 73n.
Civil Air Transport Inc. v. Central Air Transport Corp. [1953] A.C. 70,
    P.C. .... 76n.
Civilian War Claimants' Assoc. Ltd. v. The King [1932] A.C. 14
    (H.L.) .... 53n., 160n.
Clipperton Island Arbitration, 26 A.J.I.L. 390 (1932) 83
Colozza and Rubinat, Eur.Ct. H.R., ser. A, Vol. 89, Judgment of Feb. 12,
    1985 .... 184n.
Continental Shelf (Libyan Arab Jamahiriya v. Malta) Case, I.C.J. Rep.
    1985 148
—— (Tunisia v. Libyan Arab Jamahiriya) Case; Request by Malta to
    intervene, I.C.J. Rep. 1981, p. 3 .... 249, 252
—— v. (Libya) Case, I.C.J. Rep. 1982, p. 18 .... 149, 244
Cook v. U.S., 288 U.S. 102 (1933) .... 43n.
Corfu Channel Case (Preliminary Objection), I.C.J. Rep. 1948, p. 15 244
—— (Merits), I.C.J. Rep. 1949, p. 4 .... 130, 157
—— (Assessment of Compensation), I.C.J. Rep. 1949, p. 244 .... 252n.
Cristina Case, The [1938] A.C. 485 .... 35, 109

Danzig Railway Officials Case, P.C.I.J. Rep., ser. B, No. 15, p. 4 (1928) 66
Delimitation of the Maritime Boundary in the Gulf of Maine Area, I.C.J.
    Rep. 1984, p. 246 .... 142, 149
Diggs v. Schultz, 420 F (2d) 461 (1972) 43
Diversion of Water from the Meuse Case, P.C.I.J. Rep., ser. A/B, No. 70,
    pp. 76–77 (1937) .... 21n.
Duff Development Co. v. Government of Kelantan [1924] A.C. 797 (H.L.) ... 40
Dunhill, Alfred v. Republic of Cuba, 425 U.S. 682 (1976) 49

Eastern Carelia Case, P.C.I.J. Rep., ser. B, No. 5 (1923) 253
Eastern Greenland Case. *See* Legal Status of Eastern Greenland.
E.C. Commission v. E.C. Council (ERTA) Case. *See Re* the European Road
    Transport Agreement: E.C. Commission v. E.C. Council.
Edye v. Robertson, 112 U.S. 580 (1884) 42
Eichmann Case. *See* Attorney-General of the Government of Israel v.
    Eichmann.
El Oro Mining & Railway Co. Case (G.B. v. Mexico), 5 R.I.A.A. 191
    (1931) .... 173n.
Empson v. Smith [1966] 1 Q.B. 426 (C.A.) 115
English Channel Arbitration, 18 I.L.M. 397 (1979) 149
ERTA Case. *See Re* the European Road Transport Agreement E.C.
    Commission v. E.C. Council.

European Road Transport Agreement, the: E.C. Commission *v.* E.C. Council *Re* [1971] E.C.R. 263; [1971] C.M.L.R. 335 64
Exchange of Greek and Turkish Populations Case, P.C.I.J. Rep., ser. B, No. 10, p. 6 (1925) .... 33n.
Expenses Case. *See* Certain Expenses of the United Nations Case.

Fabiani Case, 10 R.I.A.A. 83 (1896) .... 20n.
Fagernes, The [1927] P. 311 40
Fenton Textiles Assoc. *v.* Krassin (1922) 38 T.L.R. 259 .... 75n.
Filartiga *v.* Pena-Irala, 630 F (2d) 876 (1980); 19 I.L.M. 96 (1980) ...... 106, 176n.
Finnish Ships Arbitration, 3 R.I.A.A. 1479 (1934) .... 173n.
Fisheries Jurisdiction Case (Jurisdiction), I.C.J. Rep. 1973, p. 3 .... 211, 212, 252
—— (Merits), I.C.J. Rep. 1974, p. 3 .... 13, 24n., 140
Foster & Elam *v.* Neilson, 27 U.S. (2 Pet.) 253 (1829) .... 43, 44n.
Free Zones of Upper Savoy & the District of Gex, P.C.I.J. Rep., ser. A/B, No. 46 (1932) .... 33n., 155n.

Gdynia Ameryka Linie Zeglugowe Spolka Akcyjna *v.* Boguslawski Case [1953] A.C. 11 75
Golder Case, Eur.Ct. H.R. ser. A, Vol. 18, Judgment of Feb. 21, 1975; 1 E.H.R.R. 524 .... 183, 184n.
Gulf of Maine Case. *See* Delimitation of the Maritime Boundary in the Gulf of Maine Area.
Gut Dam Arbitration, 8 I.L.M. 118 (1969) 97

Haile Selassie *v.* Cable & Wireless Ltd. (No. 2), [1939] Ch. 182 75
Hawaii, Territory of *v.* Ho, 41 Hawaii 565 (1957); 26 I.L.R. 557 .... 45n.
Hesperides Hotels *v.* Aegean Holidays Ltd. [1978] Q.B. 205 (C.A.) 77
Home Missionary Society Claim, 6 R.I.A.A., p. 42 (1920) 157

I Congreso del Partido [1981] 3 W.L.R. 329 (H.L.) 110
I'm Alone Case, 3 R.I.A.A. 1609; 29 A.J.I.L. 326 (1935) 136n., 160
Interhandel Case (Preliminary Objection), I.C.J. Rep. 1959, p. 6 ... 173n., 247n.
International Status of South West Africa Case, I.C.J. Rep. 1959, p. 128 .... 59n.
Ireland *v.* United Kingdom, Eur.Ct. H.R. ser. A, Vol. 25, Judgment of Jan. 18, 1978; 2 E.H.R.R. 25 183
Island of Palmas Case, 2 R.I.A.A. 829 (1928) 23, 54n., 81n., 82n., 84, 239

Janes Claim (U.S. *v.* Mexico), 4 R.I.A.A. 82 (1926) .... 163n.
Johnson *v.* Browne, 205 U.S. 309 (1907) .... 43n.
Joyce *v.* D.P.P. [1946] A.C. 347 (H.L.) .... 104n.

Kaur *v.* Lord Advocate, 1981 S.L.T. 322 .... 39n.
Kjeldsen, Busk Medsen & Pedersen Case, Eur. Ct. H.R. ser. A, Vol. 23, Judgment of Dec. 7, 1976; 1 E.H.R.R. 711 .... 184n.
Krajina *v.* Tass Agency [1949] 2 All E.R. 274 109

Lauritzen *v.* Larsen, 345 U.S. 571 (1953) .... 33n.
Legal Consequences for States of the Continued Presence of South Africa in Namibia (South West Africa) Notwithstanding Security Council Resoln. 276 (1970), I.C.J. Rep. 1971, p. 16 .... 59, 196, 242
Legal Status of Eastern Greenland Case, P.C.I.J. Rep., ser. A/B, No. 53 (1933) 83n., 197
Liamco Case, 20 I.L.M. 1 (1981) 165

Lotus Case, P.C.I.J. Rep., ser. A, No. 10 (1927) .... 15, 23, 102n., 106, 133n.
Lovelace Case, 1981 Report of the Human Rights Committee, p. 166 191
Lusitania Case (U.S. *v.* Germany), 7 R.I.A.A. 32, 38–44 (1956) 160
Luther *v.* Sagor [1921] 3 K.B. 532 (C.A.) 73n., 74

Madzimbamuito Case [1969] (P.C.) 1 A.C. 645 .... 76n.
Marckx Case, Eur. Ct. H.R. ser. A, Vol. 31, Judgment of June 13, 1979; 2
    E.H.R.R. 330 183
Maret, The, 145 F (2d) 431 (1944); (1943–45) 12 A.D. Case No. 9 .... 78n.
Martini Case (Italy *v.* Venezuela), 2 R.I.A.A. 975 (1930) .... 159n.
Massey Case (U.S. *v.* Mexico), 4 R.I.A.A. 155 (1927) .... 158n.
Mauritian Women Case, 1981 Report of the Human Rights Committee,
    p. 134 191
Mavrommatis Palestine Concessions Case, P.C.I.J. Rep., ser. A, No. 2
    (1924) .... 53n., 161n.
McWhirter *v.* Attorney-General [1972] C.M.L.R. 382 .... 38n.
Mergé Claim, 22 I.L.R. 443 170
Mighell *v.* Sultan of Jahore [1894] 1 Q.B. 149 108
Military & Paramilitary Activities in and against Nicaragua Case, I.C.J. Rep.
    1984, p. 392 .... 246, 249
Minquiers & Ecrehos Case, I.C.J. Rep. 1953, p. 47 .... 84, 244
Missouri *v.* Holland, U.S. 416 (1920) 45n., 46, 47
Monetary Gold Case, I.C.J. Rep. 1954, p. 19 .... 244n.
Mortensen *v.* Peters, 8 F (J) 93 (1906) Court of Justiciary Scotland 32n., 36
Mosul Boundary Case, P.C.I.J. Rep., ser. B, No. 12, 32 (1925) .... 20n.
Murray *v.* Schooner Charming Betsy, 6 U.S. (2 Cranch) 64 (1804) .... 33n.

Naim Molvan *v.* Attorney-General for Palestine [1948] A.C. 351 132
Namibia (South West Africa) Case. *See* Legal Consequences for States of the
    Continued Presence of South Africa in Namibia.
Nanni *v.* Pace and the Sovereign Order of Malta, 8 A.D. 2 (1935–37) .... 68n.
Nationality Decrees in Tunis & Morocco Case, P.C.I.J. Rep., ser. B, No. 4
    (1923) .... 57, 169n.
National Union of Belgian Police Case, Eur.Ct. H.R. ser. A, Vol. 19,
    Judgment of Oct. 27, 1975; 1 E.H.R.R. 578 183
Naulilaa Case, 2 R.I.A.A. 1012 (1928) .... 226n.
Neer Claim, 4 R.I.A.A. 60 (1962) .... 162n.
Nercide, The, 9 Cr. 388 (U.S. 1815) 41
Nold *v.* Commission of the European Communities [1974] E.C.R. 491; [1974]
    2 C.M.L.R. 338 .... 185n.
North American Dredging Co. Case, 4 R.I.A.A. 26 (1926) ..... 53n., 161n., 169n.
North Sea Continental Shelf Cases, I.C.J. Rep. 1969, p. 3 .... 9, 11, 14, 15, 17, 21,
                                                                                  55, 148, 237
Norwegian Loans Case, I.C.J. Rep. 1957, p. 9 .... 168, 247
Norwegian Shipowners Claim, 1 R.I.A.A. 307 (1922) .... 160n.
Nottebohm Case, I.C.J. Rep. 1955, p. 4 .... 23, 57, 169, 170
Noyes Claim (U.S. *v.* Panama), 6 R.I.A.A. 308 (1933) .... 158n., 163n.
Nuclear Tests Cases (Australia *v.* France), I.C.J. Rep. 1974, p. 253; (New
    Zealand *v.* France), I.C.J. Rep. 1974, p. 457 .... 132, 197, 198, 250

Offshore Mineral Rights (B.C.), *Re* [1967] S.C.R. 792 48
Opinion 1/76, [1977] E.C.R. 741; [1977] 2 C.M.L.R. 279 64

Paquete Habana, The, 175 U.S. 677 (1900) .... 41n.

Parlement Belge Case (1878–79) 4 P.D. 129 .... 38, 109
Philippine Admiral, The [1977] A.C. 373 (J.C.) 110
Polish Upper Silesia, P.C.I.J. Rep., ser. A, No. 7 (1926) .... 34n.
Pope Case, 8 Whiteman 709 .... 163n.
Porto Alexandre [1920] P. 30 109
Post Office v. Estuary Radio Ltd. [1968] 2 Q.B. 740 (C.A.) 33n., 40

Quintanilla Claim (Mexico v. U.S.), 4 R.I.A.A. 101 (1926) .... 162n.

R. v. Chief Immigration Officer, ex p. Bibi [1976] 1 W.L.R. 979 .... 39n.
—— v. Markus [1974] 3 All E.R. 705 .... 103n.
—— v. Secretary of State for the Home Dept. & Another, ex p. Bhajan Singh
    [1976] Q.B. 198 .... 39n.
Rann of Kutch Arbitration, 50 I.L.R. 2 21
Re Al-Fin Corp.'s Patent [1970] Ch. 160 .... 78n.
Reel v. Holder [1981] 1 W.L.R. 1226 (C.A.) .... 78n.
Reparation for Injuries Suffered in the Service of the United Nations, I.C.J.
    Rep. 1949, p. 174 .... 19, 23, 52n., 62n., 68n., 253
Republic of Italy v. Hambros Bank Ltd. [1950] Ch. 314 .... 38n.
Reservations to the Convention on Genocide Case, I.C.J. Rep. 1951, p. 15 200
Rights of Minorities in Polish Upper Silesia, P.C.I.J. Rep., ser. A, No. 15
    (1928) .... 244n.
Rights of Nationals of the United States in Morocco Case, I.C.J. Rep. 1952,
    p. 176 57
Robert E. Brown Case, 6 R.I.A.A. 120 (1923) .... 173n.
Roberts Claim, 4 R.I.A.A. 77 (1926) .... 162n.
Rustomjee v. The Queen [1876] 1 Q.B.D. 487 .... 53n.

Sabbatino Case. *See* Banco Nacional de Cuba v. Sabbatino.
Salem Case (Egypt v. U.S.), 2 R.I.A.A. 1161 (1932) 170
Salimoff v. Standard Oil Co., 186 N.E. 679 (1933); (1933–34) A.D. Case No.
    8 78
Salomon v. Commissioners of Customs & Excise [1967] 2 Q.B. 116
    (C.A.) 33n., 40
Sambaggio Case (Italy v. Venezuela), 10 R.I.A.A. 499 (1903) .... 158n.
Schmidt & Dahlström Case, Eur. Ct. H.R. ser. A, Vol. 21, Judgment of Feb.
    6, 1976 182
Schroeder v. Bissell, U.S. District Court D. Conn., 5 F (2d) 838 (1925) .... 41n.
Sei Fujii v. State of California, 242 P (2nd) 617 (1952) .... 44, 176n.
Sokoloff v. National City Bank, 145 N.E. 917 (1924); (1923–24) 2 A.D. Case
    No. 19 .... 78n.
State, The v. C. Kramer & Others, Cases 3, 4 & 6/76, [1976] E.C.R. 1279;
    [1976] 2 C.M.L.R. 440 .... 64n.
Steiner & Gross v. Polish State, 4 A.D. 291 (1928) .... 67n.
Sunday Times Case, Eur. Ct. H.R. ser. A, Vol. 30, Judgment of April 30,
    1979; 2 E.H.R.R. 245 184
Sunday Times Cases (Monetary Award), Eur. Ct. H.R. ser. A, Vol. 38,
    Judgment of Nov. 6, 1980; 3 E.H.R.R. 317 184

Temple Case, I.C.J. Rep. 1962, p. 6 .... 20n., 159n., 208, 249
Territory of Hawaii v. Ho. *See* Hawaii, Territory of v. Ho.
Texaco Case, 53 I.L.R. 389 .... 166n., 168n.
Thakrar v. Home Secretary [1974] 1 Q.B. 684 36
Toscanino Case. *See* U.S. v. Toscanino.

Trail Smelter Arbitration, 3 R.I.A.A. 1905 (1938/41) 23, 97
Treacy *v.* D.P.P. [1971] A.C. 537 (H.L.) .... 103n.
Treatment in Hungary of Aircraft of the U.S.A. Cases, I.C.J. Rep. 1954, pp.
    90–103 .... 245n.
Trendtex Trading Corp. *v.* Central Bank of Nigeria [1977] Q.B. 529; [1977] 1
    All E.R. 881, 902 .... 25n., 36, 37, 110
Triquet *v.* Bath [1764] 3 Burr. 1478 (K.B.) .... 34n.
Tyrer Case, Eur.Ct. H.R. ser. A, Vol. 26; (1978) 58 I.L.R. 339 .... 48n.

Underhill *v.* Hernandez, 168 U.S. 250 (1897) .... 48n.
Upright *v.* Mercury Business Machines, 13 A.D. 2d 36; 213 N.Y.S. (2d) 417
    (1961) .... 78n.
U.S. *v.* Belmont, 301 U.S. 324 (1937) 45
—— *v.* Germany (Administrative Decision No. V). *See* Administrative
    Decision No. V.
—— *v.* Guy W. Capps Inc., 204 F (2d) 655 (1953) (U.S. Ct. of Appeals, 4th
    Circ.) .... 45n.
—— *v.* Percheman, 32 U.S. (7 Pet.) 51 (1833) .... 44n.
—— *v.* Pink, 315 U.S. 203 (1942) 45
—— *v.* Sisson, 294 F. Supp. 515 (D. Mass. 1968) .... 50n.
—— *v.* Toscanino, 500 F (2d) 207 (1945) (U.S. Ct. of Appeals, 2nd Circ.) 107

Vagrancy Cases, Eur. Ct. H.R. ser. A, Judgment of Nov. 18, 1970 (Question
    of Procedure) 183
Voting Procedure on Questions Relating to Reports & Petitions Concerning
    the Territory of South West Africa, I.C.J. Rep. 1955, p. 67 26

Walker *v.* Baird [1892] A.C. 491 .... 38n.
Weinberger Case, 1981 Report of the Human Rights Committee, p. 114 191
Western Sahara Case, I.C.J. rep. 1975, p. 12 .... 26n., 29n., 58, 81, 82n., 84, 253
West Rand Central Gold Mining Co. *v.* R. [1905] 2 K.B. 391 (K.B.) 34
Wimbledon Case, P.C.I.J. Rep., ser. A, No. 1 (1923) 18
Wulfsohn *v.* R.S.F.S.R., 138 N.E. 24 (1923); (1923–24) 2 A.D. Case No. 16 .. 78n.

Youmans Claim, 4 R.I.A.A. 110 (1926) 158
Young, James and Webster Case, Eur. Ct. H.R., ser. A, Vol. 44, Judgment
    of Aug. 13, 1981; 4 E.H.R.R. 38 184
—— (Monetary Compensation) Eur. Ct. H.R., ser. A, Vol. 55, Judgment of
    Oct. 18, 1982; 5 E.H.R.R. 201 184

Zafiro Case, 6 R.I.A.A. 160 (1925) .... 158n., 162n.

ABBREVIATIONS

A.C.	Appeal Cases (U.K.) 1891–
A.D.	Appellate Division, New York Supreme Court
A.D. 2d	Appellate Division Reports, New York Supreme Court, Second Series
A.J.I.L., Supp.	American Journal of International Law, Supplement
All E.R.	All England Reports, 1935–
B.F.S.P.	British and Foreign State Papers, 1812–
Burr.	Burrow's Reports (King's Bench, U.K.), 1757–71
Cd., Cmd., Cmnd.	U.K. Command Papers 1900–18, 1919–56, 1956– respectively
Ch.	Chancery Reports (U.K.), 1891–
C.M.L.R.	Common Market Law Reports
Cranch.	United States Supreme Court Reports, 1801–15
C.W.I.L.J.	Californian Western International Law Journal
D.P.P.	Director of Public Prosecution
ECOSOC	Economic and Social Council
E.C.R.	European Court Reports, 1954–
ECSC	European Coal and Steel Community
E.E.Z.	Exclusive Economic Zone
E.H.R.R.	European Human Rights Reports

E.R.	English Reports
EURATOM	European Atomic Energy Community
Eur. Court H.R.	European Court of Human Rights
F (2d)	Federal Reporter, Second Series (U.S.), 1924–
F (J)	Fraser, Justiciary Cases (Scotland), 1898–
F Supp.	Federal Supplement (U.S.), 1932–
G.A.	General Assembly (United Nations)
G.A.O.R.	General Assembly Official Records
Hague Recueil	Recueil des cours de l'Academie de droit international
Hudson	International Legislation
Hudson World Court Reports	(4 Vols., 1934–43)
I.C.J. Rep.	International Court of Justice Reports, 1947–
I.C.L.Q.	International and Comparative Law Quarterly
I.L.M.	International Legal Materials, 1962–
I.L.R.	International Law Reports, 1950–
J.L.S.S.	Journal of the Law Society of Scotland
K.B.	King's Bench (U.K), 1901–52
L.I.E.I.	Legal Issues of European Integration
L.N.O.J.	League of Nations Official Journal
L.N.T.S.	League of Nations Treaty Series, 1920–45
L.Q. Rev.	Law Quarterly Review, 1885–
Moore Int. Arb.	International Arbitration, 5 Vols., 1898

NATO	North Atlantic Treaty Organisation
N.E.	North Eastern Reporter, 1885–1936
N.Y.S.	New York Supplement Reporter, 1888
N.Y.S. 2d	New York Supplement, Second Series, 1937–
O.J.	Official Journal of the European Communities
Oppenheim	L. Oppenheim, International Law, Vols. 1 and 2
P.	Court of Probate
P.C.	Privy Council
P.C.I.J.	Permanent Court of International Justice
P.C.I.J. Rep., ser. A	Permanent Court of International Justice, Judgments and Orders, 1922–30
P.C.I.J. Rep., ser. A/B	Advisory Opinions, Judgments and Orders, 1931–40
P.C.I.J. Rep., ser. B	Advisory Opinions, 1922–30
P.D.	Probate Division Reports (U.K.), 1875–90
Pet.	Peter's, United States Supreme Court Reports, 1828–42
Q.B.	Queen's Bench Reports (U.K.), 1891–1901, 1952–
Q.B.D.	Queen's Bench Division Reports (U.K.), 1875–90
R.I.A.A.	Reports of International Arbitral Awards, 1948–
S.C.O.R.	Security Council Official Records
S.C.R.	Supreme Court Reports (Canada), 1876–
S.L.T.	Scots Law Times

T.I.A.S.	Treaties and Other International Acts Series (U.S.), 1950–
T.L.R.	Times Law Reports (U.K.), 1841–1952
U.K.T.S.	United Kingdom Treaty Series
UN	United Nations
UNCLOS III	Third United Nations Conference on the Law of the Sea
U.N.T.S.	United Nations Treaty Series, 1946–
U.S.	United States Supreme Court Reports, 1875–
U.S.C.	United States Code
U.S. Dept. State Bull.	United States Department of State Bulletin
U.S.T.	United States Treaties
U.S.T.S.	United States Treaty Series
Ves.	Vesey Junior's Chancery Reports (U.K.), 1789–1816
Whiteman	Digest of International Law, 14 Vols., 1936–73
W.L.R.	Weekly Law Reports (U.K.), 1953–
Y.B.I.L.C.	Yearbook of the International Law Commission

Chapter One

INTRODUCTION

The subject-matter of this text is international law, that is, public international law as distinct from private international law (conflict of laws).[1]

DEFINITION

Today international law[2] refers to those rules and norms which regulate the conduct of states and other entities which at any time are recognised as being endowed with international personality, *e.g.* international organisations and individuals, in their relations with each other. Such a definition takes account of international law's "youthfulness" and recognises that new actors may be required to participate on the international stage. States, although they remain the primary subjects of international law,[3] are no longer its exclusive subjects as they once were. International law was initially concerned exclusively with regulating inter-state relations and then only in respect of diplomatic relations and the conduct of war. This is no longer true.

International law has expanded both in terms of its subjects and its content. Major problems of international concern have been tackled collectively by states. This has proved, for example, more resource effective than attempting individual state action. The consequence has been a proliferation in the number of international organisations in the years since 1945. Modern technology has brought states and their populations into closer and more frequent contact with each other and rules have evolved to regulate such contact. The subject-matter of international law has correspondingly expanded and international law now has within its ambit issues which were traditionally regarded as being exclusively within a state's domestic jurisdiction, *e.g.* treatment of one's own nationals.

---

[1] Private international law (conflict of laws) is a system of law which is part of states' domestic law and which is utilised to determine how conflicts of jurisdiction are to be resolved.

[2] The term international law is something of a misnomer as statehood and nationhood are not necessarily synonymous.

[3] International personality is dealt with in Chapter 4.

This has had repercussions for individuals. They are now recognised as possessing some, albeit limited, international personality. The traditional definition of international law, namely a body of rules governing the relations of independent states in times of peace and war, is too rigid and outmoded. A definition of international law must accommodate the developments which the international legal system has witnessed in the twentieth century and must reflect international law as it is today.

NATURE AND CHARACTERISTICS OF INTERNATIONAL LAW

Is International Law Law?

The question is not one which the author intends to explore. Any analysis of the question presupposes a definition of law and is therefore one more suited for a jurisprudence class than an international law class. It is sufficient to say here that international law is law. States acknowledge it as such. Some states refer to international law in their constitutions. States like to be seen acting in accordance with it and legal advisers are employed to formulate, present and defend their state's position in international law.

Others, while recognising international law, purport to deny its effectiveness. What those who are derogatory of international law fail to appreciate is that their expectations of international law may be unrealistic. Law cannot coerce states in matters which are primarily political. International law cannot of itself and by itself dictate the policies of states. If hostilities break out international law is criticised for not maintaining international peace, yet international law cannot prevent its own violation any more than the municipal criminal law can prevent crimes being committed or contract law can prevent contracts being broken. In other words, the fact that law is violated does not in itself negate a legal system's effectiveness. Law is not a solution in itself, but is rather a means of handling a particular situation. International law is concerned with promoting international co-operation and achieving co-existence amongst states. When international law breaks down the fault lies not with international law itself, but with those who operate within the international legal system.

International law receives a bad press, especially when it breaks down. The issues involved are internationally politically sensitive, and so are newsworthy. International law, however, functions very effectively on a day to day level. Today we can switch on the television and see events "live" from anywhere in the world. Mail is sent and delivered throughout the world, international travel is an everyday occurrence. Such happenings are taken for granted, but they are only made possible through the efficient functioning of international law, whose "low-key" operation is generally overlooked, especially as the media do not regard it as newsworthy.

What are the Characteristics of International Law?

International law is not imposed on states—there is no international legislature. The international legal system is decentralised and founded essentially on consensus. International law is made primarily in one of two ways: through the practice of states (customary international law) and through agreements entered into by states (treaties).[4] Once international rules are established they have an imperative character and cannot be unilaterally modified at will by states. The absence of a strong enforcement machinery is highlighted by sceptics as a weakness of international law. There is no international police force nor is there an international court with compulsory jurisdiction to which states are required to submit. That is not to say, however, that international law is not effective. Sanctions are available which may be employed and which may affect a state's conduct. If international law is violated there are a number of self-help measures which the victim state may adopt, *e.g.* a treaty may be suspended or terminated, or the assets of an offending state may be frozen. The United Nations Security Council may authorise economic sanctions. Force may be used in defined circumstances.

Public opinion can also be an effective sanction. States want to be seen to be adhering to international law: why otherwise do they go to considerable efforts to justify their particular position in international law?

There is an international court to which states can refer their disputes for settlement. States, however, must agree to submit to the court; there is no legal compulsion on them to do so.

The role of reciprocity in international law observance should not be undermined. It is in a state's own interest to respect, for example, the territorial sovereignty of other states as they in their turn will respect its territorial sovereignty.

The international legal system is intrinsically different from municipal law. The principal participants of the international legal system, states, are all treated as equally sovereign.[5] The international community is composed not of a homogeneous grouping of states, but rather a heterogeneous group of some 159 states, which differ politically, economically, culturally and ideologically.

---

[4] See Chapter 2, "Sources."
[5] This is a legal fiction as obviously some states carry more weight than others in the international community.

States need to co-exist. International law was conceived and born out of such a need and thus is designed to promote international peace and harmonisation. A system which sought to characterise one state as "guilty" and one as "innocent" would not facilitate the realisation of international peace. International law must be conciliatory rather than adversary.

The international legal system is a young, immature system which is constantly evolving and developing. It is not simply lawyers' law. Politics plays an influential role. Consequently, the study of international law facilitates a greater comprehension and gives an insight into the functioning of the international community.

THE DEVELOPMENT OF INTERNATIONAL LAW

Some Observations

International law as a system is of recent origin.[6] Modern international law stems from the rise of the secular sovereign state in Western Europe. As in any community, law was required to regulate the relations of states with each other. The rules of war and those on diplomatic immunity were the earliest expression of international law. The Age of Discovery in the sixteenth and seventeenth centuries necessitated the evolution of rules governing the acquisition of territory. At the same time, the principle of the freedom of the seas was articulated. International law grew out of necessity, *viz.* as already said, in response to the need of states to co-exist.

International law set the perimeters of state action; within these perimeters establishing national competence, states enjoyed freedom of action. International law continued to expand as international intercourse increased and by the nineteenth century had become, geographically at least, a universal system. It remained, however, rooted in Western European traditions and values and in its concept and content it maintained this European bias. The twentieth century has witnessed major changes which have had repercussions for the international legal system. The sovereign independent state has been challenged; universal war has brought devastation twice; previous colonial territories have attained independence. The twentieth century has seen a greater emphasis on international co-operation, whereby states work together rather than individually. Matters once considered exclusively within domestic jurisdiction are now susceptible to international regula-

---

[6] Although the embryo of international concepts was apparent within Greek city states, *e.g.* it was recognised that citizens of states in other territories had rights, there was, however, no concept of an international community as such.

tion. The use of force has been prohibited except in defined circumstances.

International law is no longer the preserve of some 50 states, but rather some 159 states: it is no longer an exclusive western club. The "new" states have ideas contrary to those held by the "old" states. They do not challenge the existence of international law *per se*, but they do challenge the substantive content of some of these rules, *e.g.* the measure of compensation to be awarded in respect of the expropriation of an alien's property. The European bias of international law has been destroyed. Political ideologies other than that of the capitalist are now heard within international fora, *e.g.* the communist and socialist. Modern technology has not only brought states into more frequent contact with each other, but has created new areas for international regulation, *e.g.* the deep sea-bed and outer space.

The twentieth century for international law has been one of unparalleled expansion. It is on the international legal system as it exists today that this text focuses.

FURTHER READING

Cases and Materials

D.J. Harris, *Cases and Materials on International Law* (1983), Chapter 1.

L. Henkin, R. Pugh, O. Schachter and H. Smit, *International Law: Cases and Materials* (1980), Chapter 1.

J. Sweeny, C. Oliver and N. Leech, *The International Legal System: Cases and Materials* (1981), Chapter 18.

Specialised Texts

J.E.S. Fawcett, *The Law of Nations* (1971).
R. Fisher, *Points of Choice* (1980).
R. Fisher, *Improving Compliance with International Law* (1981).
W. Friedmann, *The Changing Structure of International Law* (1964).
L. Henkin, *How Nations Behave* (1972).
J.G. Merrills, *Anatomy of International Law* (1976).
G. Schwarzenberger, *The Dynamics of International Law* (1976).

General Texts

M. Akehurst, *A Modern Introduction to International Law* (1982), Chapters 1 and 2.

L. Green, *International Law: A Canadian Perspective* (1984), Part I, §§1–6.

D.W. Greig, *International Law* (1976), Chapter 1, pp. 1–5.

J.G. Starke, *An Introduction to International Law* (1984), Chapter 1.

Chapter Two

SOURCES

Rules and norms of any legal system derive authority from their source.[1] The "sources" articulate what the law is and where it can be found. In a developed municipal legal system, sources may be readily identifiable in the form, for example, of Parliamentary legislation and judicial decisions. However, on the international plane there is neither an international legislature which passes international legislation, nor is there an international court to which all members of the international community must compulsorily submit. Furthermore, the international legal system does not, unlike the majority of municipal legal systems, possess a written constitution. There is no international constitution identifying the principal organs of government investing them with authority and defining the scope of their power and the procedures by which such power may be executed.

In the absence of such "law-giving" sources, how is the legal quality of alleged rules of international law assessed?

A pragmatic response to the question has been found in the provisions of Article 38 of the Statute of the International Court of Justice. Article 38 does not mention the word "sources," but rather spells out how the Court is to decide disputes which may come before it for settlement. The Statute provides that the Court is to apply:

"(a) international conventions, whether general or particular, establishing rules expressly recognised by the contesting States;

(b) international custom, as evidence of a general practice accepted as law;

(c) the general principles of law recognised by civilised nations;

(d) subject to the provisions of Article 59, judicial decisions and the teachings of the most highly qualified publicists

[1] "Sources" may be interpreted in a variety of ways, *e.g.* the underlying reason why laws develop, but here its meaning is confined to that given in the text.

of the various nations, as subsidiary means for the determination of rules of law."

Sources may be characterised as formal or material. Briefly, formal sources constitute what the law is whereas material sources only identify where the law may be found. Hence Article 38(1)(a)-(c) (treaties, custom and general principles) are formal sources, whereas Article (38)(1)(d) (judicial decisions and juristic teachings) are material sources.[2]

Article 38 is therefore primarily a direction to the International Court of Justice on how disputes coming before it should be tackled. Nevertheless, in spite of the absence of the term "sources," Article 38 is regarded as an authoritative statement on the sources of international law. Article 38 does not stipulate that it is establishing a hierarchy, but it is self-evident that Article 38 is nonetheless establishing a hierarchy of procedure for the application of international law in the settlement of international disputes. Initially, existing relevant treaty provisions between the parties to the dispute must be applied. In the event of no prevailing provision, a custom which is accepted as legally binding, should be applied. If neither a treaty provision nor a custom can be identified then "general principles as recognised by civilised nations" may be invoked; while finally, at least under Article 38, judicial decisions and judicial writings may be utilised as a means of determining the rules of international law.

Each category of law spelt out in Article 38 will be examined. Custom, although cited second in Article 38 is, as it historically preceded treaties, considered initially.

CUSTOM

In any society rules of "acceptable" behaviour develop at an early stage and the international community was no exception. States in their relations with each other did, for whatever motives, what they wanted to do rather than what they agreed to do. However, with the increase of international intercourse certain norms of behaviour crystallised into rules of customary international law. Custom, through the absence of an international executive and legislature, has exercised an influential role in the formation of international law. In a mature legal system, custom is considered cumbersome and relatively unimportant, whereas in the international field it has, until at least recently, been a dynamic source of law and its

---

[2] For a fuller exposition, see Harris, pp. 20–21.

contribution is still witnessed in the provisions of many treaties which mirror previously established rules of international customary law.

Definition of Custom

What is meant by custom? Custom in international law is a practice followed by those concerned because they feel legally obliged to behave in such a way. Custom must be distinguished from mere usage, such as behaviour which may be done out of courtesy, friendship or convenience rather than out of legal obligation or a feeling that non-compliance would produce legal consequences, *e.g.* sanctions imposed by other members of the international community.

How is custom differentiated from behaviour that is motivated by reasons other than legal obligation? A rule of customary international law derives its law hallmark through the possession of two elements: (i) a material and (ii) a psychological element. The material element refers to the behaviour and practice of states, whereas the psychological element is the subjective conviction held by states that the behaviour in question is compulsory and not discretionary.

Accordingly, any alleged rule of customary international law must be assessed as to its (i) material and (ii) psychological element.

Material Element

The material element refers to the behaviour of states, but does that behaviour itself have to satisfy certain criteria? Has it to be practised for a certain length of time? Must it be indulged in frequently or is one act sufficient? Must the behaviour be consistently practised or may there be some divergences from the norm? Must the behaviour be universally practised by all states? Finally, what, for the purposes of customary international law, constitutes state practice?

Duration of Practice. There is no set time limit and no demand that the practice should be engaged in since "time immemorial." The fact that a practice has been engaged in only for a brief period of time will not in itself be a bar to the formation of a customary rule, provided that the other requirements of custom are met. The relative unimportance of time if other criteria are satisfied was highlighted by the International Court of Justice in the *North Sea Continental Shelf Cases*[3] in which it stated that:

[3] I.C.J. Rep. 1969, p. 3.

" . . . although the passage of only a short period of time is not necessarily, or of itself, a bar to the formation of a new rule of customary international law . . . an indispensable requirement would be that within the period in question, short though it might be, State practice . . . should have been both extensive and virtually uniform in the sense of the provision invoked; and should moreover have occurred in such a way as to show a general recognition that a rule of law or legal obligation is involved."[4]

The length of time required to establish a rule of customary international law will depend upon other factors pertinent to the alleged rule. If, for example, the rule is dealing with subject-matter in which there are no previously established rules, then the duration of the practice will require to be less than if there is an existing rule to be overruled. Time has also become less important as international communication has improved. It is now much easier to assess a state's response to an alleged rule than it was in the past. Time is the least important characteristic of state behaviour and as to how important it is in any given case depends on other factors peculiar to the activity concerned and these will now be looked at below.

Extent of State Practice. The International Court of Justice in the *Asylum Case*[5] held that before state practice could be acknowledged as law, it had to be "in accordance with a constant and uniform usage practised by the States in question."[6] Of course, although a particular pattern of behaviour may be engaged in frequently, it does not follow that the conduct is being practised out of any legal obligation. Similarly, an activity engaged in, albeit infrequently, may be practised because of a legal compulsion to do so. The importance of frequency of practice will depend upon the circumstances surrounding each alleged rule. For instance, a state which is able to cite two examples of state practice to support its contention that the practice is law, will be in a better position than the state which can cite no such examples. However, a more significant factor than frequency is the consistency of practice. In other words, do those states engaging in the practice in question behave in a like manner, thus demonstrating conformity?

The Court's judgment in the *Asylum Case* is again instructive. In that case the Court maintained that there was too much fluctuation and discrepancy in both the practice of and the views expressed

---

[4] *Ibid.* p. 43.
[5] I.C.J. Rep. 1950, p. 266.
[6] *Ibid.* p. 277.

regarding diplomatic asylum for a rule of custom to have been established. Consequently, the Court concluded that it was impossible to find "any constant and uniform usage accepted as law."[7] The existence of diverging practice proved to be the stumbling block in that particular practice's evolution into law.

Inconsistency *per se*, however, is not sufficient to negate the crystallisation of a rule into customary international law. Any inconsistency must be analysed and assessed in the light of factors such as subject-matter, the identity of the states practising the inconsistency, the number of states involved and whether or not there are existing established rules with which the alleged rule conflicts. Inconsistency of practice is explored in greater depth below when the question of how customary international law may be amended or modified is discussed.

How many states must be involved in a particular activity before the practice is accepted as law? Universal practice is fortunately not necessary. Article 38(1)(b) speaks not of universal practice, but a general practice. A practice can be general even if it is not universally followed, and there is no precise formula indicating how widespread a practice must be. What in fact is of more importance than the number of states involved is the attitude of those states whose interests are actually affected. It is the stance adopted by such states which is relevant and which has to be considered, a fact which was emphasised in the *North Sea Continental Shelf Cases*:

"... an indispensable requirement would be that within the period in question ... State practice, including that of States whose interests are specially affected should have been both extensive and virtually uniform ... "[8]

Thus it transpires that the number of states is less consequential than is the identity of the states involved. Each alleged rule must therefore be examined and assessed in context. In every activity certain states carry more weight than others—their interest is greater than that of other states and their attitude to an alleged rule is of importance. If an alleged rule is to attain legitimacy, a favourable response from "leading" states is pre-requisite. Hence, for example, Britain's contribution in the nineteenth century to sea law and currently the role of both the United States and the Soviet Union in the law of outer space. In any given area, the participation

---

[7] *Supra.* n. 5 at p. 277.
[8] *Supra.* n. 3 at p. 43.

of certain states is needed more than others before an alleged rule
may be transformed into customary international law.

Numbers are more important when the custom is a local, regional
one and involving fewer states than general customary law. A
regional custom is of a more contractual nature than a general one
and therefore requires to be positively acknowledged and supported
by all the states involved. Hence, the International Court's emphasis
on a "constant and uniform usage" in the *Asylum Case*.

Can a state choose not to be bound by a rule of customary
international law? If a state opposes a rule of customary international law and shows its opposition to that rule from the time of the
rule's inception, then the state will not be bound. Opposition,
however, must be demonstrated from the outset. Only then can the
state concerned not incur liability. In the *Anglo-Norwegian Fisheries
Case* the Court held that if the particular rule in question was one of
international law, it would be "inapplicable as against Norway
insomuch as she has always opposed any attempt to apply it to the
Norwegian coast."[9]

Dissent which is expressed only after the rule has become
established is too late to prevent the state from being bound and,
likewise, early opposition by a state to a rule, if abandoned, loses its
effectiveness. Dissention, of course, only prevents a rule from
becoming binding on the dissenter and does not affect the rule's
application on other states.

Why is dissent important? Expression of dissent is vital because
attaining a state's consent is in reality fictitious. Being difficult to
prove, consent is inferred and silence, although it may stem from
indifference, will be regarded as acquiescence and will serve to
reinforce the practice in question as law.

A state which enters the international system after a practice has
ripened into an established rule is bound by it, regardless of whether
it agrees with it or not. Such a state may seek though to amend or
modify the rule in question.

How may this occur? Initially, it can be said that it is easier for
custom to develop if there are no pre-existing conflicting rules; *e.g.*
in the exploitation of outer space rules of behaviour quickly evolved
because not only were there no pre-existing norms regulating
behaviour, there were only two States, the United States and the
Soviet Union, who were actively employed in that exploitation. The
position is different and more complicated if there exists established
rules of behaviour. The "new" rule's future will depend on the
number indulging in the behaviour contrary to the established rule

---

[9] I.C.J. Rep. 1951, p. 116 at p. 131.

relative to the number protesting against the creation of the new rule.

This naturally raises the question of how customary international law may be amended or modified if conflicting behaviour acts as a hindrance to the crystallisation of an alleged rule into law. Contradictory behaviour has the effect of throwing uncertainty on the apparently established rule, which in turn produces ambiguity regarding the entire law on the subject-matter, a fact which was highlighted in the *Fisheries Jurisdiction Case (United Kingdom* v. *Iceland) Merits*,[10] heard by the International Court of Justice in 1974, when in a Joint Separate Opinion Judges Forster, Bengzon, Aréchaga, Singh and Rudha expressed the view that:

> "If the law relating to fisheries constituted a subject on which there were clear indications of what precisely is the rule of international law in existence, it may then have been possible to disregard altogether the legal significance of certain proposals which advocate changes or improvements in a system of law which is considered to be unjust or inadequate. But this is not the situation. There is at the moment great uncertainty as to the existing customary law on account of the conflicting and discord practice of States. Once the uncertainty of such a practice is admitted the impact of the aforesaid official pronouncements, declarations and proposals most undoubtedly have an unsettling effect on the crystallisation of a still evolving customary law on the subject."[11]

It is also possible as is reflected in the above Opinion, that while states may behave in contradiction to an established rule, the conflicting behaviour may itself be inconsistently expressed. In such circumstances, change, if it is to come about, will take longer than if the states are united in what they want the new rule to be. If support for the rule is wide and consistent, then the acceptance of it as law will be relatively smooth and rapid. Similarly, if there is substantial opposition to the "new rule," the established accepted rule will retain its law character. However, if the numbers in favour of the established rule and the new rule are evenly divided, then a period of ambiguity as characterised by the Court and as illustrated in the law relating to fishing limits will follow. Indeed, there may be a time when two rules of customary law may exist side by side. International customary law can accommodate change, but how

---

[10] I.C.J. Rep. 1974, p. 3.
[11] *Ibid* p. 48.

quickly that change will occur is dependent upon the response of states to the proposed alteration of the law. There may well be a period in the change process when the established rule and the new rule will be seen to exist simultaneously, a situation which can make it difficult to determine where the old law ends and the new begins.

This has the advantage, particularly if states are agreed upon the change they want, of allowing flexibility, but the disadvantage of creating uncertainty as to what the law is at any given time.

State Practice. Finally, what, for the purposes of establishing customary international law, constitutes evidence of state practice? Treaties, diplomatic correspondence, statements by national legal advisers in domestic and international fora are amongst the indicators of state practice. This view, although a majority one, has been refuted on the grounds that only an overt act can constitute evidence of state practice, *e.g.* by D'Amato.[12]

Practice in itself does not establish custom. An alleged rule of customary international law has to manifest not only a material element, but a psychological element, otherwise known as *opinio juris*.

Opinio Juris Sive Necessitatis

States in their relations with each other engage in behaviour other than that which is required of them legally. If certain rules are to evolve into law, it is necessary to distinguish rules which are regarded as legally obligatory from those which are not. *Opinio juris* was introduced as a legal formula in an attempt to distinguish legal rules from mere social usage, and it refers to the subjective belief maintained by states that a particular practice is legally required of them. A practice which is generally followed but which states feel they are legally free to disregard at any time cannot be characterised as law. In the words of the International Court of Justice:

> "... Not only must the acts concerned amount to a settled practice, but they must also be such, or be carried out in such a way, as to be evidence of a belief that this practice is rendered obligatory by the existence of a rule of law requiring it. The need for such a belief, *i.e.*, the existence of a subjective element, is implicit in the very notion of the *opinio juris sive necessitatis*. The States concerned must therefore feel that they are conforming to what amounts to a legal obligation."[13]

[12] *The Concept of Custom in International Law* (1971), p. 88.
[13] *Supra* n. 3 at p. 44.

The problem with *opinio juris* is one of proof. It is frequently difficult to determine when the transformation into law has taken place. How can a state's conviction be proved to exist? Essentially what must be proved is the state's acceptance, recognition or acquiescence in the binding character of the rule in question. The onus of proof is on the state relying upon the custom—it is the party alleging the existence of custom which must demonstrate that the custom is so established that the other party is bound by it—and insufficient evidence of *opinio juris* is fatal to a case, as for example in the *Lotus Case*[14] and the *North Sea Continental Shelf Cases.*

In the *Lotus Case* although France identified previous instances where in practice the victim's flag state had refrained from criminal prosecution, France, in the Court's view, failed to demonstrate that states restrained from prosecuting because they had been conscious of a duty requiring them so to do.

Similarly, in the *North Sea Contintental Shelf Cases* the International Court of Justice maintained that, although the principle of equidistance was employed in the delimitation of the continental shelf between adjacent states, there was no evidence:

> "that they so acted because they felt legally compelled to draw them in this way by reason of a rule of customary law obliging them to do so—especially considering that they might have been motivated by other factors."[15]

Opinio juris and state practice are complementary in the creation of customary international law.

How may customary international law accommodate change if *opinio juris* demands behaviour in accordance with the law? How may new rules evolve if activity contrary to the established rules is prohibited?

If too rigid a view was taken of *opinio juris*, then obviously the law would become stunted and in time deficient. States, however, do act contrary to established rules and do so in the belief that the new behaviour, if not already law, is about to become law. What will determine the future of such behaviour—whether it in fact does become law or withers—is the response of other states. Their reaction determines whether the new practice gains the necessary *opinio juris*.

Finally, mention must be made of a new type of custom known by the somewhat anomalous term of "instant custom." The term is

[14] P.C.I.J. Rep., ser. A, No. 10 (1927).
[15] *Supra.* n. 3 at pp. 44–45.

anomalous being as it is self-contradictory, but what it is used to describe certainly defies classification as traditional custom. It refers not to behaviour, which is constant, uniform and frequently engaged in, but rather to spontaneous activity practised by a *great* number of states acting as they want to act. Instant custom is relatively rare. Two examples of "instant customary law" are the doctrine of the continental shelf originating from President Truman's Proclamation in 1945 and the unilateral seaward extension throughout the 1970s by coastal states. The doctrine of the continental shelf became established as customary international law on the basis of assertions (*i.e.* claims of exclusive rights and denial of access to others) and general acquiescence although in fact there was an absence of much actual practice since for a long time continental shelf mining was neither technologically nor economically feasible. The exclusive economic zone became established as customary international law in the 1970s as coastal states particularly concerned with controlling the exploitation and conservation of fishery resources increasingly, rather than wait for agreement within UNCLOS III,[16] took unilateral action and extended their sovereign rights beyond their territorial sea to a maximum limit of 200 miles.[17] Instant custom may appear an unsatisfactory term, but the activity it describes, while not fitting into the mould of traditional custom, still falls under the general umbrella of custom, rather than under any "new" source of law and, accordingly, the term in the absence of any other will have to suffice. As stressed already, instant custom is an exception from the norm.

Concluding on custom, therefore, it is seen that the character of customary international law is such that uncertainty and ambiguity may prevail regarding the law on any given subject at a particular time. Today, the number of states participating on the international plane has increased some three-fold over the last two decades and the subject-matter of international law now extends beyond the traditional realm of diplomatic relations and the rules of warfare and has broken through the national hold on such issues as human rights and welfare law.

In the light of this, coupled with the desire of states to know what they have agreed to, treaties are increasingly utilised as the means for regulating international relations.

---

[16] Third United Nations Conference on the Law of the Sea.
[17] The E.E.Z. (Exclusive Economic Zone) has been recognised in the 1982 Convention on the Law of the Sea: Article 55 defines the E.E.Z. and Article 56 defines the rights of coastal states within the E.E.Z. See below, Chapter 7.

TREATIES

Article 38(a) does not mention the term "treaties," but refers to "any international conventions, whether general or particular establishing rules expressly recognised by the contesting States." The effect of this direction to the Court is that, if an existing treaty provision pertains between the parties to the dispute before the Court, then, if relevant, the treaty provision must be applied.

A treaty, although it may be identified as comparable in some degree to a Parliamentary Statute within municipal law, differs from the latter in that it only applies to those states which have agreed to its terms, and normally a treaty does not have universal application. In other words, opting out, which is not available to individuals under national law, is available to the members of the international community.

Treaties are only examined here in so far as they constitute a source of law.[18] Treaties, as Article 38(a) infers, may be between two states (bipartite) or between several states (multipartite).[19]

A distinction is sometimes drawn between law-making treaties ("traité-lois") and "treaty contracts" ("traité-contracts"). The essence of the distinction lies apparently in the fact that "treaty contracts," being agreements between relatively few parties can only create particular law between the signatories, whereas treaties to which there are many signatories create law *per se*. However, all treaties involve a contractual obligation for the parties concerned and, consequently, create law for all parties agreeing to the terms of the treaty. In other words, a bilateral[20] treaty does not create a *lesser* law than does a multilateral treaty. Multilateral treaties may admittedly have a wider effect and, as such, may be regarded as law-making, in that not only do they have a greater number of signatories, but the provisions of such a treaty may become customary international law, as the Netherlands and Germany attempted unsuccessfully to argue in the *North Sea Continental Shelf Cases*. Multilateral treaties may, although they may never have the truly legislative effect of municipal legislation, have a quasi-legislative effect which is at least *prima facie* denied to bilateral treaties. Conversely, a multilateral or a bilateral treaty may merely spell out what has been accepted as customary international law, and a provision contained repeatedly in bilateral treaties may

---

[18] The technicalities of treaty law are examined in Chapter 10.
[19] Participation in a treaty is not confined exclusively to states, but states are the only entities which have *locus standi* before the I.C.J. in contentious cases.
[20] Although the terms "bipartite" and "multipartite" are strictly correct, the terms "bilateral" and "multilateral" are more commonly used.

provide evidence that a particular rule of customary international law exists.

Treaties represent the most tangible and most reliable method of identifying what has been agreed between states, and those of the Soviet school of thought particularly see treaties as the most important source of international law. Treaties, accordingly, regulate a diverse and extensive subject-matter including *inter alia* drug control, space exploitation, the establishment of organisations, extradition and safety regulations in the air and at sea.

Customary law and law made by treaty have equal authority as international law, but if a treaty and a customary rule exist simultaneously on the issue in dispute, then the treaty provisions take precedence as is illustrated by the *Wimbledon Case*.[21] In that case the Permanent Court of International Justice, whilst recognising that under customary international law it was prohibited to allow the passage of armaments through the territory of a neutral state to the territory of a belligerent state, upheld Article 380 of the Treaty of Versailles which provided that the Kiel Canal was to be "free and open to the vessels of commerce and of war of all nations at peace with Germany on terms of entire equality." In stopping a vessel flying the flag of a state with which she was at peace, Germany was, the Court maintained, in breach of her treaty obligations under the Treaty of Versailles.

In other words, unless the parties have expressed otherwise, a rule established by agreement supersedes for them a previous conflicting rule of customary international law. Generally, in the event of inconsistency, the latter, be it custom or treaty, prevails as between the same parties. Parties to a treaty may agree to adhere to the treaty obligations even in the light of subsequent general custom. Nevertheless, though modification of customary law by treaty is common there are few instances of rules of customary law developing in conflict with earlier agreements and in such cases the principle that the latter in time prevails will be applied on the presumption that the parties to the treaty have impliedly given their consent.[22]

A presumption exists though against the replacement of customary rules by treaty and *vice-versa*. Treaties are not intended to derogate from customary law, and a treaty which seemingly modifies or alters established custom should be construed so as to best conform to, rather than derogate from, accepted principles of international law, unless, of course, the treaty in question is clearly

---

[21] P.C.I.J. Rep., ser. A., No. 1 (1923).
[22] One such example was the acceptance as law of the 200 mile exclusive economic zone in conflict to the 1958 Geneva Conventions on the Law of the Sea.

intended to alter the existing rules of custom. A treaty will not however prevail over prior customary law if the latter is *jus cogens.*[23]

Whatever their legislative effect, treaties generally do not, unlike municipal legislation, have universal application. This statement must be qualified. There are two types of treaties which, because of their purpose, do produce consequences which non-signatories cannot ignore, *viz.* (i) those establishing a special international regime and (ii) those establishing an international organisation.

In 1920 a Committee of Jurists was appointed by the League of Nations to determine whether Finland, as successor state to Russia, was bound by the 1856 Convention under which Russia had agreed with France and Great Britain to the non-fortification of the Aaland Islands.[24] The Committee concluded that the treaty extended beyond the three contracting parties. The islands enjoyed "a special international status" and that until the 1856 Convention was replaced, every state interested had a right to insist upon it being complied with, while "any State in possession of the Islands must conform to the obligations binding upon it."[25] Treaties of this type are, however, very exceptional.

Constitutive treaties establishing international institutions, *e.g.* the United Nations, have created organisations which have subsequently been held to possess varying degrees of international personality,[26] a personality which has enabled such entities to operate on the international stage and which has, in certain instances, been enforced against non-member states, *e.g.* in the *Reparations Case.*[27]

"General Principles of Law as Recognised by Civilised Nations"

International law as a legal system would be undermined if the International Court of Justice, because of an apparent absence of relevant legal rules, was unable to give a decision based on law (such a situation is referred to as *non liquet*). In a municipal system, such a situation would be tackled by the deducing of relevant rules from already existing rules, or from basic legal principles, such as justice and equity. A *"non-liquet"* situation is, or at least was, more

[23] See below p. 28 and Chapter 10.
[24] *League of Nations Official Journal* (1920), Sp.Supp. No. 3, p. 3.
[25] See also Harris, p. 222.
[26] International personality is covered in Chapter 4.
[27] *Reparation for Injuries Suffered in the Service of the United Nations, Advisory Opinion,* I.C.J. Rep. 1949, p. 185.

likely to arise in international law[28] than in a developed mature legal system. Accordingly, "general principles of law . . ." was inserted to plug the gaps and to avoid an undermining of international law which an inability to render judgment through an insufficiency of law would undoubtedly incur.

General principles were those as understood by "civilised nations". "Civilised nations" has today, for obvious reasons, been dropped. Its colonial connotations are unacceptable in today's international community.

What then is understood by general principles? It is not clear whether general principles refers to those of the international legal system or those of municipal legal systems. Such ambiguity is advantageous as it imposes no restraint on the principles which may be applied.

Rather than dwell on the conceptual arguments that have raged over the definition of general principles, it is more advantageous here to identify instances of when general principles have been employed. What has happened is that legal principles have been drawn from the developed municipal legal systems. This does not mean that judges have to have expertise in every legal system of the world, because of course legal systems can be divided into families and, consequently, common elements may be identified within legal systems. The general principles are therefore those which are common to the major legal systems of the world.

Most of the parallels drawn from municipal law have related to procedural, administrative and jurisdictional situations. Principles applied by international tribunals and the International Court and its predecessor, have been those of a state's responsibility for the acts of its agents,[29] the principle of estoppel (personal bar),[30] no one must be a judge in his own case,[31] and the principle of reparation.[32] Analogies with municipal legal systems have been utilised in recent years in the new areas of international law, *e.g.* commercial and administrative law. In the *Barcelona Traction Case*[33] the International Court of Justice emphasised that if:

"the Court were to decide the case in disregard of the relevant

---

[28] It should always be borne in mind that the Statute of the I.C.J. is the direct successor of the Charter of the Permanent Court of International Justice and that in the 1920s international law was certainly less developed than it is today.

[29] *Fabiani Case*, 10 R.I.A.A. 83 (1896).

[30] *Temple Case*, I.C.J. Rep. 1962, p. 6.

[31] *Mosul Boundary Case*, P.C.I.J. Rep., ser. B, No. 12, p. 32 (1925).

[32] *Chorzów Factory Case (Indemnity) (Merits)*, P.C.I.J. Rep., ser. A, No. 17, p. 29 (1928).

[33] I.C.J. Rep. 1970, p. 3.

institutions of municipal law it would without justification invite serious legal difficulties. It would lose touch with reality, for there are no corresponding institutions of international law to which the Court could resort. . . . It is to rules generally accepted by municipal legal systems . . . and not to the municipal law of a particular State, that international law refers."[34]

No precise definition either to the extent or scope of general principles has been universally agreed. The importance of general principles, however they may be defined, is that recourse to them has prevented a case from being shelved on the grounds that international law as it exists lacks, or is inadequate for dealing with the particular issue raised.[35]

Whether a particular general principle is eligible for absorption by international law will depend upon the development of international law at the time in question, *e.g.* the prohibition on the use of torture is now conceivably part of international law based on the fact that the prohibition is at least *prima facie* common to all legal systems.

EQUITY[36]

"The Court has not been expressly authorised by its Statute to apply equity as distinguished from law. . . . Article 38 of the Statute expressly directs the application of 'general principles of law recognised by civilised nations,' and in more than one nation principles of equity have an established place in the legal system. . . . It must be concluded, therefore, that under Article 38 of the Statute, if not independently of that Article, the Court has some freedom to consider principles of equity as part of the international law which it must apply." [37]

In the *Rann of Kutch Arbitration,*[38] equity was identified as constituting part of international law while the International Court of Justice in the *North Sea Continental Shelf Cases* directed the

---

[34] *Supra.* n. 33 at p. 37.
[35] Possible general fundamental principles of international law are considered under "*jus cogens*" below at p. 28.
[36] Equity is sometimes treated separately as a possible independent source of law, but it is considered here in keeping with, *e.g.* Professor Harris' scheme of presentation which is in line with this author's thinking.
[37] Separate Opinion of Judge Hudson in *The Diversion of Water from the Meuse Case,* P.C.I.J. Rep., ser. A/B, No. 70, pp. 76–77 (1937).
[38] 50 I.L.R. 2.

parties involved to seek a solution by reference to "equitable principles."

Principles of equity in the sense of fairness, justice and reasonableness are akin to general principles, and it may be wondered why they should not always be considered under the umbrella of general principles. Equity differs from the general principles most frequently applied in that, while the latter has related mainly to procedural techniques, equity as a concept reflects values, values which may be hard to define, but which may profoundly affect the application of the law. Equity in itself cannot be a source of law in that it does not contribute to substantive law, but it can, nevertheless, affect the way substantive law is administered and applied.

Equity plays a subsidiary role in supplementing existing rules. Equity as understood above must be distinguished from the International Court's power "to decide a case *ex aequo et bono*, if the parties agree thereto,"[39] *i.e.* the Court may apply equity in precedence over all other rules. A judge can only exercise his power under Article 38(2) if he has been expressly authorised so to do.[40]

In the event of the International Court of Justice being unable to solve a dispute by reference to treaty law, custom or general principles, Article 38 provides that the subsidiary means of "judicial decisions and the teachings of the most highly qualified publicists of the various nations" may be employed. Judicial decisions and writings are subsidiary means of determining what the law is on a given issue. They constitute the material sources of international law as distinct from the formal sources. They are not the law as such, but are rather where the law may be found. However, the increasing growth of, in particular, treaty law has witnessed a decline in the employment of both judicial decisions and writings, as will be seen as each is considered individually below.

JUDICIAL DECISIONS

Judicial decisions may be applied "subject to the provisions of Article 59." Article 59 states that " . . . the decision of the Court has no binding force except between the parties and in respect of that particular case." There is no rule of *stare decisis* in international law whereby the Court is obliged to follow its previous decisions. Nevertheless, in spite of the absence of *stare decisis* in international law, the International Court of Justice and international tribunals

[39] Article 38(2).
[40] Article 38(2) has never been invoked before the I.C.J. though some international arbitration awards have been decided *ex aequo et bono*.

examine previous decisions and do take them into account when seeking the solution to a subsequent dispute. There is obviously value in judicial consistency—it will promote some degree of certainty for those participating in the legal system as to what the law is on a particular issue. Although, strictly speaking, the International Court of Justice is only to apply the law and not to make law, it has delivered a number of judgments and advisory opinions which have been influential in their contribution to the development of international law, *e.g. Reparations Case*[41] (legal personality of the United Nations), the *Nottebohm Case*,[42] (genuine link between individual and claimant state) and the *Anglo-Norwegian Fisheries Case*[43] (baselines from which the territorial sea may be drawn). Similarly, arbitration decisions have contributed to the growth of international law, *e.g.* the *Alabama Arbitration Awards*[44] (duties of a neutral state), the *Island of Palmas Case*[45] (evidence of territorial sovereignty).

Caution should be exercised when assessing the contribution of a particular decision, *e.g.* the Court may be equally divided and the casting vote of the President may be necessary for a decision as in the *Lotus Case*. Similarly, the importance of an arbitration decision will depend, for example, on the subject-matter involved and the parties concerned.

Before assessing the contribution of any arbitration decision to the development of international law, reference should be made to the contents of the *compromis*; *viz.* the agreement concluded between the parties to the arbitration which may specify, for instance, the tribunal's jurisdiction and the law to be applied. Law, other than international law, or in addition to international law, may be employed by an arbitration tribunal and if this is the intention of the parties it must be stipulated in the *compromis*.[46] In the *Trail Smelter Arbitration*,[47] for example, the Tribunal was instructed to "apply the law and practice followed in dealing with cognate questions in the United States of America, as well as international law and practice." It is therefore necessary to remember that an arbitration tribunal, in settling a dispute between two states, may not necessarily be applying international law or, at least, exclusively international law.

---

[41] *Reparation for Injuries Suffered in the Service of the United Nations, supra.* n. 27.
[42] I.C.J. Rep. 1955, p. 4.
[43] *Anglo-Norwegian Fisheries Case, supra.* n. 9.
[44] Moore, 1 Int. Arb. 495 (1872).
[45] 2 R.I.A.A. 829 (1928).
[46] In the absence of any stipulation, international law will be applied.
[47] 3 R.I.A.A. 1905 (1938/41).

A judicial decision by the International Court of Justice may give the stamp of law to an alleged rule of custom. Again, caution must be exercised. For instance, the International Court of Justice in 1974 pronounced that:

> " ... two concepts have crystallised as customary law in recent years arising out of the general consensus revealed at that Conference [1960 Law of the Sea Conference]. The first is the concept of the fishery zone. ... The second is the concept of preferential rights of fishing in adjacent waters in favour of the coastal State in a situation of special dependency on its coastal fisheries. ... "[48]

The evidence produced by the Court in support of its contention was unconvincing. The Court took existing instances of preferential rights at face value and considered neither the reasons why preferential treatment was granted, nor whether the parties concerned felt any legal obligation to provide preferential treatment for coastal states. The evidence produced in Court illustrated that relatively few states put preferential rights into practice—21—and that the practice was confined to a single geographical area (the North Atlantic). The Court did not attempt to demonstrate that states felt any legal obligation to act in the way they had done. Nor has state practice since the Court's judgment supported the view that the Court was giving "judgment *sub specie legis ferendae*" and was anticipating "the law before the legislator had laid it down."[49]

DECISIONS OF MUNICIPAL COURTS

Article 38 does not limit the judicial decisions that may be employed to those of international tribunals. Thus, if a municipal court decision is relevant, it may be applied. The weight attached to a decision of a national court will depend upon the standing of the court concerned. The United States Supreme Court is held in high regard and, in its decisions dealing with individual state boundaries, it has not only applied but played a role in developing the relevant principles of international law. Similarly, decisions of the English Prize Courts contributed to the growth of prize law—law relating to vessels captured at sea during war.

---

[48] *Fisheries Jurisdiction Case (Merits), supra* n. 10 at p. 23.
[49] That this is what the Court may have been seeking to do is borne out by Judge Ignacio-Pinto's declaration (at p. 37) that the Court gave him the impression that it was "anxious to indicate the principles on the basis of which it would be desirable that a general international regulation of rights of fishing should be adopted."

A municipal court decision may also serve as evidence of a state's position on a particular issue. Nevertheless, it must always be borne in mind that although a national court is apparently applying international law, it may in reality be applying a rule of national law, *e.g.* as in questions of sovereign and diplomatic immunity.

WRITERS

"Teachings of the most highly qualified publicists of various nations" may be referred to as a subsidiary means in an attempt to settle a dispute.

Writers have played a considerable role in the development of international law. Their influence has been due, in part, to the absence of an executive and a legislative body and, in part, to the "youthfulness" of the international legal system. Especially in its formative period, writers were, because of insufficient state practice, able to help determine, mould and articulate the scope, content and basic principles of international law, *e.g.* Grotius—"freedom of the seas"—in the early seventeenth century. However, as the substantive law of international law increased via, for example, state practice and the growth of customary international law, the role of writers declined. Nevertheless, international law is still a relatively young system and its boundaries are constantly being extended; writers may still make a contribution in identifying and highlighting areas where international regulation should be introduced, *e.g.* environmental pollution. Writers may also prompt an assessment of the aims and values of international law. Writings, though they have receded in importance, are utilised not as a source of law in themselves, but as a means of ascertaining what the law actually is on a given subject.[50] They are subsidiary means of determining what the law is on a particular issue at a particular point in time, and in the absence of any rule of *stare decisis* in international law, writings do not necessarily carry less weight than judicial decisions. Obviously, though, which publicists are "the most highly qualified" cannot be conclusively proved.

The international community of today is very different from the one to which Article 38(1) and its predecessor were introduced. It is relevant, therefore, after having examined all the possible "sources" identified by reference to Article 38(1), to ask whether these are the only sources? Article 38(1) does not profess to be exhaustive and it

---

[50] See, for instance, reference by Lord Stephenson in *Trendtex Trading Corporation* v. *Central Bank of Nigeria* [1977] 1 All E.R. 881, 902.

is, especially because of the developing character of international law, quite legitimate to look beyond Article 38(1).

OTHER POSSIBLE SOURCES OF INTERNATIONAL LAW

Acts of International Organisations

The multiplication of international organisations is a phenomenon of the last 30 years. The best known, enjoying almost universal membership, is the United Nations. Every member state of the United Nations (159 members) possesses one vote within the General Assembly. Voting on important questions requires a two-thirds majority, whilst on all other questions a simple majority will suffice. Only those Resolutions adopted by the Assembly on procedure and budgetary questions are legally binding on members. All other Resolutions are recommendations, statements on a given issue. However, certain General Assembly Resolutions, namely those which are "Declarations of Principle," although they carry no legal obligation, do have considerable moral force, e.g. G.A. Resolution 1514 (XV), "Declaration on the Granting of Independence to Colonial Countries and Peoples."[51] However, other Resolutions cannot be dismissed as being of no legal significance. In the words of Judge Lauterpacht:

> "It would be wholly inconsistent with sound principles of interpretation as well as with highest international interest, which can never be legally irrelevant, to reduce the value of the Resolutions of the General Assembly—one of the principal instrumentalities of the formation of the collective will and judgment of the community of nations represented by the United Nations—and to treat them, . . ., as nominal, insignificant and having no claim to influence the conduct of the Members. International interest demands that no judicial support, however indirect, be given to any such conception of the Resolutions of the General Assembly as being of no consequence."[52]

The legal effect of General Assembly Resolutions remains uncertain and if General Assembly Resolutions, in themselves, are to be

---

[51] G.A. Resolution 1514 (XV) December 14, 1960; see *Advisory Opinion—Western Sahara*, I.C.J. Rep. 1975, p. 12, pp. 31 *et seq.* for the effect of G.A. Resolutions in the evolution of the principle of self-determination.

[52] Separate Opinion in Voting Procedure on Questions Relating to Reports and Petitions Concerning the Territory of South West Africa, I.C.J. Rep. 1955, p. 67 at p. 122.

recognised as law-creating, a consistent approach would have to be adopted towards them, rather than the current selective approach where their impact is dependent upon such factors as the subject-matter of the Resolution, how large a majority the Resolution commands and to what extent it receives the support of the principally affected states in the given field. However, as it is, a vote in the General Assembly is cast by a state's representative and as such will reflect a particular state's position on a given issue. How a state votes can be the means of providing evidence of state practice. Thus, voting within an organisation may be a useful link in the international law-making process, *i.e.* it may provide the evidence necessary for "law" to be attributed to usage. The voting on General Assembly Resolutions may provide an indication of what the law is, or possibly what the law should be on a particular topic at a given time.

Regional Organisations

Regional organisations such as the Council of Europe, the European Communities, the Organisation of American States and the Organisation for African Unity can, via their internal measures demonstrate what they, representing a particular regional grouping of states, consider to be the law. Regional organisations enjoy varying degrees of legal personality (discussed in Chapter 3) and if this should extend to a treaty-making competence, the organisation in question may shape substantive international law by participating in treaties.

The International Law Commission

A criticism levelled against custom is that it is diffuse and lacking in precision. In the light of this, attempts have been made at codification—the Hague Conferences 1899 and 1907 produced Conventions on the law of war and neutrality and in 1930 the Hague Convention on Certain Questions Relating to the Conflict of Nationality Law was drawn up. Codification essentially involves a stream-lining of all existing law on a particular subject and it is distinct from consolidation which is simply a drawing together of all material on a particular subject. In 1946 the International Law Commission was established and charged with the task of furthering the progressive development and codification of international law. "Progressive development" is defined in Article 15 of the International Law Commission's Statute as "the preparation of draft conventions on subjects which have not yet been regulated by international law or in regard to which the law has not yet been sufficiently developed in the practice of States." Codification, however, is defined as "the more precise formulation and systemisation of rules of international law in fields where there already has been extensive state practice, precedent and doctrine." All codification has, accordingly, since 1946, been effected via the International Law Commission.

The Commission has 25 members[53] who sit as individuals rather than as representatives of their governments.[54] The Commission may be invited by the General Assembly to look at a particular field of law. However, this is rare and the Commission as a rule normally initiates its work programme for itself. Draft articles are prepared and subsequently submitted to Member States for their comments. A conference is convened which will, on the basis of the draft articles, produce a Convention, which will eventually be opened for signature.[55]

The value of the International Law Commission's work lies not only in that a multilateral treaty may be produced, but that in its preparatory work state practice may be identified and, as such, may assist the formation of customary international law. Again, the interrelation of treaty law and customary international law and *vice versa* is illustrated.

Other agencies apart from the International Law Commission are engaged in attempts to clarify existing law on given subjects, *e.g.* the United Nations Commission on International Trade Law, the International Labour Organisation and independent bodies such as the International Law Association.

Mention, albeit brief, must be made of *jus cogens*.[56]

Jus Cogens

Jus cogens is the technical term given to those norms of general international law which are of a peremptory force and from which, as a consequence, no derogation may be made except by another norm of equal weight. A treaty, for instance, which conflicts with such a norm is void[57] and should a new peremptory norm develop any existing conflicting treaty becomes void and terminates.[58]

---

[53] Increased from 15 members to 21 in 1956 and to 25 in 1961.
[54] Elections are by the General Assembly from lists of national groups and are elected with regard, *e.g.* to equitable geographical distribution.
[55] Conferences may span a number of years, *e.g.* United Nations Conference on the Law of the Sea had its opening session in New York in 1973, but it was not until December 10, 1982 that a Convention was open for signature. Apart from the Law of the Sea, the Commission has considered such topics as the law of treaties, diplomatic and consular relations and state succession.
[56] *Jus cogens* is looked at more closely within the context of treaty law—Chapter 10.
[57] Vienna Convention on the Law of Treaties, 1969, Article 53.
[58] *Ibid.* Article 64.

How does an international rule gain status as a peremptory norm? The Vienna Convention defines[59] a peremptory norm of general international law as one which is "accepted and recognised by the international community of States as a whole. . . ." A peremptory norm may, it would appear, be derived from a custom or a treaty, but not, it is submitted, from any other source.

Jus cogens is the label for what are essentially the "public policy" rules of the international legal system. There is, as might be anticipated, considerable uncertainty as to the scope and extent of *jus cogens*. Aggression—the use of force in contravention of the United Nations Charter—is probably the most likely candidate, though others suggested include the prohibition on genocide and the principle of self-determination.[60]

Of course, the almost universal recognition and acceptance of certain basic principles as fundamental, would represent an advancement and refinement in the international legal system, and the system for this step forward does not depend upon itself, but rather upon its principal participants, states.

---

[59] For the purposes of the Convention.
[60] Commentary International Law Commission, Y.B.I.L.C., 1966, II, pp. 247–248; *Western Sahara Case, supra.* n. 51.

FURTHER READING

Cases and Materials

D.J. Harris, *Cases and Materials on International Law* (1983), Chapter 2.
L. Henkin, R. Pugh, O. Schachter and H. Smit, *International Law: Cases and Materials* (1980), Chapter 2.

Specialised Texts

C. Parry, *The Sources and Evidence of International Law* (1965).
G.J.H. Van Hoof, *Rethinking the Sources of International Law* (1983).

General Texts

M. Akehurst, *A Modern Introduction to International Law* (1982), Chapter 3.
I. Brownlie, *Principles of Public International Law* (1979), Chapter 1.
L. Green, *International Law: A Canadian Perspective* (1984), Part I, §§7–31.
D.W. Greig, *International Law* (1976), Chapter 1, pp. 5–51.
J.G. Starke, *An Introduction to International Law* (1984), Chapter 2.

Chapter Three

INTERNATIONAL LAW AND MUNICIPAL LAW

International law today is not confined to regulating the relations between states. The scope of international law continues to extend and is no longer exclusively concerned with the rules of warfare and diplomatic relations. Today matters of social concern such as health, education and economics fall within the ambit of international regulation. International law is more than ever aimed at individuals.

But, can individuals invoke international law before domestic courts? Can they gain rights under international law which they can enforce within the municipal legal system?

Essentially, the issue which is to be examined in this chapter is the extent to which municipal courts will give effect within the domestic system to rules of international law which are contrary, or not contrary, to domestic law. The approach of a particular state's municipal courts to international law will be characterised by that state's attitude to and reception of international law—an attitude which may and does differ according to the type of international law in question—treaty law or customary international law. There is no universal uniform practice stipulating how states should incorporate international law into their domestic legal systems and it is a state's perception of international law which determines the way in which international law becomes part of municipal law. In other words, states differ in the way that their municipal courts are either required or allowed to give effect to international obligations.[1]

Before looking at what happens in practice, mention, albeit brief, must be made of the theories which have evolved on the relationship of municipal law to international law. The theorists traditionally have divided themselves into two principal schools—(i) the monistic school and (ii) the dualistic school.

MONISTIC SCHOOL

Monists have a unitary concept of law and see all law, and

---

[1] Strictly the way in which a state makes international law part of its domestic legislation is a matter of municipal law rather than international law.

consequently international law and municipal law, as an integral part of the same system. In the event of a conflict between international law and municipal law, most monists would contend that international law should unquestionably prevail.

DUALISTIC SCHOOL

Dualists see domestic law and international law as independent of each other. The two systems, it is maintained, regulate different subject-matter. International law regulates the relations of sovereign states while municipal law regulates affairs internal to the state, *e.g.* the relations of the executive *vis-à-vis* its citizens and the relations of individual citizens *vis-à-vis* each other. Accordingly, dualists hold that the two systems are mutually exclusive and can have no contact with and no effect on each other. If international law is applied within a state it is only because it has been expressly incorporated into municipal law. The question of primacy is not one to which dualists address themselves. Dualism, as formulated, does not admit that a conflict can arise between the international legal system and a municipal legal system.

Sir Gerald Fitzmaurice stepped into the debate between monists and dualists in the mid-fifties when he submitted what has become popularily known as the "Fitzmaurice compromise."[2] Fitzmaurice acknowledged that international law and municipal law have for the most part separate fields of operation and that each is supreme in its own domain. Nevertheless, on occasion they have a common field of application and, should a conflict arise, what is involved, Fitzmaurice concluded, is not a conflict of legal systems, but rather a conflict of obligations. If a state is, by its municipal law, unable to act in the manner required by international law, it is not its internal law which the municipal courts will uphold, which is called into question, but rather the state's liability on the international plane for the non-fulfilment of its international obligations.[3]

In practice the differences between international law and a particular municipal system are minimised and every effort is made to achieve a harmonisation between the two systems. In the United Kingdom there exists, for example, a presumption in statutory interpretation that Parliament does not intend to infringe interna-

---

[2] Fitzmaurice, "The General Principles of International Law Considered from the Standpoint of the Rule of Law," 92 *Hague Recueil* 5.
[3] As illustrated in *Mortensen* v. *Peters* (1906) 8 F. (J.) 93—see below p. 36.

tional law.[4] In the United States such a presumption is an established principle of interpretation.[5]

What is meant if it is said that a country is monistic or dualistic in its approach to international law? Simply it is monistic if it accepts international law automatically as part of its municipal law and does not demand an express act of the legislature, whereas if a state is dualistic international law will only become part of its municipal law if it has been expressly adopted as such by way of a legislative act.

MUNICIPAL LAW IN INTERNATIONAL LAW

On the international scene international law is unequivocably supreme, as is borne out by both arbitral and judicial decisions and international conventions which reflect accepted international law.

In the *Alabama Claims Arbitration*[6] the arbitration tribunal concluded that neither municipal legislative provisions, nor the absence of them, could be pleaded as a defence for non-compliance with international obligations, whilst the Permanent Court of International Justice in an advisory opinion held that:

"... a State which has contracted valid international obligations is bound to make in its legislation such modifications as may be necessary to ensure the fulfilment of the obligations undertaken."[7]

Article 13 of the Draft Declaration on Rights and Duties of States 1949 provides that:

"Each State has the duty to carry out in good faith its obligations arising from treaties and other sources of international law, and it may not invoke provisions in its constitution or its laws as an excuse for failure to perform this duty."[8]

---

[4] *E.g. Salomon* v. *Commissioners of Customs and Excise* [1967] 2 Q.B. 116 (C.A.)—Lord Diplock at 143; also *Post Office* v. *Estuary Radio Ltd.* [1968] 2 Q.B. 740 (C.A.)

[5] *Murray* v. *Schooner Charming Betsy* 6 U.S. (2 Cranch.) 64 at 118 (1804). Also *Lauritzen* v. *Larsen* 345 U.S. 571 at 578 (1953). For Canadian authority see, for example, *Bloxem* v. *Favre* 8 P.C. 101 at 107 (1883).

[6] Moore, 1 Int. Arb. 495 (1872).

[7] *Exchange of Greek and Turkish Populations Case*, P.C.I.J. Rep., ser. B, No. 10, p. 6 at p. 20. (1925) See also *Free Zones of Upper Savoy and Gex*, P.C.I.J. Rep., ser. A/B, No. 46 (1932).

[8] This was prepared by the International Law Commission—Y.B.I.L.C., 1949, pp. 286, 288.

Article 27 of the Vienna Convention on the Law of Treaties[9] stipulates that "a party may not invoke the provisions of internal law as justification for its failure to perform a treaty."

The overriding conclusion to be extracted from the foregoing is that a state may not evade fulfilling an international obligation because of either the presence or absence of an internal legislative provision. Such must be the standpoint on the international level if international law is to succeed and maintain credibility.

International tribunals may, of course, choose to look at municipal legislation. Domestic legislation may be employed as evidence of a state's compliance or non-compliance with international obligations. Consideration of municipal law may make it possible to ascertain what a state's stance is on a particular issue at a given time.[10]

Turning to the municipal scene, what is the position when municipal tribunals are confronted with international law? How do they apply it? What happens in the event of a conflict between international law and municipal legislation?

INTERNATIONAL LAW BEFORE MUNICIPAL COURTS

United Kingdom Practice

There is no written constitution defining the internal status within Britain of international law.[11]

Customary International Law

Britain essentially adopts a monistic approach to customary international law. This is, however, an over simplification. Although it was maintained by Lord Talbot in *Buvot* v. *Barbuit*[12] the true British view was best presented by Lord Alverstone in the *West Rand Central Gold Mining Co. Case*[13]:

"It is quite true that whatever has received the common

---

[9] U.K.T.S. 58 (1980) Cmnd. 7964; 8 ILM 679 (1969). See also Chapter 10 below.
[10] Highlighted by the Permanent Court of International Justice in *Polish Upper Silesia*, P.C.I.J. Rep., ser. A, No. 7, p. 22 (1926) and *Brazilian Loans Case*, P.C.I.J. Rep., ser. A, No. 21, pp. 124–125 (1929).
[11] *C.f.* F.R.G.—Article 25 German Constitution. "The general rules of public international law are an integral part of federal law. They shall take precedence over the laws and shall directly create rights and duties for the inhabitants of the federal territory." See also Articles 65 and 66 Dutch Constitution 1953 and 1956.
[12] (1737) Cases t. Talbot 281, "That the law of nations, in its full extent was part of the law of England" and reaffirmed by Lord Mansfield in *Triquet* v. *Bath* (1764) 3 Burr. 1478. Court of King's Bench.
[13] [1905] 2 K.B. 391. (K.B.D.).

consent of civilised nations must have received the assent of our country, and that to which we have assented along with other nations in general may properly be called international law, and as such will be acknowledged and applied by our municipal tribunals when legitimate occasion arises for those tribunals to decide questions to which the doctrines of international law may be relevant. But any doctrine so invoked must be one really accepted as binding between nations, and the international law sought to be applied must, like anything else, be proved by satisfactory evidence, which must shew either that the particular proposition put forward has been recognised and acted upon by our own country, or that it is of such a nature, and has been so widely and generally accepted, that it can hardly be supposed that any civilised State would repudiate it . . . that the law of nations forms part of the law of England, ought not to be construed so as to include as part of the law of England opinions of text-writers upon a question as to which there is no evidence that Great Britain has ever assented, and *a fortiori* if they are contrary to the principles of her laws as declared by her Courts."[14]

Lord Alverstone's emphasis was on assent and the need to demonstrate the existence and scope of any particular alleged rule of customary international law—an emphasis which has been reflected consistently in subsequent cases. In *The Cristina Case*[15] Lord Macmillan held that municipal courts before acknowledging customary international law as part of domestic law should initially be satisfied that it (*i.e.* custom) had the hallmark of consent.[16] In *Chung Chi Cheung* v. *The King*[17] Lord Atkin said:

"It must always be remembered that, so far, at any rate, as the courts of this country are concerned, international law has no validity save in so far as its principles are accepted and adopted by our own domestic law. There is no external power that imposes its rule upon our own code of substantive law or procedure. The Courts acknowledge the existence of a body of rules which nations accept amongst themselves. On any judicial issue they seek to ascertain what the relevant rule is, and, having found it, they will treat it as incorporated into the

[14] *Ibid.* at 406.
[15] [1938] A.C. 485.
[16] *Ibid.* at 490. See also Lord Wright at 502.
[17] [1939] A.C. 160.

domestic law, so far as it is not inconsistent with rules enacted by Statutes or finally declared by their tribunals."[18]

Lord Denning in *Thakrar* v. *Home Secretary*[19] said that "In my opinion, the rules of international law only become part of our law in so far as they are accepted and adopted by us."[20] However, three years later in *Trendtex Trading Corporation* v. *Central Bank of Nigeria*[21] in considering the two schools, incorporation or transformation, Lord Denning concluded that the doctrine of incorporation was correct. However, that case dealing with sovereign immunity predated the 1978 Sovereign Immunity Act and therefore was governed by judicial decisions. The real question was whether the rules of precedent applying to rules of English law incorporating customary international law meant that any change in international law could only be recognised by the English courts (in the absence of legislation) within the scope of the doctrine of *stare decisis*. Lord Denning concluded otherwise and held that:

> "International law knows no rule of *stare decisis*. If this court today is satisfied that the rule of international law on a subject has changed from what it was 50 or 60 years ago . . . it can give effect to that change—and apply the change in our English law—without waiting for the House of Lords to do it."[22]

The decision in *Trendtex* would appear to allow an exception from an application of the principle of *stare decisis* in cases where international law has changed since the earlier decision was delivered. In the light of the *Trendtex Case* it seems that if international law has changed then the "new" international law may be applied in spite of the earlier municipal decision.

Rules of Customary International Law Inconsistent with Municipal Law

Any rule of customary international law which is inconsistent with a British Statute will not be enforced in the British courts. The domestic legislation will be upheld while the state will incur liability on the international scene as in *Mortensen* v. *Peters*,[23] when the Court quashed an appeal against a conviction made under a

---

[18] *Ibid.* at 167.
[19] [1974] 1 Q.B. 684.
[20] *Ibid.* at 701.
[21] [1977] Q.B. 529.
[22] *Ibid.* at 554.
[23] (1906) 8 F. (J.) 93.

domestic legislative provision which allegedly contravened customary international law. The Court in dismissing the appeal unanimously held, *inter alia*, that the relationship of municipal legislation and international law was one of construction and "of construction only" and that it was not the function of the Court:

> "to decide whether an Act of the Legislature is *ultra vires* as in contravention of generally acknowledged principles of international law . . . an Act of Parliament duly passed by Lords and Commons and assented to by the King, is supreme, and we are bound to give effect to its terms."[24]

The Court concluded that whilst there was a presumption against Parliament violating international law:

> " . . . it is only a presumption, and as such it must always give way to the language used if it is clear, and also to all counter presumptions which may legitimately be had in view in determining, on ordinary principles, the true meaning and intent of the legislation. Express words will of course be conclusive, and so also will plain implication."[25]

Customary international law will be treated as part of United Kingdom law provided that there is no contrary judicial decision of a higher court, save possibly the exception admitted by the *Trendtex Case*, or contrary statutory provision.

Treaties

A treaty does not become part of British domestic law unless and until it is specifically incorporated as such by a legislative measure, an enabling Act. The United Kingdom adopts therefore a dualistic approach to treaty law.

Why is an enabling Act required? Treaty-making power is an executive function coming within the royal prerogative. The legislature does not participate and its consent is not required before Britain can undertake international obligations. An enabling Act is a safeguard against the possible abuse of executive authority as it prevents the executive from using its treaty-making competence to introduce domestic legislation without going through the necessary

[24] *Ibid.* at 100.
[25] *Ibid.* at 103.

Parliamentary procedures. Treaties regulating the conduct of war and the cession of territory do not demand an Enabling Act.[26]

In practice, the Enabling Act to give internal effect to a treaty will be passed before the treaty is ratified and the opportunity will be taken then to bring municipal law into accordance with international law. There is also the practice known as the Ponsonby Rule whereby a treaty is, following signature, laid for 21 days before both Houses of Parliament before ratification, publication and circulation in the United Kingdom Treaty Series.[27] Although expedient to provide this opportunity for discussion, it is not legally required.[28] The reason for the requirement of an Enabling Act was spelt out in the *Parlement Belge Case*[29] by Sir Robert Phillimore when he concluded that to recognise the immunity granted by a Convention[30] to a vessel other than a public war ship as being enforceable in the municipal courts would be " ... a use of the treaty-making prerogative of the Crown which I believe to be without precedent, and in principle contrary to the laws of the constitution."[31]

In the event of a conflict between a domestic statute and a treaty the domestic legislative measure will prevail. Such is the case with the European Convention on Human Rights[32] which is not part of British municipal law and although domestic legislation should be construed to be in conformity with the Convention if an Act of Parliament should contain provisions contrary to the Convention, then it would prevail. As Lord Denning said in 1975 when considering the position of the Convention in English law:

> "[T]he Court can and should take the Convention into account. They should take it into account whenever interpreting a statute which affects the rights and liberties of the individual. It is to be assumed that the Crown, in taking its part in legislation,

[26] Treaties involving the cession of territory may be an exception to the principle that Parliamentary consent is not required for a treaty. See McNair, *Treaties*, p. 97, "it is unlikely that the Crown will agree to cede any territory without being sure that Parliament would approve, or, if in doubt, without inserting a clause making the cession dependent upon Parliamentary approval."

[27] *Hansard*, H.C.Deb., Vol. 171, cols. 2003–2004 (April 1, 1924.)

[28] *E.g.* the Rule was not applied when the United Kingdom accepted the compulsory jurisdiction of the I.C.J. there being no requirement of ratification—*Hansard*, H.C.Deb., Vol. 578, cols. 1145–1146 (November 27, 1957.)

[29] (1878–79) 4 P.D. 129. Probate, Divorce and Admiralty Division.

[30] Postal Convention Regulating Communications by Post (Belgium and Britain) 1876.

[31] *Supra* n. 29 at 154. See also *Walker* v. *Baird* [1892] A.C. 491; *The Republic of Italy* v. *Hambros Bank Ltd.* [1950] Ch. 314 and *McWhirter* v. *A.G.* [1972] C.M.L.R. 882, also illustrate the need for an Enabling Act.

[32] Dealt with in more detail in Chapter 9 below.

would do nothing which was in conflict with treaties. So the Court should now construe the Immigration Act 1971 so as to be in conformity with a Convention and not against it."[33]

British courts do not enjoy the power to deem a statute unconstitutional, a fact reaffirmed by Lord Denning in the above case when he took the opportunity to correct what he had suggested in an earlier case, namely that if an Act of Parliament did not conform to the Convention he would be inclined to hold it invalid.[34] Such a suggestion, he conceded, "was a very tentative statement, but it went too far."[35] A more rigid dualistic approach is demonstrated by the Scottish courts:

"If the Convention does not form part of the municipal law, I do not see why the Court should have regard to it at all. It was His Majesty's government in 1950 which was a High Contracting Party to the Convention. The Convention has been ratified by the United Kingdom, but ... its provisions cannot be regarded as having the force of law ... Under our Constitution, it is the Queen in Parliament who legislates and not Her Majesty's government, and the Court does not require to have regard to acts of Her Majesty's government when interpreting the law."[36]

There is, therefore, within Britain judicial support for both a broad approach allowing unimplemented treaties persuasive effect and a narrow restrictive approach whereby only implemented treaties may be referred to by the Courts. A Statute, even one arising from an international treaty, will always prevail over a rule of international law.[37]

Nevertheless, there is a presumption in the United Kingdom that the Crown does not intend to violate international law and domestic

---

[33] *R. v. Secretary of State for the Home Department and Another, ex p. Bhajan Singh* [1976] Q.B. 198 at 207. See *R. v. Chief Immigration Officer, ex p. Bibi* [1976] 1 W.L.R. 979 at 984 (A.C.)

[34] This was said in *Birdi v. Secretary of State for Home Affairs*, 1975, unreported, but quoted in *Singh, ibid.* at 207.

[35] *Ibid.*

[36] *Kaur v. Lord Advocate*, 1981, S.L.T. 322. Lord Ross at 329. See also W. Finnie, "The European Convention on Human Rights. Domestic Status," 25 *J.L.S.S.* 434 and Note 98 *L.Q.Rev.* 183 (1982).

[37] *Callco Dealings Limited v. Inland Revenue Commrs.* [1962] A.C. 1 at 19 (H.L.) Lord Simonds at 19. See also Lord Reid at 22 where it was held that the only person entitled to complain against such a breach of treaty is the other party, even if the rights of private persons are adversely affected by violation.

legislation will be construed as being in conformity with international law.[38]

Membership of the EEC

The relationship between European Community law and British domestic law is no different in kind from the general problem of international treaty law and domestic law. Britain joined the European Communities when she signed a treaty with the six original members and the other applicant states. Community law, however, did not become part of British law until the 1972 European Communities Act was passed. As an Act it is not of "superior" force and it enjoys no more legal weight than any other domestic Statute.[39]

Executive Certificate

The executive certificate is a statement issued by the Foreign Office relating to "certain categories of questions of fact in the field of international affairs."[40] A certificate may stipulate, for instance, whether a particular foreign state or government is recognised by Britain, whether a particular person is entitled to diplomatic immunity or the existence and scope of British jurisdiction in a foreign country. An executive certificate is accepted as conclusive by the courts as was held in *The Fagernes*,[41] *Duff Development Co.* v. *Government of Kelantan*[42] and *Post Office* v. *Estuary Radio Ltd.*[43] The Courts still, however, determine what is the effect of such a factual situation, although they may not examine the basis on which the Foreign Office made its decision.

United States Practice

American law, with its roots in the English legal system, adopts a similar attitude to international law as that adopted by Britain, that is, with respect to customary international law, the United States is monistic in its approach and dualistic in respect of treaties.

---

[38] *Salomon* v. *Commissioners of Customs and Excise* [1967] 2 Q.B. 116 (C.A.), Lord Diplock at 143, and *Post Office* v. *Estuary Radio Ltd.* [1968] 2 Q.B. 740 (C.A.)

[39] The relationship of European Community law to British law, the provisions of the European Communities Act and the possible outcome of a conflict between a subsequent domestic legislative measure and earlier Community provisions are all thoroughly explored by L. Collins, *European Community Law in the United Kingdom* (3rd ed., 1984)

[40] L. Oppenheim, *International Law* (1967) Vol. I, para. 357(a).

[41] [1927] 311, 324.

[42] [1924] A.C. 797 (H.L.).

[43] [1968] 2 Q.B. 740.

Customary International Law

Judicial decisions confirm that customary international law is part of United States law.

Chief Justice Marshall in *The Nercide*[44] declared that in the absence of an Act of Congress the Court was bound by the law of nations which was part of the law of the land, while Justice Gray in 1900 pronounced:

> "International law is part of our law, and must be ascertained and administered by the courts of justice of appropriate jurisdiction, as often as questions of right depending upon it are duly presented for their determination."[45]

This acceptance of customary international law was, however, qualified:

> "[T]his rule of international law is one which prize courts, administering the law of nations, are bound to take judicial notice of, and to give effect to, in the absence of any treaty or other public act of their own government in relation to the matter."[46]

Customary international law is accepted without any legislative measure as part of American law provided there is neither a domestic judicial decision or a domestic legislative measure to the contrary. In the event of a conflict between alleged international law and municipal legislation, the domestic courts will uphold the municipal provisions:

> "International practice is law only in so far as we adopt it, and like our common law or statute law it bends to the will of the Congress. . . . There is one ground only upon which a federal court may refuse to enforce an Act of Congress and that is when the act is held to be unconstitutional. The act may contravene recognised principles of international law, but that affords no more basis for judicial disregard of it than it does for executive disregard of it."[47]

What is the internal status of customary international law?

---

[44] 9 Cr. 388 (U.S. 1815).
[45] *The Paquete Habana* 175 U.S. 677, 700 (1900).
[46] *Ibid.* at 708.
[47] *Schroeder* v. *Bissell* 5 F (2d) 838 (1925) (U.S. Dist. Court D. Conn).

Customary international law is accepted as federal law and its determination by the federal courts is binding on the state courts.[48]

Treaty Law

Under the American Constitution, the President has "Power by and with the Advice and Consent of the Senate, to make Treaties, provided two-thirds of the Senators present concur."[49]

Unlike in Britain, the American legislature participates in the treaty-making process. The President, in the light of the Constitution, has the power to make a treaty, but he may only ratify a treaty after the Senate has given its advice and approval. "All treaties made or which shall be made under the Authority of the U.S. shall be the supreme law of the land."[50]

What is the status of a treaty within the United States? "Supreme" only places treaties on an equal footing with Federal Statutes.[51] In the event of a conflict between a treaty and a subsequent statute, the latter prevails. This was made quite clear by the Supreme Court in *Edye* v. *Robertson*,[52] when it refuted the contention that an Act of Congress which conflicted with an earlier United States treaty should be declared invalid. The Court unanimously held that a treaty was a law of the land, as an Act of Congress was, and that there was nothing which made a treaty "irrepealable or unchangeable" and that the Constitution gave "it no superiority over an Act of Congress in this respect, which may be repealed or modified by an Act of a later date . . . " Congress, of course, does not enjoy the competence to act on the treaty itself and thus Congress cannot repeal a treaty. What Congress may do, however, is to enact legislation which will subsequently be determined as being inconsistent with the law as previously represented.

A treaty provision cannot "be rendered negatory in any part of the United States by municipal ordinances or State laws."[53] However, a later treaty provision will not be treated as having repealed by implication an earlier Statute unless "the two are absolutely incompatible and the Statute cannot be enforced without

---

[48] A.L.I. Restatement of the Law Foreign Relations Law of the United States (Revised) Tentative Draft No. 1 (1980) p. 51, 131 at 3. This is the prevailing view. It has not always been so. State and federal courts decided international law issues for themselves and consequently issues of international law were determined differently by courts in different states and the federal courts.

[49] Article II (2).

[50] Article 6 U.S. Constitution.

[51] *Edye* v. *Robertson* 112 U.S. 580 at 599 (1884).

[52] *Ibid.*

[53] *Asakura* v. *City of Seattle* 265 U.S. 332 at 341 (1924).

antagonising the treaty."[54] A treaty is not repealed or modified by a subsequent federal Statute unless that is the clearly expressed intention of Congress.[55]

The presumption exists when interpreting domestic legislation that Congress did not intend to infringe international law and that acts of Congress should be construed as conforming to international law. Congress strives to interpret acts of Congress so that they do not conflict with earlier treaty provisions. Nevertheless, in *Diggs* v. *Schultz*,[56] although recognising that the Byrd Amendment allowing imports contrary to the U.N. Security Council embargo on Rhodesian products was in blatant disregard of United States treaty obligations, the Court, nevertheless, concluded that under the American constitutional scheme Congress could denounce treaties if it saw fit to do so and that there was nothing other branches of government could do about it.

In the United States a distinction is made between *self-executing treaties* and *non self-executing treaties*.

Self-executing treaties are automatically part of American domestic law—*i.e.* no implementing legislation is required—whereas *non self-executing treaties* are not incorporated into domestic law until the necessary enabling legislation has been passed. Some provisions of an international agreement may be self-executing, while other provisions in the same agreement may be non self-executing. The distinction was initially made in *Foster and Elam* v. *Neilson*[57] when Chief Justice Marshall submitted:

> "A treaty is in its nature a contract between two nations, not a legislative act. It does not generally effect of itself, the object to be accomplished, especially so far as its operation is intra-territorial; but is carried into execution by the sovereign power of the respective parties to the instrument.
>
> In the United States a different principle is established. Our Constitution declares a treaty to be the law of the land. It is, consequently, to be regarded in courts of justice as equivalent to an act of the legislature, whenever it operates of itself without the aid of any legislative provision. But when the terms of the stipulation import a contract, when either of the parties engages to perform a particular act, the treaty addresses itself to the political, not the judicial department; and the legislature

---

[54] *Johnson* v. *Browne* 205 U.S. 309 at 321 (1907).
[55] *Cook* v. *The United States* 288 U.S. 102 at 119–120 (1933).
[56] 470 F (2d) 461 (1972).
[57] 27 U.S. (2 Pet.) 253 at 314 (1829).

must execute the contract before it can become a rule for the court."[58]

Similarly, in *Sei Fujii* v. *California*[59] it was said that in order to determine whether a treaty is self-executing, courts must look to "the intent of the signatory parties as manifested by the language of the instrument, and, if the instrument is uncertain, recourse may be had to the circumstances surrounding its execution" and that "for a treaty provision to be operative without further implementing legislation and have statutory effect and force, it must appear that the framers of the treaty intended to prescribe a rule that, standing alone, would be enforceable in the courts."

The determining factor as to whether a treaty provision will be self-executing within the United States is the intention of the treaty framers. If the agreement is silent and the intention of the United States is unclear, account must be taken of relevant circumstances surrounding its conclusion such as any statement issued by the President or any views expressed by the Senate. A treaty provision, to be self-executing, must therefore be:

unambiguous,
certain, and
not forward-looking

(*i.e.* legally complete and not dependent on subsequent legislation for its implementation).[60]

Generally, agreements which can be readily given effect by executive or judicial bodies, federal or state, without further federal legislation are deemed self-executing, unless a contrary intention is manifest. Treaties covering issues on which Congress has regulated extensively are more likely to be interpreted as non self-executing.

Self-executing treaties are advantageous in that they prevent delay in the execution of obligations and they obviate the need (i) to include the participation of the House of Representatives (excluded from the treaty-making process by the Constitution), and (ii) to further consult the Senate after having received its consent under the two-thirds majority rule.

Although there is no hard and fast rule as to what may and may

---

[58] The treaty in *Foster* v. *Neilson* which Chief Justice Marshall held not to be self-executing was later held by him to be self-executing, after the Spanish text was placed before the Court. *United States* v. *Percheman* 32 U.S. (7 Pet.) 51 (1833).

[59] 242 P (2d) 617 (1952); 19 I.L.R. 312 (1952) Supreme Court of California.

[60] Hence in *Sei Fujii, supra*, the provisions of the Preamble and Articles 1, 55 and 56 of the United Nations were held not to be self-executing as they lacked "the mandatory quality and definitions which would indicate an intent to create justiciable rights in private persons immediately upon ratification," but rather were "framed as a promise of future action by member nations."

not be the subject of a self-executing treaty, there nevertheless appears to be a generally assumed principle that "an international agreement cannot take effect as domestic law without implementation by Congress if the agreement would do what lies within the exclusive law-making power of Congress under the Constitution."[61]

Executive Agreements[62]

Executive agreements are international agreements entered into by the President without the advice and consent of Senate. Executive agreements are nevertheless regarded as being of the same force as a treaty and thereby, under international law, can effectively bind the United States. The validity of an executive agreement was upheld in *U.S.* v. *Belmont*[63] and in *U.S.* v. *Pink*.[64] In the latter case, it was held that "A treaty is a law of the Land under the supremacy clause (Article VI, cl. 2) of the Constitution. Such international compacts and agreements as the Litvinoff Agreement have a similar dignity."[65] Executive agreements may be superseded by subsequent federal legislation, but whether an executive agreement can supersede a prior treaty or Act of Congress is unclear.[66] The argument against such an effect is based essentially on the view that it would be inconceivable that the act of a single person, the President, could repeal an Act of Congress. However, an executive agreement is federal law and there are not varying degrees of status for federal law. "All constitutional acts of power, whether in the executive or the judicial department, have as much legal validity and obligation as if they proceeded from the legislature."[67] If an executive agreement was held to supersede a statute, Congress could re-enact the statute and thereby supersede the intervening executive agreement as domestic law.[68]

Attempts have been made to subject executive agreements to greater congressional control, *e.g.* the abortive Bricker Amendment

---

[61] A.L.I. Restatement—Tentative Draft No. 1, § 131 i—*cf. Missouri* v. *Holland* 252 U.S. 416 (1920). See below.

[62] For definition of executive agreement see letter of January 26, 1973 from C. Browne, Acting Legal Adviser to Carl Marcy, Chief of Staff of the Committee on Foreign Relations of the United States Senate—*Digest of U.S. Practice in International Law* 1973 at 187.

[63] 301 U.S. 324 (1937).

[64] 315 U.S. 203 (1942).

[65] *Ibid.* at 230.

[66] See, *e.g. United States* v. *Guy W. Capps Inc.*, 204 F (2d) 655 (1953) (U.S. Court of Appeals, 4th Circuit).

[67] *The Federalist* No. 64 (Jay) cited in *U.S.* v. *Pink, supra,* n. 64.

[68] A.L.I. Restatement (Revised) Tentative Draft No. 1, § 135 6. An executive agreement has been held to prevail over a subsequent inconsistent state law—*Territory of Hawaii* v. *Ho*, 41 Hawaii 565 (1957); 26 I.L.R. 557.

1953–54, Department of State Circular 175, 1955 (as amended 1966)[69] and more recently, the Case Act 1972, as amended 1977 and 1978. In 1972, the Case Act[70] required that "all international agreements other than treaties, thereafter entered into by the U.S., be transmitted to the Congress within 60 days after the execution thereof." The 1977 amendment requires that the procedure laid down in the Case Act be applied to agreements made by any department or agency of the United States Government and in 1978 this was extended to cover oral as well as written agreements.

Executive Congressional Agreements

An executive congressional agreement is an international agreement made by the President with the backing of a simple majority in both Houses of Congress. Such agreements have an advantage over the treaty as prescribed by the Constitution in that their use can simplify the legislative process. For example, a treaty goes to the Senate for consent and, then subsequently often, to the Senate again as well as to the House for implementation, whereas a congressional executive agreement can go to both houses in the first instance, and thus "consent" and implementation are achieved simultaneously.

Problems Peculiar to a Federal State

In a unitary state the authority to enter into international agreements and the competence (subject to legislative approval) to give internal effect to such legislation lies with the central government. This is not the case in a federal state where legislative competence is divided between the federal government and the individual states' governments. *Missouri* v. *Holland*[71] illustrates how legislation may be introduced by a back door. A 1913 Act of Congress designed to protect migratory wild fowl was declared to be outwith the legislative competence of the federal government, and within the residual power of the states' legislatures. In 1916 the United States concluded the Migratory Bird Act with Britain (acting on Canada's behalf) and the Act was given internal effect within the United States by the Migratory Bird Treaty Act 1918. Appeal was made to the Supreme Court following a district court's dismissal of a suit brought by the State of Missouri attempting to prevent Holland, a game warden, from enforcing the Migratory Bird Act. The Supreme Court held that the Act of Congress being challenged was valid as:

---

[69] Foreign Affairs Manual Vol. II.
[70] P.L. 92–403, 86 Stat. 619; 1 U.S. C.A. 112b.
[71] 252 U.S. 416 (1920).

> "[T]he power of the Federal Government to make and enforce treaties is not a limitation on the reserved powers of States, but is the existence of a power not reserved to the States under the 10th Amendment being both expressly granted to the United States and prohibited to the States."[72]

In other words, there was no limitation on what could be the subject-matter of a treaty and the enforcement of a treaty, regardless of subject-matter, falls within the exclusive competence of the federal government.

Missouri v. *Holland* may be contrasted with *Attorney-General for Canada* v. *Attorney-General for Ontario*.[73] Canada, like the United States, is a federal state and in 1937 the Judicial Committee of the Privy Council was required to give its opinion on what was the position when the federal government did not have the competence to give internal effect to international obligations which it had undertaken.[74] The Committee advised:

> "there is no such thing as treaty legislation as such. The distribution is based on classes of subjects; and as a treaty deals with a particular class so will the legislative power of performing it be ascertained;... the Dominion cannot, merely by making promises to foreign countries, clothe itself with legislative authority inconsistent with the Constitution."

and:

> "... so that while in a unitary State whose legislative possesses unlimited powers the problem is simple. Parliament will either fulfil or not treaty obligations imposed upon the State by its executive.
> The nature of the obligation does not affect the complete authority of the Legislature to make them law if it chooses ... in a federal State where legislative authority is limited ... or is divided up between different Legislatures ... the problem is complex.... The question is not how the obligation is

---

[72] *Ibid.* at 431.

[73] [1973] A.C. 326.

[74] Legislation designed to give effect within Canada to draft conventions adopted by the International Labour Organisation of the League of Nations was claimed to be invalid as the Dominion Parliament did not possess the competency to legislate on the subject-matter concerned.

formed, that is the function of the executive; but how is the obligation to be performed . . ."[75]

It may also happen in a federal state that the federal government will undertake an international obligation which is inconsistent with the law of a particular constituent part of the federation. As far as possible the "offending" legislation will be interpreted as being consistent with international law, but the general principle regarding such a conflict is that it is the central government and not the constituent state which will have to answer to the international community.[76]

Suggestion

The State Department's "suggestion" is the American counterpart of the British executive certificate. However, the suggestion does not confine itself to merely giving the facts, but may include comments on the situation and indicate the executive's attitude. Although not regarded as conclusive, the suggestion will be accepted as persuasive by the courts.

Act of State Doctrine[77]

What if a measure of a foreign state is contrary to international law? The act of state doctrine precludes the Court from inquiring into the validity of the public acts of a recognised foreign sovereign power within its own territory, "the Judicial Branch will not examine the validity of a taking of property within its own territory by a foreign sovereign government."[78]

The essence of the act of state doctrine is that the act of one independent government cannot be successfully questioned by the courts of another; redress of grievances by reason of such acts must be obtained through the means open to be availed of by sovereign powers as between themselves.[79] In other words, the judiciary abstains from giving a decision in deference to the executive so as not to embarrass the conduct of the executive foreign relations by questioning the acts of foreign states. Strict adherence to the act of

[75] *Supra*, n. 73 at 351, 352 and 347. The limited internal competence of the federal government was why Canada did not accede to the U.N. 1966 Covenants on Economic, Social and Cultural Rights and Civil and Political Rights until 1976.

[76] Reference *Re Offshore Mineral Rights* (B.C.) [1967] S.C.R. 792 at 821, *cf. Tyrer Case* (1978) 58 I.L.R. 339.

[77] Act of State has a different connotation in British constitutional law—an alien, who is injured abroad by an act authorised or subsequently approved by the Crown, has no remedy in English courts.

[78] *Banco Nacional de Cuba* v. *Sabbatino* 376 U.S. 398 at 428 (1964).

[79] *Underhill* v. *Hernandez* 168 U.S. 250 at 252 (1897).

state doctrine was maintained by the United States Supreme Court in the *Sabbatino Case*, even when the State Department had described the Cuban legislative measure as:

> "manifestly in violation of those principles of international law which has long been accepted by the free countries of the West. It is in its essence discriminatory, arbitrary and confiscatory."[80]

The outcome of the *Sabbatino Case* was that the Court gave effect to the Cuban decree in spite of its having been contrary to international law.

The act of state doctrine as understood in the *Sabbatino Case* has its basis in the separation of powers and the *raison d'être* of the *Sabbatino* position was the need to avoid conflict between the judiciary and the executive on decisions regarding the legal nature of foreign actions.

The *Sabbatino* decision prompted a response from Congress in the form of the "Hickenlooper Amendments" to the Foreign Assistance Act, whereby:

> "no court in the United States shall decline on the ground of the ... Act of State doctrine to make a determination on the merits giving effect to the principles of international law in a case in which a claim of title or other right to property is asserted by any party including a foreign State (or a party claiming through such State) based upon (or traced through) a confiscation or other taking ... by an act of that State in violation of the principles of international law."[81]

Accordingly, American courts may review the acts of foreign governments which violate international law and which affect property owned by American citizens. The State Department can express in a "suggestion" that the act of state is to apply in a particular case.

Judicial determination of the legality of the foreign act of state will not necessarily interfere with the executive's conduct of foreign affairs.[82]

In *Alfred Dunhill* v. *Republic of Cuba*,[83] the Legal Adviser to the

---

[80] *Ibid.* at 403.
[81] s. 620(e)(2) of the Foreign Assistance Act of 1965, Pub. L. No. 89–171; 301(d)(2), 79 Stat. 653, 659 as amended.
[82] See *Banco Nacional de Cuba* v. *First National City Bank* U.S. Supreme Court, 406 U.S. 759 (1972); 92 S.L.T. 1808.
[83] 425 U.S. 682 (1976).

State Department submitted a letter in which he stated that in the State Department's experience there was little support for the presumption "that adjudication of acts of foreign States in accordance with the relevant principles of international law would embarrass the conduct of foreign policy." Accordingly, he concluded that it would not cause embarrassment to the conduct of United States foreign policy if the Court demanded to overrule the holding in the *Sabbatino Case*.[84]

The act of state doctrine would not apply in respect of war crimes or offences over which there is universal jurisdiction. The act of state doctrine should be distinguished from the political question doctrine, *viz.* that there are certain national issues so sensitive that they are non-justiciable.[85] Cases which raise the political question doctrine are dismissed by the courts, unlike those involving the act of state doctrine which are adjudicated.

The act of state doctrine is one of American municipal law. There is no rule of international law which requires the application of the act of state doctrine.

---

[84] *Ibid.* Letter of Monroe Leigh, Legal Adviser, Department of State—printed as Appendix 706, 709, 710–11.

[85] *U.S.* v. *Sisson* 294 F. Supp. 515 (D. Mass. 1968) in which the Court concluded that a domestic tribunal was incapable of ascertaining facts pertaining during war and that the defendant had submitted an issue of a political character not within the jurisdiction of the Court. The defendant had invoked as his defence to a charge of refusing to serve in the United States armed forces that the United States operations in Vietnam were contrary to international law. On non-justiciability of political questions, see also *Baker* v. *Carr* 369 U.S. 186 (1962).

FURTHER READING

Cases and Materials

D.J. Harris, *Cases and Materials on International Law* (1983), Chapter 3.

L. Henkin, R. Pugh, O. Schachter and H. Smit, *International Law: Cases and Materials* (1980), Chapter 3.

J. Sweeny, C. Oliver and N. Leech, *The International Legal System: Cases and Materials* (1981), Chapter 1.

General Texts

M. Akehurst, *A Modern Introduction to International Law* (1982), Chapter 4.

I. Brownlie, *Principles of Public International Law* (1979), Chapter II.

L. Green, *International Law: A Canadian Perspective* (1984), Part I, §§32–47.

D.W. Greig, *International Law* (1976), Chapter 2.

J.G. Starke, *An Introduction to International Law* (1984), Chapter 4.

Chapter Four

INTERNATIONAL PERSONALITY

The possession of international personality means that an entity is a subject of international law and is "capable of possessing international rights and duties, and that it has the capacity to maintain its rights by bringing international claims."[1]

A subject of international law owes responsibilities to the international community and enjoys rights, the benefits of which may be claimed, and which, if denied, may be enforced to the extent recognised by the international legal system, via legal procedures, *i.e.* the entity will have procedural capacity.

Which entities have international legal personality?

The concept of international personality is neither static nor uniform:

> "The subjects of law in any legal system are not necessarily identical in their nature or in the extent of their rights, and their nature depends upon the needs of the community. Throughout its history, the development of international law has been influenced by the requirements of international life, and the progressive increase in the collective activities of States has already given rise to instances of action upon the international plane by certain entities which are not States."[2]

As international law has developed and expanded in scope, so "new" entities have been admitted as "actors" on the international scene. The personality enjoyed by such actors varies considerably.

States were once considered the exclusive subjects of international law:

> "Since the law of nations is based on the common consent of individual States, and not of individual human beings, States solely and exclusively are the subjects of international law."[3]

---

[1] *Reparations for Injuries Suffered in the Service of the United Nations*, I.C.J. Rep. 1949 p. 174.

[2] *Ibid.* at p. 178.

[3] L. Oppenheim, *International Law* (2nd ed., 1912).

Today, however, although they remain its primary subjects, they are no longer the exclusive subjects of the international legal system. Throughout this century, the scope of international legal personality has widened considerably as a consequence of the proliferation of international organisations and the greater international awareness of human rights. However, whilst states possess full international legal personality as an inherent attribute of their statehood, all other entities possessing personality do so only to the extent that states allow. Their personality is derived via states.

The personality of states may thus be characterised as *original* and that of other entities as *derivative*.

STATES

States are the principal persons of international law. International law is essentially the product of relations between states, be it through practice forming customary international law, or through international agreements (treaties). States alone may be parties to contentious cases before the International Court of Justice.[4] States alone enjoy the discretion as to whether or not to espouse a claim on behalf of a national who has allegedly been aggrieved by another state; and once a state does take up a claim the dispute is raised to the international level and becomes one between two states.[5] An individual cannot denounce his state's right to espouse a claim on his behalf should it choose to do so[6] and a state does not act as the agent of its nationals when negotiating a treaty.[7]

What is a State?

A "state" under international law is an entity which has a defined territory, a permanent population, is under the control of a government and engages in, or has the capacity to engage in, formal relations with other entities.[8]

The definition reflects the indices of statehood enunciated in the 1933 Montevideo Convention on Rights and Duties of States.[9] The Convention regarded as representing in general terms the requirements of statehood demanded by customary international law, was

---

[4] Article 34(1) Statute of the International Court of Justice.

[5] See, *e.g. Mavrommatis Palestine Concessions Case* P.C.I.J. Rep., ser. A, No. 2 (1924).

[6] *North American Dredging Company Case* 4 R.I.A.A. 26 at pp. 29 *et seq.* (1926).

[7] See, *e.g. Rustomjee* v. *The Queen* (1876) 1 Q.B.D. 487 at 492; and *Civilian War Claimants' Association Ltd.* v. *The King* [1932] A.C. 14 at 26 (H.L.).

[8] The American Law Institute: *Restatement of the Law, Foreign Relations Law of the United States (Revised) Tentative Draft No. 2* at §201.

[9] 164 L.N.T.S. 19; U.S.T.S. 881; 28 A.J.I.L., Supp., 75 (1934).

adopted by the Seventh International Conference of American States (15 Latin American and the United States):

> "The State as a person of international law should possess the following qualifications: (a) a permanent population; (b) a defined territory; (c) government; and (d) capacity to enter into relations with other States."[10]

Permanent Population

States are aggregates of individuals and accordingly a permanent population is a prerequisite condition of statehood. No minimum population is, however, required. Naura, with a population of 6,500 has been considered a state, as has Liechtenstein with a population of 20,000.

Defined Territory

States are territorial units and:

> "territorial sovereignty . . . involves the exclusive right to display the activities of a State. This right has a corollary, a duty: the obligation to protect within the territory the rights of other States, in particular their right to integrity and inviolability in peace and in war, together with the rights which each State may claim for its nationals in foreign territory. Without manifesting its territorial sovereignty in a manner corresponding to circumstances, the State cannot fulfil this duty. Territorial sovereignty cannot limit itself to its negative side, *i.e.* to excluding the activities of other States; for it serves to divide between the nations the space upon which human activities are employed, in order to assure them at all points the minimum of protection of which international law is the guardian . . . "[11]

Article 9 of the Montevideo Convention provides that:

> "The jurisdiction of States within the limits of national territory applies to all the inhabitants.
> Nationals and foreigners are under the same protection of the law and the national authorities and the foreigners may not claim rights other or more extensive than those of the nationals."

[10] Article 1, Montevideo Convention.
[11] *Island of Palmas Case* 2 R.I.A.A. 829, Judge Huber at 839 (1928).

However, while territory is necessary there is no prescribed minimum geographical size. The requirement of territory may be satisfied even if the entity's territorial boundaries are not precisely defined or are to some extent in dispute, *e.g.* Israel in 1948, Kuwait in 1963. This rule, that indefinite boundaries need not defect a claim to statehood, was noted by the Court in the *North Sea Continental Shelf Cases*:

"The appurtenance of a given area, considered as an entity, in no way governs the precise determination of its boundaries, any more than uncertainty as to boundaries can affect territorial rights. There is for instance no rule that the land frontiers of a State must be fully delimited and defined, and often in various places and for long periods they are not . . . "[12]

A Government

Statehood must be evidenced by the establishment of an effective government, *i.e.* one independent of any other authority and one which enjoys legislative and administrative competence. Non-dependence was stressed by the International Committee of Jurists in 1920 in its Report on the status of Finland. The Committee highlighted the difficulty of ascertaining the actual date when Finland became in the legal sense a sovereign state, but concluded that it certainly was not one:

"until a stable political organisation had been created, and until the public authorities had become strong enough to assert themselves throughout the territories of the State without the assistance of foreign troops. It would appear that it was in May 1918, that the civil war ended and that the foreign troops began to leave the country, so that from that time onwards it was possible to re-establish order and normal political and social life, little by little."[13]

An established state's statehood will not be nullified if it is without an effective government for a period of time, *e.g.* during a civil war. Nor does military occupation, *e.g.* Germany's occupation of the European states during World War II, terminate statehood.

Capacity to Enter into International Relations

This is an important indice of statehood, but its realisation

---

[12] I.C.J. Rep. 1969, p. 3 at 32.
[13] L.N.O.J., Special Supp. No. 3, p. 3 (1920).

depends on the response of other actors on the international stage. The satisfaction of the first three criteria is essentially factual, but fulfilment of this criterion depends on recognition:

> "The political existence of the State is independent of recognition by the other States. Even before recognition the State has the right to defend its integrity and independence, to provide for its conservation and prosperity, and consequently to organise itself as it sees fit, to legislate upon its interests, administer its services, and to define the jurisdiction and competence of its courts.
> The exercise of these rights has no other limitation than the exercise of the rights of other States according to international law."[14]

In other words, an entity may have the capacity to enter into foreign relations, but should other states decline to enter into relations with it, the entity in question is denied the opportunity to demonstrate this capacity in practice. For example, Southern Rhodesia, a British self-governing territory until it declared unilateral independence from Britain in November 1965, had a population, territory, a government and the capacity to enter into relations with other states. However, no other state was willing to enter into relations with Southern Rhodesia. Southern Rhodesia was refused recognition as a state by the rest of the international community.[15] Similarly, governments have consistently refused to enter into relations with the Transkei. The Transkei territory was declared by South Africa in 1976 to be a "sovereign and independent State," but the United Nations General Assembly subsequently adopted a resolution rejecting the "independence" as "invalid."[16] An entity which possesses the ability to conduct foreign relations does not terminate its statehood if it voluntarily hands over all or part of the conduct of its foreign relations to another state, *e.g.* San Marino (Italy), Monaco (France). Another "mini" European state is Liechtenstein, which operates within the Swiss economic system

---

[14] Article 3, Montevideo Convention, *supra* n. 9.
[15] See Security Council Resolution of November 12, 1965, Resolution 216 (1965) S.C.O.R., 20th Year, Resolutions and Decisions, p. 8 and Security Council Resolution of November 20, 1965, Resolution 217 (1965) S.C.O.R., 20th Year, Resolutions and Decisions, p. 8 in which the Smith regime was characterised as illegal, the declaration of independence as of "no legal validity" and U.N. members were called upon to refrain from assisting the "illegal racist minority regime."
[16] G.A. Resolution, G.A.O.R., 31st Sesson, Supp. 39, p. 10.

and has delegated a number of sovereign powers to Switzerland, but nevertheless is still recognised as a sovereign state.[17] Similarly, the personality of a protected state which existed before the conclusion of the agreement establishing its dependent status is not extinguished. See, for example, *Nationality Decrees in Tunis and Morocco Case*[18] and *Rights of Nationals of the United States in Morocco Case*.[19] Such relationships were characteristic of the British and French Empires, and most were terminated during the decolonisation movement which gathered momentum after World War II. Nor does participation in, for instance, a regional economic organisation, *e.g.* the European Economic Community, negate the statehood of the individual members.

Existing states may refuse "statehood" to an entity which has attained a characteristic of statehood in violation of international law, *e.g.* the acquisition of territory by the use of force contrary to Article 2(4) of the United Nations Charter, or to the principle of non-intervention.[20] However, in most instances, whether or not there has been an unlawful threat or use of force will be disputed, and generally it is not an issue which will be authoritatively resolved, *e.g.* Indian intervention in Bangladesh was by many governments deemed to be illegal whilst others argued to the contrary, justifying India's action as supporting the principle of self-determination. Territory acquired by the legitimate use of force, *e.g.* in self-defence, and then annexed from the aggressor, *may* (emphasis added) be an exception to the non-recognition of conquest rule.

Political self-determination, *i.e.* the principle whereby the political future of a colony or similar non-independent territory is determined in accordance with the wishes of its inhabitants, has, particularly since the 1960s, been taken into account in issues of statehood. The principle although not one of customary international law "is a formative principle of great potency … "[21] The

---

[17] Although denied admission to the League of Nations on the grounds that she could not discharge all the international obligatons which would be imposed upon her by the Covenant, Leichtenstein has been a party to a case before the I.C.J. (the *Nottebohm Case*, 1955). Liechtenstein has not applied for UN membership.

[18] P.C.I.J. Rep., ser. B, No. 4 (1923).

[19] I.C.J. Rep. 1952, p. 176.

[20] See G.A. Resolution 2625 (XXV) "Declaration on Principles of International Law Concerning Friendly Relations and Co-operation among States in Accordance with the Charter of the United Nations," G.A.O.R., 25th Session, Supp. 28 (A/2028), p. 121 (1970); 65 A.J.I.L. 243 (1970).

[21] Schwarzenburger, *Manual of International Law* (6th ed., 1976) at p. 59.

Declaration on the Granting of Independence to Colonial Territories and Peoples[22] articulated the principle and paragraph 2 reads:

> "All peoples have a right to self-determination; by virtue of
> that right they freely determine their political status and freely
> pursue their economic, social and cultural development."

The aim of paragraph 2 was identified in the *Western Sahara Case*.[23]
It was acknowledged therein "that the application of the right of
self-determination requires a free and genuine expression of the will
of the peoples concerned."[24] Judge Dillard in a separate opinion
(though concurring in the Court's opinion) stated that:

> "It seemed hardly necessary to make more explicit the cardinal
> restraint which the legal right of self-determination imposes.
> The restraint may be captured in a single sentence. It is for the
> people to determine the destiny of the territory and not the
> territory the destiny of the people . . . "[25]

However, Resolution 1514 does not purport to negate a title to
colonial and similar non-independent territory, which does not
reflect the wishes of its people, but rather emphasises that
"immediate steps" should be taken to ensure independence is
attained in accordance with self-determination. The emergence of
self-determination, as a cardinal principle in shaping the political
future of a colonial or similar non-independent territory, means that
such territories can no longer be considered as mere adjuncts of the
administering power. They have according to the 1970 Declaration
on Principles of International Law:

> "a status separate and distinct from the territory of the State
> administering it; and such separate and distinct status under
> the Charter [i.e. U.N. Charter] shall exist until the people of the
> colony or non self-governing territory have exercised their right
> of self-determination in accordance with the Charter, and
> particularly its purposes and principles."[26]

---

[22] G.A. Resolution 1514 (XV). December 14, 1960, G.A.O.R., 15th Session, Supp. 16,
p. 66. Harris, p. 95.
[23] Advisory Opinion. I.C.J. Rep. 1975, p. 12—see also Harris, pp. 97–101 for a fuller
exposition of self-determination.
[24] *Ibid.* at p. 32.
[25] *Ibid.* at p. 122.
[26] *Supra*, n. 20.

This separate identity of an administered peoples is further reflected in several legal statements relating to the status of South West Africa (Namibia).[27]

South West Africa was placed under a "C" Mandate at the conclusion of World War I. Mandates were introduced as a novel type of administration for those territories taken from defeated powers and "inhabited by peoples not yet able to stand by themselves under the strenuous conditions of the modern world."[28] After the conclusion of World War II the mandate system was replaced by that of trusteeship.[29] South Africa, however, refused to place South West Africa under that trusteeship system and this precipitated much political and legal argument on the status of South West Africa.[30] In the 1950 Opinion, Judge McNair pronounced that the system involved a:

> "new institution—a new relationship between territory and its inhabitants on the one hand and the government which represents them internationally on the other—a new species of international government which does not fit into the old conception of sovereignty and which is alien to it."[31]

The sovereignty, Judge McNair maintained, was held to be in abeyance until the inhabitants of the territory obtained recognition as an independent State. The issues before the Court concerned the responsibilities and duties of South Africa but, against the backcloth of the self-determination movement, there was a move away from the traditional view that a mandated/trusteeship territory only achieved international recognition on attaining independence to one according such an entity at least a degree of international status; a view which was articulated by Judge Ammoun when he concluded that:

[27] For the background and details of the mandated and trusteeship systems established by the League of Nations and the United Nations respectively. See Harris, pp. 104–114.

[28] Covenant of the League of Nations, Article 22.

[29] The system applied only to 11 territories—10 former mandates and Somelia taken from Italy. No other territories were brought into the system as was envisaged by Article 77(1) UN Charter. All with the exception of the Pacific Islands north of the Equator, have become independent states or have been incorporated into independent states.

[30] *International Status of South West Africa Case*, I.C.J. Rep. 1950, p. 128; *Legal Consequences for States of the Continued Presence of South Africa in Namibia (South West Africa) Notwithstanding Security Council Resolution 276 (1970). Advisory Opinion*, I.C.J. Rep. 1971, p. 16.

[31] *Ibid.* p. 150.

"Namibia, even at the periods when it had been reduced to the status of a German colony or was subject to the South African Mandate, possessed a legal personality which was denied to it only by the law now obsolete.... It nevertheless constituted a subject of law ... possessing national sovereignty but lacking the exercise thereof.... Sovereignty ... did not cease to belong to the people subject to mandate. It had simply, for a time, been rendered inarticulate and deprived of freedom of expression."[32]

Judge Ammoun's view representing the Third World illustrates the change in international attitude, *viz.* that non-self-governing territories can no longer be dismissed as adjuncts of the administering power. They cannot, by definition, enjoy full sovereignty until independence has been attained, but they do apparently enjoy some status, be it one that falls short of full sovereignty.

States are the primary subjects of international law, but they are not the exclusive subjects. Other entities are afforded a degree of international legal personality. Of these entities, international organisations are undoubtedly the most important.

INTERNATIONAL ORGANISATIONS

International organisations have proliferated during the twentieth century. An international organisation, for the purposes of international law, is an entity established by agreement and which has states as its principal members.[33] Organisations vary considerably in their competences, importance and membership. The United Nations, for example, is a global organisation enjoying almost universal membership, whilst the European Economic Community is an example of a regional organisation.

Before an international organisation can make any impact on the international scene, it must be afforded some degree of international personality. The degree of international personality enjoyed by international organisations varies. An international organisation may enjoy certain rights, but not others, and, while all states enjoy the same degree of personality, this is not true with regard to international organisations.

Determination of Personality

International organisations frequently resemble states in the

---

[32] I.C.J. Rep. 1971, p. 68.
[33] Inter-governmental organisations are distinct from non-governmental organisations established by individuals.

personality which they possess. Their legal personality may to some extent parallel that of states. Organisations may have the capacity to own, acquire and transfer property, and to enter into contractual agreements and international agreements with states and other international organisations. They may pursue legal remedies and may enjoy rights and duties under international law. International organisations are restricted though by their constituent Charter, *i.e.* the agreement establishing the organisation. Determination of an organisation's personality thus demands that the constituent document be examined.

The constituent document may expressly provide that an organisation is to have international legal personality.[34] Alternatively, and this is more usual, personality may only be implied from the constituent document and consolidated through the practice of the organisation.

The United Nations

The United Nations Charter is silent on the Organisation's international legal personality. Only two articles in the Charter deal explicitly with legal status, and then only with the United Nations' status within the municipal systems of Member States. Article 104 provides that the United Nations is to enjoy within Member States' territory "such legal capacity as may be necessary for the exercise of its functions and fulfilment of its purposes," whilst Article 105 provides that the United Nations "shall enjoy in the territory of each of its Members such privileges and immunities as are necessary for the fulfilment of its purposes."

Articles 104 and 105 do not grant international legal personality to the United Nations. Articles 104 and 105 have been supplemented by the Convention on the Privileges and Immunities of the United Nations drawn up by the General Assembly in 1946.[35] The agreement is in force between the United Nations and every Member of the Organisation and provides for functional privileges and immunities for the United Nations. A similar convention, the Convention on the Privileges and Immunities of the Specialised Agencies[36] provides for the immunities and privileges of the specialised agencies. The United Nations has also entered into agreements with host States in which it operates, *e.g.* U.N./U.S.A.

---

[34] Exceptionally, a Constituent Document may deny an organisation personality, *e.g.* Article 4 of the Statute of the International Hydrographic Bureau.

[35] 1 U.N.T.S. 15; U.K.T.S. 10 (1950) Cmd. 7891; 43 A.J.I.L. Supp. I.

[36] 33 U.N.T.S. 261; U.K.T.S. 69 (1959) Cmnd. 855.

Headquarters Agreement.[37] Headquarters agreements are necessary as an organisation can only establish itself within a state's territory when it has that state's consent. Such agreements determine the status of the organisation's headquarters and its capacities, privileges and immunities.

The capacity of the United Nations to be a party to agreements with states helped the International Court to conclude that the Organisation indeed enjoyed international legal capacity. The Court held that the United Nations:

> "was intended to exercise and enjoy, and is in fact exercising and enjoying, functions and rights which can only be explained on the basis of the possession of a large measure of international personality and the capacity to operate on the international plane."[38]

The Court had been given the opportunity to comment on the international personality of the United Nations when it was requested by the General Assembly to give an Advisory Opinion on whether the Organisation had the capacity to espouse an international claim in respect of injury sustained by a United Nations official whilst in the service of the United Nations. The Court, before delivering its Opinion, took the opportunity to discuss the question of the United Nations' personality. The Court looked at the objectives of the Organisation—the promotion of international peace and security—and concluded that the United Nations could not fulfil the objectives for which it was established if it did not possess international personality. As to whether the Organisation could initiate an international claim, the Court arrived at an affirmative conclusion.

The Court further confirmed that the United Nations could not only espouse a claim for the damage caused to the interests of the Organisation, *i.e.* its administrative machinery, its property and assets, but could initiate a claim for reparation in respect of damage caused to the U.N. official or agent, or to persons entitled through him. In reaching this conclusion the Court again made reference to the purposes and functions of the United Nations and held that a U.N. official could only perform his duties satisfactorily if he were afforded adequate protection. Individual states could not be expected to and, indeed, were not able to offer such protection.

---

[37] 11 U.N.T.S. 11 (1947) Supplemented; 554 U.N.T.S. 308 (1966); 687 U.N.T.S. 408 (1969).

[38] *Reparations for Injuries Suffered in the Service of the United Nations*, I.C.J. Rep. 1949, p. 174 at p. 179; Harris, p. 114.

The Court upheld that the United Nations enjoyed this right of initiative against a non-Member State (in this case, Israel) because the Court maintained the United Nations possessed objective personality as opposed to subjective personality. Objective personality can be enforced *vis-à-vis* the whole world by virtue of the purposes of the Organisation and its almost universal membership.

The Court's Opinion proved to be not only a landmark for the United Nations, but for international organisations generally. The Court emphasised that the rights and duties of an organisation (*i.e.* any organisation) depend upon the purposes and functions of the organisation as specified or implied in its constituent document and developed in practice.

The administration of territories by the United Nations under the trusteeship system and the competence of the Organisation to intervene to maintain or restore international peace and security have served further to reinforce the United Nations' international personality.

One word of caution: while a treaty-making power is evidence of international personality, a general treaty-making power should not be deduced from the possession of some degree of personality. In other words, entities having a treaty-making capacity possess some international personality, but not all international entities necessarily possess a general treaty-making capacity.

The European Communities

The Treaty of the Coal and Steel Community (ECSC) 1951 expressly recognises the international personality of the Community to the extent that such capacity is necessary for it "to perform its functions and attain its objectives."[39] Article 185 of the EURATOM Treaty provides that the Organisation "may within the limits of its powers and jurisdiction, enter into obligations by concluding agreements or contracts with third States, an international organisation or a national of a third State." Article 210 of the Treaty of Rome provides that the European Community "shall have legal personality." The Treaty does not make specific mention of international personality, but does make provision for the conclusion by the Community of international agreements, *e.g.* Article 113 deals with agreements made pursuant to the Community's commercial policy and Article 238 authorises the Community to enter into agreements of association with a third state, a union of states or an international organisation. The Community's treaty-

---

[39] Article 6, E.C.S.C. Treaty 1951, Cmd. 4863.

making competence has been affirmed by the European Court of Justice in a number of cases.

In the *ERTA* decision,[40] the Court developed the Community's treaty-making competence as provided for by the Treaty of Rome by determining that:

> "Such authority may arise not only from an explicit grant by the Treaty ... but may equally flow from other provisions of the Treaty and from steps taken, within the framework of these provisions, by the Community institutions."[41]

In 1977 the Court went further and held:

> " ... whenever Community law has created for the institutions of the Community powers within its internal system for the purpose of attaining a specific objective, the Community has authority to enter into the international commitments necessary for the attainment of that objective even in the absence of an express provision in that connection. This is particularly so in all cases in which internal power has already been used in order to adopt measures which come within the attainment of common policies. It is, however, not limited to that eventuality. Although the internal community measures are only adopted when the international agreement is concluded and made enforceable, as is envisaged in the present case by the proposal for a regulation to be submitted to the Council by the Commission, the power to bind the Community *vis-à-vis* third countries nevertheless flows by implication from the provisions of the Treaty creating the internal power and in so far as the participation of the Community in the international agreement is, as here, necessary for the attainment of one of the objectives of the Community."[42]

The Court thus moved away to some extent from its position in the *ERTA* case and expounded a far wider principle, *viz.* that external competence does not depend on the actual exercise of a parallel internal competence.[43]

The European Community's role on the international plane is not

---

[40] *Re The European Road Transport Agreement : E.C. Commission* v. *E.C. Council* [1971] E.C.R. 263; [1971] C.M.L.R. 335.

[41] *Ibid.* 274; *ibid.* 354–355.

[42] Opinion 1/76, [1977] E.C.R. 741 at 755; [1977] 2 C.M.L.R. 279 at 295.

[43] See also Cases 3, 4 and 6/76, *The State* v. *C. Kramer and Others* [1976] E.C.R. 1279; [1976] 2 C.M.L.R. 440.

confined to treaty-making. The Community receives and accredits representatives. Over 100 countries have a diplomatic mission at the Community in Brussels, while the Community has eight delegations established in third countries. The Community maintains contact with international organisations and has four delegations accredited in Paris, Geneva, New York and Vienna for the purpose of maintaining contact with the organisations in these respective cities.[44]

The overriding conclusion in respect of international organisations is that no generalisation may be made regarding their international personality. Each organisation has to be looked at individually and its international legal status assessed in the light of its constituent document and the organisation's own practice. The plethora of institutions on the international scene has resulted in the growth of law pertaining specifically to them.[45] The law of international institutions is now a specialised sub-division of international law and can be treated as an autonomous subject.[46]

INDIVIDUALS

Individuals have limited international legal personality, although contemporary international law increasingly recognises that an individual may possess both international rights and duties. The greater awareness of human rights over the last 40 years has promoted the guarantee of human rights for individuals through both international and regional regulations.[47]

Simultaneously, it has been increasingly recognised that individuals may be held responsible for certain conduct. It is no longer believed that states are exclusively the perpetrators of conduct which breaches international law. The legal fiction that individuals do not participate on the international scene, and consequently could not be held responsible for their acts, has been dented. The notable exception is, of course, piracy, which has long been established under customary international law as an international crime.[48] Genocide and war crimes are now recognised as acts which

---

[44] For a series of articles on the European Communities as an International Organisation, see *Legal Issues of European Integration* 1984/1.

[45] A good general text on international institutions is D. W. Bowett, *The Law of International Institutions* (4th ed., 1982).

[46] In a number of educational institutions the law of international institutions is a separate course, independent of international law.

[47] See Chapter 9.

[48] See Chapter 6.

individuals can be held responsible for as individuals, *e.g.* as in the judgment of the International Tribunal at Nuremberg:

> "Crimes against international law are committed by men, not by abstract entities, and only by punishing individuals who commit such crimes can the provisions of international law be enforced."

The corollary of this acknowledgment that individuals may incur international responsibility is that they are under an obligation to refrain from such conduct. Individuals, therefore, have limited rights and duties on the international scene. A major handicap to individuals exercising international personality has been their lack of procedural capacity denied to them because of the reluctance of states to grant them such capacity.

Procedural Capacity of Individuals

The Permanent Court in the *Danzig Railway Officials Case*[49] recognised that exceptionally treaties could create rights for individuals, and that in certain circumstances these rights could be enforced in the municipal courts:

> "the very object of an international agreement, according to the intention of the Contracting Parties, may be the adoption by the Parties of some definite rules creating individual rights and obligations and enforceable by the national courts."[50]

The Central American Court of Justice, established in 1908, was novel in that it was envisaged that the Court would deal with disputes between states and private individuals. The Court was to have jurisdiction to hear disputes between private individuals of any one of the five Contracting Parties and any of the other Contracting Governments. The Court's importance lay in that it envisaged the potential procedural capacity of individuals. The Court itself ceased to function in 1918 after hearing only five cases—of which four were declared inadmissible while the fifth failed on the merits.

The Treaty of Versailles[51] provided for the espousal of claims by individuals against governments and nationals of the defeated states. However, as part and parcel of the peacekeeping treaty this

---

[49] P.C.I.J. Rep., ser. B, No. 15, pp. 4–47 (1928); 4 A.D. 587; Hudson, *World Court Reports*, Vol. II (1927–32), p. 237.

[50] P.C.I.J. Rep., ser. B, No. 15, p. 17 (1928); Hudson, p. 247.

[51] U.K.T.S. 4 (1919) Cmd. 153; 13 A.J.I.L. Supp. 151; 16 A.J.I.L. Supp. 207.

cannot be regarded as a major enhancement of the individual's position under general international law.

The Tribunal established under the Upper Silesian Convention was notable in that it was competent to hear cases brought by nationals of a state against their own state.[52]

Individuals can initiate claims alleging breaches of the European Convention on Human Rights by their national state provided, that is, the latter has recognised, under Article 25 of the Convention, the right of individual petition.[53] Individuals enjoy limited procedural capacity before the Court of Justice of the European Communities:

> "any natural or legal person may . . . institute proceedings against a decision addressed to that person or against a decision which, although in the form of a regulation or a decision addressed to another person is of direct and individual concern to the former."[54]

The procedural capacity of individuals on the international stage has been extended, but only to the extent that states have been willing to accord them such capacity.

OTHER ENTITIES—ANOMALIES

The Holy See

The Holy See of which the Pope is the head, is the most notable example of such an entity. Its population, which is neither permanent nor indigenous, performs an exclusively religious function, yet the Holy See has been a signatory as a member of international treaties concerning diverse subject-matter from arbitration to nuclear non-proliferation. It enjoys diplomatic relations with some 90 states and has been admitted as a full member to specialised agencies of the United Nations, *e.g.* UNESCO, WHO and ILO, which under their constituent Charters require members to be states. Although the Holy See maintains that its international personality stems from its religious and spiritual authority, this has not been acknowledged by the international community for obvious reasons. It could establish a precedent for other religious organisations to make assertions of international personality. The foundation of the Holy See's international personality has not required to be answered as there is a territory, albeit small, the City of the Vatican, over which the Holy See's exclusive sovereignty and

---

[52] See *Steiner and Gross* v. *Polish State* 4 A.D. 291 (1928).
[53] See Chapter 9.
[54] Article 173(2), EEC Treaty.

jurisdiction was recognised in Article 4 of the 1929 Lateran Treaty signed between the Holy See and Italy.[55] In Article 4 of the Lateran Treaty, Italy acknowledged "the sovereignty of the Holy See in the international domain as an attribute inherent in its nature in accordance with its traditions and requirements of its mission in the world...." A new treaty between Italy and the Holy See was concluded in June 1985.

The Holy See is an anomaly on the international scene enjoying and exercising international personality because other international actors are willing to enter into international relations with it. The same is true of the Sovereign Order of Malta which performs functions of a charitable nature from its Headquarters in Rome.[56]

CONCLUSION

There is no prototype international personality. States remain the primary subjects of international law. The international status of states is inherent in their statehood and states possess "the totality of rights and duties recognised by international law...."[57] States are no longer the exclusive subjects of international law and other entities, notably international organisations and individuals, have had to be accommodated within what is to be understood as an international person.

RECOGNITION OF STATES AND GOVERNMENTS

The international community is not static. New states may be created while existing states may become extinct. Governments come to power and are removed from power. Recognition essentially denotes a willingness on the part of the recognising entity to enter into relations with the entity that is being recognised.

Recognition is of importance as it is concerned with status, *i.e.* the status of the entity in question (i) on the international scene and (ii) within the municipal legal system of the recognising state.

Recognition is a complex issue. Factors other than legal considerations influence decisions to recognise any given entity. Recognition is accorded in the majority of cases by the executive. It is a matter of policy in which the recognising state has discretion: an entity, in other words, cannot demand recognition as of right. An

[55] 23 A.J.I.L. Supp. 187 (1929); Italy does carry out many of the functions which are normally exercised by states for the Vatican, *e.g.* police and waste disposal.
[56] *Nanni* v. *Pace and the Sovereign Order of Malta* 8 A.D. 2 (1935–37) Italian Court of Cassation; Harris, pp. 123–124.
[57] *Reparations Case, supra.* n. 1, at p. 180.

apt description of recognition is that it is a political act which produces legal consequences.

Recognition of States and Governments Distinguished

Recognition of a state is the formal acknowledgment by another state that the recognised state possesses the attributes of statehood and signifies a willingness to treat the entity as a state.

Recognition of a government is the formal acknowledgment by the recognising state that the regime in question is the effective government and signifies a willingness to treat that regime as such.

Recognition of a state is normally a one-off act—*i.e.* once an entity has been recognised as a state, that recognition will not usually be retracted if the requirements of statehood continue to be fulfilled. If these requirements cease to be fulfilled, the entity will cease to be a state but derecognition will not be necessary, *e.g.* two states may be consolidated into one single state as in 1968 when Tanganyika and Zanzibar became Tanzania. However, the governmental regime of a state may not always be accorded recognition. Refusal to accord recognition to a particular governmental regime does not negate its state's statehood. In normal circumstances, governments will be accorded recognition. The question of recognition is only raised when the regime in question has come to power by unconstitutional methods, *e.g. coup d'état*. The point to be concluded here is that while an entity may be recognised as a state, it is possible for its governmental regime not to be accorded recognition.

Before considering what happens in practice, the two principal schools of thought on recognition must be mentioned, albeit briefly.

Theories

There are two principal theories on recognition: (i) the constitutive school of thought; and (ii) the declaratory school of thought.

(i) The Constitutive School

Adherents to this school of thought emphasise the act of recognition itself. They maintain that it is the act of recognition which establishes (is constitutive of) the international personality of the entity in question. The act of recognition is regarded as a precondition to the entity's legal status or, to put it another way, it is the act of recognition which (a) creates a state and (b) determines the legal personality of a new governmental regime. The constituent theory raises two immediate problems. What is the position of unrecognised entities, are they free to act as they like on the international scene unfettered by the obligations which international law imposes? What if an entity is recognised by some states and not by others?

(ii) Declaratory (or Evidentiary) School of Thought

Adherents to the declaratory school of thought minimise the importance of the act of recognition by other entities. It is regarded as only the formal acknowledgment of already existing circumstances. In other words, the act of recognition is not regarded as one which brings into being, for example, a state which did not previously exist.

State practice supports the declaratory theory. Recognition when granted has retroactive effect—*i.e.* recognition is backdated: for example, the British accorded recognition to the *post*-revolution regime in the Soviet Union in 1921, but when recognition was granted it was backdated to 1917.

Existing states do treat unrecognised entities as having obligations under international law. They are not free to act as they wish on the international scene, *e.g.* in 1949 Britain demanded compensation from the Jewish State in respect of British aircraft shot down by Jewish airmen over Egypt; in 1957 compensation was demanded by the British from the unrecognised Taiwan Government for damage done by Taiwan forces to British vessels; and in 1968 the United States asserted that North Korea, which it did not recognise, had violated international law by attacking a United States vessel, *The Pueblo.*

Is there a Duty to Recognise?

The most notable exponent of the proposition that if an entity satisfies the formal factual requirements of a state or a government, then recognition should be awarded, was the late Sir Hersch Lauterpacht.[58] He did, however, acknowledge that recognition should be withheld if the entity had come to power through a violation of international law, *e.g.* the use of force contrary to Article 2(4) U.N. Charter. Although states do look at the factual criteria which are manifested by an entity, the act of recognition is essentially governed by political expediency. A state is not required to enter into relations with another entity if it does not wish to do so. If there was a legal duty to recognise, recognition would not be discretionary but compulsory. The non-recognition by the United States of the Peking regime as the Government of China until 1979 illustrates the possible impact of political factors on a decision of whether to recognise an entity or to withhold recognition.

---

[58] Lauterpacht, *Recognition in International Law* (1947) Chaps. 3 and 11.

Criteria for Recognition of States

The criteria of statehood have already been considered. States will generally accord recognition to an entity if the latter satisfies the requirements spelt out in the Montevideo Convention—defined territory; permanent population; independent government; capacity to engage in relations with other international persons. If the governmental regime appears effective and stable, then recognition will be accorded. Effective refers to the physical control of the territory in question. Does the regime enjoy control over most of the state's territory and is that control likely to continue? An affirmative answer will characterise the control as effective. Stable, on the other hand, refers to the political independence of the regime in question (see below, especially distinction between recognition *de facto* and recognition *de jure*). If all the criteria are fulfilled, then when recognition is actually awarded is a matter for the recognising state—and usually the timing is with regard to the recognising state's own national interests, *e.g.* commercial.

Recognition of Governments

The question of whether to recognise a government does not arise when the government comes to power by constitutional procedures. It only arises when the new governmental regime has assumed power by unconstitutional means.

British practice in the past has been not to look so much at how a government came to power, but to consider whether it displayed the criteria for recognition, *viz.* effectiveness and stability. Recognition by the United Kingdom did not imply approval of the new regime. The British adopted an "acknowledgment of the facts" stance. The United States, on the other hand, however, regarded recognition as a political weapon, not as something to be granted as a matter of international obligation. Its granting or refusal was discretionary and could be withheld to further national policy. However Britain and the United States now adopt a similar stance in respect of the recognition of governments. Both countries have undertaken to de-emphasise recognition and do not formally recognise new regimes:

> "In recent years, U.S. practice has been to de-emphasise and avoid the use of recognition in cases of changes of governments and to concern ourselves with the question of whether we wish to have diplomatic relations with the new governments."[59]

---

[59] *Digest of U.S. Practice in International Law* (1977) 19–21.

In 1980 the then British Foreign Secretary, Lord Carrington, announced that the Government had concluded that:

> "... there are practical advantages in following the policy of many other countries in not according recognition to governments. Like them, we shall continue to decide the nature of the dealings with regimes which came to power unconstitutionally in the light of our assessment of whether they are able of themselves to exercise effective control of the territory of the State concerned, and seem likely to continue to do so."[60]

In practice, little has changed in that the same tests of effectiveness and likelihood of permanence are still applied. What is different is that there is no formal acknowledgment of recognition.[61]

The general rule is that a new governmental regime will be recognised if it has effective control over the territory which it claims to represent, it has the ability to represent the state in question on the international stage and it is likely to maintain its control.

De Facto and De Jure Recognition

The practice of differentiating the recognition accorded to either a state or a government evolved in the nineteenth century. The practice was initiated by the British, but was also employed by other countries such as Canada. The United States has generally accorded only *de jure* recognition. The distinction does not appear in the Foreign Secretary's Statement on Recognition.

In reality, of course, it was not the recognition which was either *de facto* or *de jure*, but rather the entity which was being recognised. If a government was recognised as the *de facto* government, it implied that the government had effective control and that that control appeared to be permanent, *i.e.* there was a likelihood that the regime would be the permanent one. A government which was recognised as *de jure* was one which had effective control and was firmly established. An entity recognised as *de facto* was one which manifested most of the attributes of sovereignty, whereas a *de jure* entity displayed all the characteristics of sovereignty. *De facto* recognition was not a substitute for *de jure* recognition nor was it a lesser alternative. *De facto* recognition in essence meant that the recognising state recognised with reservations the entity in question. The distinction was one generally applied in respect of govern-

---

[60] *Hansard*, H.L. Deb., Vol. 408, cols. 1121–1122 (April 28, 1980); Harris, p. 127.
[61] The statement only refers to British practice in recognising governments which came to authority by unconstitutional means.

ments rather than states. The State of Israel, however, is an example of a state which was initially recognised *de facto* by some other states, *e.g.* Canada.

The benefit of the distinction was that it allowed the recognising entity to hold back and see how a particular situation was going to develop. In particular, it prevented a state from according premature recognition. To afford, for example, recognition to revolutionaries while the existing government is attempting to quell the revolutionaries is an unquestionable breach of international law. The advantage of the distinction was that it enabled cognisance to be taken of factual circumstances while still acknowledging the *de jure* government—even if that government was not in physical control of every part of a state's territory,[62] or was in exile abroad.[63] In the event of competing authority within a territory, the general rule has been to recognise that the *de facto* regime is competent within the area in which it has physical control, whereas the *de jure* authority remains competent for matters arising outwith that territory.

THE EFFECT OF RECOGNITION IN MUNICIPAL LAW

United Kingdom Practice

A recognised state or government, *de facto* and *de jure*:

(i) enjoys *locus standi* in the United Kingdom courts and it can accordingly raise an action in the United Kingdom courts;[64]

(ii) enjoys immunity from suit[65] in the United Kingdom courts and cannot be sued without its consent.

In the *Arantzazu Mendi Case*[66] the House of Lords held that as the British government recognised Franco's Nationalist Government, "a Government which at present exercises *de facto* administrative control over the larger portion of Spain,"[67] the Nationalist Government could not be impleaded without its consent. This case also illustrates the unfortunate consequences that may arise from recognising a *de facto* government and *de jure* government in respect of the same territory simultaneously. The Republican Government's action seeking repossession of the *Arantzazu Mendi*

---

[62] The United Kingdom during the Spanish Civil War 1936–39 recognised *de facto* General Franco's forces as they extended their control throughout the country, but still recognised the Republican government as the *de jure* regime.

[63] *e.g.* the Polish Government in exile in London was recognised as the *de jure* government, though it had no control over Polish territory.

[64] *The City of Berne* v. *Bank of England* 9 Ves. 347 (1804); 32 E.R. 636 (Ch).

[65] *Luther* v. *Sagor* [1921] 3 K.B. 532 (C.A.)—discussed below.

[66] [1939] A.C. 256 (H.L.).

[67] *Ibid.* at 258.

which had been requisitioned under a decree by the Nationalist Government accordingly failed.[68] The case was initiated in the English courts as the *Arantzazu Mendi* was in London at the time the Republican Government issued its writ of possession.

(iii) Its legislative and administrative acts will be given effect to within the United Kingdom. In *Luther* v. *Sagor*[69] the Court of first instance refused to give effect to a Soviet confiscation decree as the Soviet regime had not been recognised by the British Government. However, by the time the case was heard on appeal the British Government had accorded *de facto* recognition to the Soviet regime:

"The Government of this country... recognised the Soviet Government as the Government in possession of the powers of sovereignty in Russia, the acts of that Government must be treated by the Courts of this country with all the respect due to the acts of a duly recognised foreign sovereign state."[70]

(iv) Recognition once granted is retroactive. It is backdated to the establishment of the entity in question. It does not relate to the time recognition is accorded. In *Luther* v. *Sagor*, Judge Bankes concluded that the Soviet Government assumed the position of a sovereign Government as of December 1917. British recognition of the Soviet Government was therefore backdated to 1917 and all legislative and administrative acts of the Soviet Government after that date had to be recognised as valid. *Luther* v. *Sagor* therefore demonstrates that a government, be it a *de facto* or a *de jure* government, is entitled to immunity before British courts; that effect will be given to the legislative and administrative acts of a *de facto* and *de jure* regime; that recognition is retroactive; and that generally the effects of *de facto* and *de jure* recognition are essentially the same.

There are, however, two major differences between *de facto* and *de jure* recognition.

De jure recognition alone implies full diplomatic relations and

---

[68] Franco's Nationalist forces were in control of the Basque region of the country. The Republican Government issued a requisition decree in respect of all vessels registered in the Port of Bilbao. Some nine months later the Nationalist Government also issued a decree taking control of Bilbao vessels. The owners of the *Arantzazu Mendi* accepted the latter decree, but opposed that of the Republican Government.

[69] *Supra*, n. 65.

[70] *Luther* v. *Sagor*, *supra*, n. 65 at 543.

immunities and privileges for representatives.[71] Only a *de jure*
government can recover a public debt or state asset. It was
recognised in the *Haile Selassie* v. *Cable and Wireless Ltd. (No.2)*[72]
that only the ousted, but still *de jure* recognised government of a
state whose new government was only recognised *de facto*, was
entitled to sue for a debt recoverable in England. However, when
the *de facto* regime, in this case the Italian Government, was
recognised *de jure*, because recognition is retroactive, it assumed the
right as the *de jure* regime to pursue the claim, whereas the former
de jure regime of Haile Selassie was divested of any such right.

The retroactivity of recognition can create problems. What if two
governments are simultaneously recognised as the *de jure* regime of
the same state? In reality, this does not happen. One *de jure*
government will be superseded by another *de jure* government. The
effect, however, of back-dating recognition of a new regime can be
to place a state in the position of recognising measures of two *de jure*
regimes simultaneously. The question of retroactivity and its *raison
d'être* was considered in the *Gdynia Ameryka Linie Zeglugowe
Spolka Akcyjna* v. *Boguslawski Case*.[73] A new Provisional Government established itself as the *de facto* Government of Poland on
June 28, 1945 and at midnight on July 5/6 the British Government
accorded it *de jure* recognition. Prior to this the British Government
had recognised the Government in Exile in London as the *de jure*
Government of Poland. The issue which confronted the House of
Lords was the effect of the *de jure* recognition of the Provisional
Government on the validity of acts done by the Government in
London on July 3, 1945 with regard to Polish merchant marine
personnel. The Lords emphasised that English courts were required
to regard as valid not only acts done by the new Government after
recognition, but also acts done by it before its recognition in so far
as those acts related to matters under its control at the time when the
acts were performed. This did not, however, involve invalidating all
measures of the old government prior to the withdrawal of
recognition. It was, the Lords maintained "not inconsistent to say
that the recognition of the new government has certain retroactive
effects, but that the recognition of the old government remains
effective down to the date when it was in fact withdrawn."[74] What
emerges from *Gdynia Ameryka Linie* v. *Boguslawski* is that
retroactivity relates specifically to matters within the effective

---

[71] *Fenton Textiles Assoc.* v. *Krassin* [1922] 38 T.L.R. 259; see Diplomatic Privileges
   Act 1964.
[72] (1939) Ch. 182.
[73] [1953] A.C. 11.
[74] *Ibid.* at 45.

control of the new government and that the *raison d'être* of the retroactivity of recognition is to give validity to the acts of a former unrecognised regime, but may *not* (emphasis added) to invalidate the acts of the formerly recognised *de jure* authority.[75]

EFFECT OF NON–RECOGNITION

International Law

At the international level, as already stated, non-recognition does not give an entity "carte blanche" to act as it wishes. An unrecognised entity has responsibilities which the international community requires it to discharge.

Municipal Law

United Kingdom Practice

As far as the United Kingdom is concerned[76] the effect of non-recognition is the converse of the consequences of recognition.

An unrecognised state or government does not have *locus standi* in the British courts; does not enjoy immunity from the jurisdiction of the British courts; its legislative and administrative measures will be denied effect by British courts.

The non-recognition of legislative and administrative measures, *e.g.* those of a private law nature, can produce severe repercussions for "innocent" persons. Britain withheld recognition from the Smith regime which declared unilateral independence in 1965 and accordingly refused to recognise judicial decrees made by judges appointed by the Smith regime. The consequences of this were, for example, that English law refused to recognise a divorce granted by a Rhodesian court in 1970.[77] The Rhodesian situation was, of course, a unique one for the British courts. They were confronted with a regime which was in rebellion to the British Crown; hence the strict enforcement of non-recognition.

The consequences of applying non-recognition to its logical conclusion were identified by Lord Reid in the *Carl Zeiss Stiftung* v. *Rayner and Keeler Ltd. (No. 2) Case*.[78] Non-recognition of the measures adopted by the German Democratic Republic would mean that:

---

[75] See also *Civil Air Transport Inc.* v. *Central Air Transport Corp.* [1953] A.C. 70, Judicial Committee of the Privy Council.

[76] And also, for instance, Canada.

[77] *Adams* v. *Adams* [1971] P. 188. This decision prompted the introduction of an Order-in-Council to give effect to Rhodesian decrees which were concerned with personal status. See also the earlier *Madzimbamiuto Case* [1969] 1 A.C. 645. (P.C.).

[78] [1967] A.C. 855.

"...the incorporation of every company in East Germany
under any new law made by the Democratic Republic or by the
official act of any official appointed by its Government would
have to be regarded as a nullity, so that any such company
could neither sue nor be sued in this country. And any civil
marriage under any such new law, or owing its validity to the
act of any such official, would also have to be treated as a
nullity, so that we should have to regard the children as
illegitimate. And the same would apply to divorces and all
manner of judicial decisions, whether in family or commercial
questions. And that would affect not only status of persons
formerly domiciled in East Germany but property in this
country the devolution of which depended on East German
law."[79]

The House of Lords in the above case employed a legal fiction
and successfully sidestepped, for that particular case, the problem of
non-recognition. The respondents argued that as Britain did not
recognise the German Democratic Republic, all enactments of
the G.D.R. should be considered nullities before the British courts.
The House of Lords, however, maintained that as Britain recognised the Soviet Government as the *de jure* authority in East
Germany, the acts of the unrecognised East German regime could
be recognised as those of a subordinate body acting under the
authority of the Soviet Union. The German Democratic Republic
became irrelevant for the House of Lords. For them the German
Democratic Republic was merely a subordinate, dependent administrative body—created by the *de jure* regime. The House of Lords
adopted a pragmatic approach.

Mitigation of the strict non-recognition rule has been favoured
where necessary by Lord Denning. He said *obiter dicta* in
Hesperides Hotels v. *Aegean Holidays Ltd.*[80] that effect should be
given to laws of a body in effective control even if not recognised by
the British Government which "regulate the day to day affairs of
the people, such as their marriages, their divorces, their leases, their
occupations and so forth."[81]

The 1980 Statement on Recognition has brought the judiciary
into the arena of determining the status of the entity in question.
Prior to 1980 recognition was exclusively an act of the executive
which was binding on the courts. Now recognition of governments
which assume power by unconstitutional means is to be inferred

[79] *Ibid.* at 907.
[80] [1978] Q.B. 205 (C.A.).
[81] *Ibid.* 218.

through the dealings which the British Government may have with the new regime. If the courts are in doubt as to the status of a particular regime, they will have to assess the evidence available to them and exercise their judgment in deciding whether the regime is unrecognised or recognised. The courts may still obtain certificates from the Foreign Office and accordingly a certificate may include, *inter alia*, confirmation of the dealings which the British Government has with the new regime and, of course, an explicit statement of non-recognition.[82] The courts when interpreting the term "state" or "government" in a statute or another document, such as a commercial one, look of course to the intention of the draftsmen or that of the parties.[83]

United States Practice

If the Executive unequivocally denies recognition, the courts must accept this as binding.[84] An unrecognised state or government cannot sue in the American courts. An unrecognised government may be entitled to immunity from the jurisdiction of the American courts, if the regime in question can be shown to exist.[85] The Executive may deny recognition, but may nevertheless in its "suggestion" indicate to the courts that cognisance may be taken of the measures promulgated by the unrecognised regime. Thus, in *Salimoff* v. *Standard Oil Co.*,[86] although the United States Government's non-recognition of the Soviet regime was confirmed in the State Department Certificate it was nevertheless acknowledged that the Soviet regime was exercising control and power in the territory of the former Russian Empire and that such a fact could not be ignored. In the absence of either explicit or implied direction to the court, the American courts have shown a willingness to modify the legal consequences of non-recognition being carried to their logical conclusion. In other words, common sense and fairness may demand that legal cognisance be accorded.[87]

---

[82] See Colin Warbrick, "Britain and the Recognition of Governments," 39 I.C.L.Q. 568 (1981).

[83] *e.g. Re Al-Fin Corporation's Patent* [1970] Ch. 160; *Reel* v. *Holder* [1981] 1 W.L.R. 1226 (C.A.).

[84] *e.g.* as in *The Maret*, 145 F. (2d) 431 (1944); (1943–5) 12 A.D. Case No. 9.

[85] *Wulfsohn* v. *R.S.F.S.R.* 138 N.E. 24 (1923); (1923–4) 2 A.D. Case No. 16.

[86] 186 N.E. 679 (1933); (1933–4) A.D. Case No. 8.

[87] See *Sokoloff* v. *National City Bank* 145 N.E. 917 (1924); (1923–4) 2 A.D. Case No. 19; *Upright* v. *Mercury Business Machines* 13 A.D. (2d) 36; 213 (N.Y.S.) (2d) 417 (1961).

MODES OF ACCORDING RECOGNITION

Recognition may be expressed or implied. In the absence of an express formal declaration of recognition, the establishment of diplomatic relations between a state and the entity concerned will be taken to infer recognition. Similarly, the conclusion of a bilateral treaty on a general topic implies recognition. A bilateral treaty for a specific purpose does not imply recognition, nor does participation in a multi-lateral treaty such as the United Nations Charter. It is possible for parties to be signatories to a multi-lateral treaty, even though one party does not recognise the other party. Admission to the United Nations is an acknowledgment of statehood for the purposes of the Organisation. It does not constitute collective recognition by the international community, or recognition of the entity by individual Member States of the United Nations.[88] The most salient factor at all times remains intention—*i.e.* the intention of the recognising state. The intentions of the United Kingdom in respect of regimes which have come to power through unconstitutional means is, as already seen, now to be deduced from the dealings that the British Government has with the regime concerned—*i.e.* recognition by the British Government is to be implied rather than explicit and thus, of course, it may be denied.

---

[88] Admission of Members is effected by a two-thirds vote of the General Assembly.

FURTHER READING

Cases and Materials

D.J. Harris, *Cases and Materials on International Law* (1983), Chapter 4.

L. Henkin, R. Pugh, O. Schachter and H. Smit, *International Law: Cases and Materials* (1980), Chapter 4.

J. Sweeny, C. Oliver and N. Leech, *The International Legal System: Cases and Materials* (1981), Chapters 10, 11, 12 and 14.

Specialised Texts

D.W. Bowett, *The Law of International Institutions* (1982).

C.A. Cosgrove and K. Twitchett, *The New International Actors: The UN and the EEC* (1970).

J. Crawford, *The Creation of States in International Law* (1977).

H. Lauterpacht, *Recognition in International Law* (1947).

Legal Issues of Integration 1984/1 (Special Issue), *The European Communities as an International Organisation.*

General Texts

M. Akehurst, *A Modern Introduction to International Law* (1982), Chapters 5 and 6, pp. 69–74.

I. Brownlie, *Principles of Public International Law* (1979), Chapters III, IV, V and XII.

L. Green, *International Law: A Canadian Perspective* (1984), Part II.

D.W. Greig, *International Law* (1976), Chapters 3 and 4.

J.G. Starke, *An Introduction to International Law* (1984), Chapters 3, 4, 6 and 20.

Chapter Five

TERRITORY

Territory is a tangible attribute of statehood and within that particular geographical area which it occupies, a state enjoys and exercises sovereignty. Territorial sovereignty may be defined as the "right to exercise therein, to the exclusion of any other State, the functions of a State."[1] A state's territorial sovereignty extends over the designated land-mass, sub-soil, the water enclosed therein, the land under that water, the sea coast to a certain limit[2] and the airspace over the land-mass and territorial sea. The means whereby title to territory may be established is essentially of academic interest—until, that is, a dispute arises and competing claims have to be assessed. Then the mode by which the parties claim to have established sovereignty over the territory will gain new relevance.

Historically, the need to demonstrate the existence of a valid title became imperative during the "Age of Discovery" when the European powers set sail in quest of new lands. Discovery alone was not sufficient to establish a superior title. Occupation was also necessary.

OCCUPATION

Occupation gives a state original title to territory. It is the means of establishing title to territory which is *terra nullius, i.e.* owned by no one and therefore susceptible to acquisition. Regarding settlement by natives this was of no consequence provided the indigenous peoples were not administratively so well organised that they could be said to have a recognisable government. In the *Western Sahara Case* it was said that state practice of the late nineteenth century was such to indicate:

> "... that territories inhabited by tribes or peoples having a social and political organisation were not regarded as *terrae*

---

[1] Arbitrator Max Huber in the *Island of Palmas Case*, Permanent Court of Arbitration, 2 R.I.A.A. 829 at 838 (1928).
[2] 12 miles is the maximum allowed under the 1982 U.N. Convention on the Law of the Sea—Article 3.

nullius. It shows that in the case of such territories the acquisition of sovereignty was not generally considered as effected unilaterally through 'occupation' of *terra nullius* by original title but through agreements concluded with local rulers . . . such agreements with local rulers, whether or not considered as an actual 'cession' of the territory, were regarded as derivative roots of title, and not original titles obtained by occupation of *terrae nullius.*"[3]

Occupation is preceded by discovery. Discovery, *per se*, does not establish a good title, giving only an inchoate and not a definite title of sovereignty. An inchoate title must be completed within a reasonable period by the effective occupation of the territory in question.[4] Publication of discovery can, of course, intimate to the international community a discovering state's prior interest and such a discovery is good against any subsequent title founded on alleged discovery. An inchoate title does not prevail over the continuous and peaceful display of authority by another state.

Effective Occupation

Effective occupation applies to the actual exercise of sovereignty. What will be regarded as sufficient to establish a good title will vary in each particular instance:

"Manifestations of territorial sovereignty assume, . . ., different forms, according to conditions of time and place. Although continuous in principle, sovereignty cannot be exercised in fact at every moment on every point of a territory. The intermittence and discontinuity compatible with the maintenance of the right necessarily differ according as inhabited or uninhabited regions are involved, or regions enclosed within territories in which sovereignty is incontestably displayed or again regions accessible from, for instance, the high seas."[5]

Max Huber was the sole arbitrator in a sovereignty dispute regarding the Island of Palmas between the United States and the Netherlands. The Island of Palmas, the United States believed, was included in the cession of the Philippines to them by the Spanish in 1898 at the conclusion of the Spanish American War. The Dutch claimed the island on the basis of the exercise of sovereignty over a considerable length of time.

---

[3] *Western Sahara Case*, I.C.J. Rep. 1975, p. 12 at p. 39.
[4] *Island of Palmas Case, supra* n. 1 at 846.
[5] *Ibid.* at 840.

The display of sovereignty required to establish title by occupation, for example, over territory inhospitable to habitation may, therefore, be minimal and in certain circumstances may be little more than symbolic. Assessing the respective claims of Norway and Denmark to East Greenland, the Permanent Court of International Justice[6] highlighted the relative test to be utilised in establishing occupation and observed:

> "It is impossible to read the records of the decisions in cases as to territorial sovereignty without observing that in many cases the tribunal has been satisfied with very little in the way of the actual exercise of sovereign rights, provided that the other State could not make out a superior claim. This is particularly true in the case of claims to sovereignty over areas in thinly populated or unsettled countries."[7]

Minimal overt action may be sufficient to establish effective occupation over small, uninhabited territory.

An important and necessary condition of occupation is "the actual, and not the nominal, taking of possession."[8] The form of the actual taking is dependent on factors such as the geographical and geological terrain of the particular territory. In the *Clipperton Island Arbitration*[9] a declaration of sovereignty made on behalf of France communicated to the French Consulate in Honolulu and transmitted to the Government of Hawaii along with publication of the French claim in the Honolulu journal, *The Polynesian* (in English), was sufficent to establish a good title to the island for France.

Discovery must be reinforced by an intention (*animus*) or will to act as sovereign. How that intention will be inferred depends on the facts in any particular case. Normally, the exercise of exclusive authority is evidenced when the state establishes an organisation capable of making its law respected; however, in respect of the Clipperton Island it was held that France had done sufficient and had made it apparent in a precise and clear manner that she considered the island French territory. France had never had the *animus* of abandoning the island, and the fact that she had not exercised authority in a positive manner did not imply the forfeiture

---

[6] *Eastern Greenland Case*, P.C.I.J. Rep., ser. A/B, No. 53 (1933) pp. 22–147; Hudson, *World Court Reports*, Vol. III (1932–35) 151.

[7] *Eastern Greenland Case* (*supra*) at p. 46; Hudson (*supra*) at 171.

[8] *Clipperton Island Case*, 26 A.J.I.L. 390 at 393 (1932).

[9] The Arbitrator established that the Island at the date relevant to the dispute was "*territorium nullius* and, therefore, susceptible of occupation."

of an acquisition already definitively perfected. The French title was further substantiated by the absence of any French intention to abandon the territory.

Characteristics of Effective Occupation

Max Huber's articulation of effective occupation is still regarded as the leading statement on the issue.

In the *Island of Palmas Case*, effective occupation must, it was established, be open and public and involve the continuous, peaceful display of state authority extending over a long period of time. An inchoate title based on such a display of state authority would be regarded as superior to any other claim to title whatever its basis.

Max Huber went to great lengths to attribute the acts of the Dutch East India Company to the Netherlands state thereby emphasising that occupation must be exercised on behalf of a state if it is to be effective. Private individuals cannot legitimately purport to act on behalf of the state of which they are a national without, that is, that state's authorisation.[10] In international law:

> " ... the independent activity of private individuals is of little value unless it can be shown that they have acted in pursuance of a licence or some other authority received from their Governments or that in some other way their Governments have asserted jurisdiction through them."[11]

The exercise of state functions was similarly emphasised in the *Minquiers and Ecrehos Case*.[12] The continuous display of state sovereignty must be the basis of the British claim to sovereignty over the Falkland Islands, 1833–1982.

Critical Date

The critical date in a territorial claim is the date on which the location of territorial sovereignty is decisive, as the state which can demonstrate an effective title in the period immediately preceding the critical date has the superior claim, *e.g.* in the *Island of Palmas Case* the critical date was 1898; in the *Western Sahara Case* it was 1884. The responsibility of deciding when the critical date is lies with the adjudicating body charged with the task of deciding the

---

[10] See Harris, p. 159 for the example of the cession of Sarawak to Sir J. Brooke, a British national, by the Sultan of Borneo in 1842.
[11] *Anglo-Norwegian Fisheries Case*, I.C.J. Rep. 1951—Lord McNair at p. 184.
[12] I.C.J. Rep. 1953, p. 47.

territorial dispute. There is no general rule governing the selection of the critical date and selection, if indeed it is made, is made in the context of the relevant circumstances peculiar to each case.

PRESCRIPTION

Claimants to title of territory based initially on discovery and occupation may invoke the principle of prescription to consolidate their claim.

Prescription is the acquisition of title by a public peaceful and continuous control of territory. Prescription involves a *de facto* exercise of sovereignty. It is distinct from occupation in that the latter can only arise in respect of virgin territory (*terra nullius*), whilst prescription can work to establish a title over any territory. Prescription can validate an initially doubtful title provided that the display of state authority is public. It must be public as a title acquired via prescription implies the acquiescence of any other interested claimant. Protest from such a claimant or a dispossessed sovereign[13] can bar the establishment of title by prescription. What form must such protest take? Previously, force could legitimately be used. Today, diplomatic protests would have to be expressed and probably formally registered in the appropriate international fora.

As to the length of time required before prescription will give good title, there is no accepted prescribed period and much will depend on the circumstances of each particular case, such as the geographical nature of the territory and the existence or absence of any competing claims. There has to date been no decision of an international tribunal conclusively acknowledging title founded on prescription.

CONQUEST

Conquest is a mode of acquisition peculiar to the international community. It has no counterpart in municipal law. Conquest is the taking possession of enemy territory by military force in time of war. To be effected there had to be not only the actual taking over (*factum*), but an intention to take over (*animus*), *i.e.* the conqueror only acquired the territory if he intended to do so. Frequently, the vanquished power would cede territory to the conqueror under treaty. In the absence of a treaty the territory could only be annexed if hostilities between the belligerent parties had ceased.

The sharp-eyed reader will have noted the use of the past tense.

---

[13] *Chamizal Arbitration (1911)*, 5 A.J.I.L. 782 (1911); Harris, p. 167.

Why has it been used? Simply because, although in earlier centuries there were no rules restricting a state's use of force, this is no longer true. The twentieth century has witnessed the denunciation of war as legitimate, *e.g.* Article 10, Covenant of the League of Nations, the 1928 Kellogg Briand Pact and Article 11 of the 1949 Draft Declaration on Rights and Duties of States, which imposes a duty on every state "to refrain from recognising any territorial acquisition by another State in violation of Article 9."[14]

The 1970 Declaration of Principles of International Law concerning Friendly Relations and Co-operation among States in accordance with the Charter of the United Nations, para. X, provides that:

> "... The territory of a State shall not be the object of acquisition by another State resulting from the threat or use of force. No territorial acquisition resulting from the threat or use of force shall be recognised as legal."

This has been interpreted as meaning that territory cannot be acquired legitimately through the use of force, even if the use of that force is in accordance with the United Nations Charter (*i.e.* in self-defence). The Security Council's denunciation of Israel's retention of territory taken during the 1967 War as unlawful is founded on the principle that force cannot give a good title.[15] Nevertheless, it must be acknowledged that *de jure* recognition by other states may validate titles based on conquest, *e.g.* Indian control over Goa, Dañao and Diu (Portuguese territories on the Indian subcontinent invaded and taken by India in December 1961). The United States, however, does continue to refuse recognition of the incorporation of Estonia, Latvia and Lithuania into the Soviet Union, though the Baltic States were conquered before World War II.

Conquest is no longer a valid means of acquiring territory, but what of territories acquired by conquest when the use of force was accepted under international law? The law applicable when title was allegedly established will be applied. To do otherwise and to require new doctrines to be of retroactive effect would be extremely disruptive, *e.g.* Britain's claim to the Falkland Islands is based on conquest in 1833.

---

[14] *i.e.* prohibition on the use of war as an instrument of national policy and the use of force contrary to Article 2(4), U.N. Charter. Chapter 11 deals with the use of force in international law.

[15] *e.g.* Security Council Resolution on the Middle East, November 22, 1967—Security Council Resolution 242 (XXII), S.C.O.R., 22nd Yr., *Resolutions and Decisions* 1967, p. 8 and Harris, pp. 175 *et seq.*

CESSION

This, the transfer of territory by one sovereign to another, is the most usual form of acquiring derivative title to land. Cession is always effected by treaty—most frequently in a peace treaty at the conclusion of a war as in the Treaty of Versailles 1919 and the Treaty of Peace with Japan 1951.[16] To some extent the cession may be forced on the defeated power, in which case the latter's consent to the transfer of sovereignty will be recorded in the cession treaty. Cession requires that one party assumes sovereignty and another relinquishes it. One sovereign state is replaced by another. The acquiring sovereign cannot possess greater rights than those possessed by its predecessor, and, should a third state have acknowledged rights in the territory, *e.g.* a right of passage, then these must be respected. In the past, land has been ceded under an exchange agreement, *e.g.* in 1890 Britain and Germany exchanged Zanzibar and Heligoland, or purchased, *e.g.* as in the case of Louisiana from France and Alaska from the Soviet Union. The emergence of the principle of self-determination has made the cession of territory between states less likely.

ACCRETION AND AVULSION

Both accretion and avulsion refer to geographical processes. They refer to relatively rare occurrences and are of minor importance.

Accretion involves the gradual increase in territory through the operation of nature, *e.g.* the gradual shifting of a river's course leading to additional territory through the formation of alluvial deposits. Avulsion refers to a violent change, *e.g.* a sudden alteration in a river's course, or the emergence by volcanic action of an island in territorial waters, *e.g.* the Island of Scutsey which appeared in Icelandic territorial waters in 1963.

If accretion occurs on a boundary river (*i.e.* between two states) then the international boundary changes, whereas with cases of avulsion the international boundary will remain where it was originally established. If the river is navigable, the boundary will follow the *thalweg, viz.* the centre of the navigable channel. If a river is not navigable, the middle of the river stream will constitute the boundary.

NEW STATES

The attainment of independence, in accordance with the principle of self-determination or the constitutional granting of independence

---

[16] 112 B.F.S.P. 1 and 136 U.N.T.S. 45.

to former colonial possession, involves the replacement of one sovereign by another and thus gives a derivative title to territory. The recognition of title to territory by an entity which comes to "statehood" by unconstitutional means, *e.g.* by revolt, will depend on recognition by the other members of the international community, and title may finally only be established when an "acknowledgment of the facts" stance is adopted.

POLAR REGIONS

The Arctic

The Arctic consists largely of ice rather than land. It is incapable of occupation in the accepted sense of the term, and below the frozen masses navigation by submarines is possible. Sovereignty over such land, *e.g.* Eastern Greenland, can be established by minimum overt acts. Greenland belongs to Denmark, while Norway exercises sovereign rights over Spitzbergen. The Soviet Union and Canada, both anxious to eliminate any potential foreign and possibly hostile settlement, have made claims in the area. Both have utilised a modification of the contiguity principle (principle whereby the occupying state may claim territory which is geographically pertinent to its area of lodgment), *viz.* the sector principle. By this, the sector principle, all land falling within the triangle between the east-west extremities of a state contiguous to the Pole and the Pole itself should be the territory of that state, unless another state has a previously recognised established title. Both the Soviet Union and Canada have asserted sovereignty over extensive areas in the Arctic region.[17] The other Arctic States, Norway, Denmark, Finland and the United States have not utilised the sector principle. The major argument against claims in the Arctic is that what lies beneath the frozen wastes is high seas and not land and is, therefore, not capable of national appropriation.

Antarctica

All of Antarctica has been the subject of territorial claims, though that made by Admiral Byrd on behalf of the United States has never been officially adopted. The United States favours an internationalisation of the area and has not recognised any of the claims made by other states (Argentina, Australia, Chile, France, New Zealand, Norway and the United Kingdom). The sectors

[17] See Harris, p. 183.

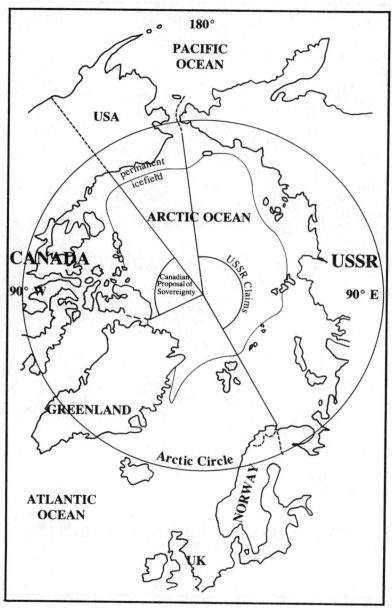

EFFECTS OF CANADIAN
PROPOSALS ON POLAR
WATERS

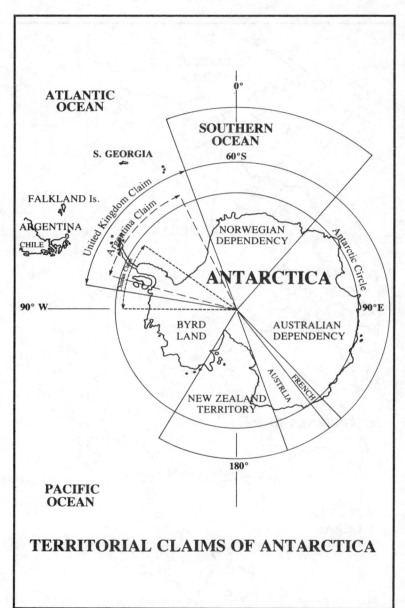

TERRITORIAL CLAIMS OF ANTARCTICA

claimed by Argentina, Chile and the United Kingdom overlap to some extent.[18] The other states involved appear to have recognised each other's respective claims. However, in an attempt to avoid a "scramble for Antarctica" the Antarctic Convention was drawn up in Washington in 1959,[19] and entered into force in 1961. The Treaty designates Antarctica exclusively for peaceful purposes and prohibits any measures of a "military nature."[20] Territorial claims have been put into abeyance for the life span of the treaty.[21] (No party may withdraw from the Convention during the first 30 years, *i.e.* until 1991.) Nor should anything done during that time be considered an assertion of, support for, or a denial of a claim to territorial sovereignty in the area.[22] Freedom of movement throughout the Antarctic is provided for all designated observers. Such observers remain, however, under the jurisdiction of their sending state rather than that of the "host" state. Thus, the possibility of disputes over jurisdiction is minimised.

AIRSPACE

Every state enjoys exclusive sovereignty over the airspace above its territory to a height once thought to be indeterminable. In the wake of outer space exploitation, it is now recognised that there is an upward limit to airspace, but what this limit is has yet to be established. State sovereignty over airspace quickly became customary international law in the early part of this century and was crystallised in the 1919 Paris Convention on the Regulation of Aerial Navigation,[23] and Article I of the 1944 Chicago Convention on International Civil Aviation.[24] International law does not give a right of innocent passage through airspace, and entry into a state's airspace requires the permission of the host state.

The Chicago Convention, which entered into force in 1947, replaced the 1919 Paris Convention rules on navigation. The Chicago Convention recognises the exclusive sovereignty of *all* states over their airspace, *i.e.* regardless of whether or not they are

---

[18] The United Kingdom did in 1955 initiate proceedings seeking a declaration from the International Court of Justice, but the latter struck the case from its list in 1956 as it had not received any response from either Argentina or Chile.
[19] Antarctic Treaty 1959, U.K.T.S. 97 (1961) Cmnd. 1535; 402 U.N.T.S. 71; A.J.I.L. 477 (1960); Harris, p. 181.
[20] Antarctic Treaty (*supra*) Article 1.
[21] *Ibid.* Article 4(1).
[22] *Ibid.* Article 4(2).
[23] 11 L.N.T.S. 173; U.K.T.S. 2 (1922) Cmd. 1609.
[24] U.K.T.S. 8 (1953) Cmd. 8742; 15 U.N.T.S. 295; Harris, p. 184.

Contracting Parties of the Convention. The Convention applies
only to civil aircraft and not state aircraft, which, for the purposes of
the Convention, are defined as "aircraft used in military, customs
and police services."[25] Such aircraft require authorisation by special
agreement.[26] The primary stipulation of the Convention is that
contained in Article 6, *viz.* that the scheduled international aircraft
of a Contracting State must, before flying into or over the territory
of a Contracting State, have that state's permission and comply with
any conditions of the said authorisation.

The Chicago Conference failed to reach agreement on the
granting of reciprocal rights of overflight or of transportation of
passengers and cargo.

Two further supplementary agreements were adopted, *viz.* (i) the
International Air Services Transit Agreement (the "Two Freedoms"
Agreement),[27] and (ii) the International Air Transport Agreement
(the "Five Freedoms" Agreement).[28] The "Two Freedoms" Agreement refers only to transit rights. The state granted the freedom
enjoys no commercial rights in the territory of the grantor state. The
"Five Freedoms" Agreement embraces the two freedoms plus three
additional freedoms. The latter are traffic rights. The third and
fourth freedoms are usually granted in conjunction. The right to
carry traffic from the territory of the state granted the right to the
grantor state is guaranteed by the third freedom, while the fourth
freedom is the right to carry traffic from the grantor state's territory
to the territory of the state granted the right. The fifth freedom
which is the right to carry traffic between the grantor state and
another state's territory has, because it is more extensive, not been
so readily granted.

The "Two Freedoms" Agreement thus provides that each
Contracting State grants to all other Contracting States (1) the
privilege of flying across its territory without landing; and (2) the
privilege of landing for non-traffic purposes (*e.g.* refuelling or
maintenance).

The state granting the freedoms may require (i) transit flights to
follow designated routes,[29] (ii) airlines of states granted the freedoms
to provide reasonable services at the airports they use,[30] and (iii)
payment for the use of airports.[31] A "host" state may revoke

[25] Chicago Convention (*supra*) Article 3(b).
[26] *Ibid.* Article 3(c).
[27] U.K.T.S. 8 (1953) Cmd. 8742; 84 U.N.T.S. 389; Harris, p. 186.
[28] 171 U.N.T.S. 387; 149 B.F.S.P. 1.
[29] The Two Freedoms Agreement, *supra* n. 27, Article 1(4).
[30] *Ibid.* Article 1(3).
[31] *Ibid.* Article 1(4).

permission granted "to an air transport enterprise of another State in any case when it is not satisfied that substantial ownership and effective control is vested in nationals of a Contracting State." Permission may also be revoked when an air enterprise fails to comply with the laws of the territorial state, or when it fails to perform its obligations under the agreement.[32]

The "Five Freedoms" Agreement requires Contracting Parties to grant to each other the Two Freedoms as well as the privilege of putting down passengers, mail and cargo taken on in the territory of the state whose nationality the aircraft possesses; the privilege of taking on passengers, mail and cargo destined for the territory of the state whose nationality the aircraft possesses; and the privilege of taking on passengers, mail and cargo destined for the territory of any other Contracting State and the privilege to put down passengers, mail and cargo coming from any such territory.

Only relatively few states have adhered to the Five Freedoms. The Agreement has thus been of minimal significance. Instead, Bermuda type bilateral agreements (*i.e.* based on that negotiated by the United Kingdom and the United States at Bermuda in 1946) have been adopted for the regulation of scheduled international air flights.

Aircraft in Distress

Contracting Parties are required by Article 25 of the Convention to render assistance to civil aircraft (of other Contracting Parties) which find themselves "in distress" in their airspace.

There are no established rules of international law as to what response a "host" state should make on the appearance of an unauthorised civil aircraft in its airspace. Although, arguably, such an aircraft, not being "in distress", does not come within the ambit of Article 25, it would be untenable to allege that the "host" state could take whatever action it wished. If the host state is not a party to the Convention, there is still, on humanitarian grounds, no reason for a distinction to be made between its position and that of a party to the Convention. Injury and death inflicted on innocent air passengers will not be readily accepted by the international community. Unfortunately, though, the violation of air sovereignty has precipitated some states to shoot first and ask questions later, *e.g.* the 1953 Aerial Incident in which an Israeli aircraft was shot down in Bulgarian airspace; the 1973 shooting down of a Libyan aircraft by Israel; and the shooting down in 1983 of a South Korean aircraft by the Soviet Union. Such a response, in particular from a

[32] *Ibid.* Article 1(5).

Contracting Party of the Convention, is especially regrettable when, under Article 4, Contracting States undertake that civil aviation is not to be used for any purpose inconsistent with the aims of the Convention. The Convention does not identify any sanctions which are to be adopted against "offending" Contracting Parties, and states are left to take whatever measures they see fit in the circumstances. Thus, following the shooting down of the South Korean aircraft a number of states refused, for a time, the Soviet airline landing rights and cancelled flights by their own aircraft to the Soviet Union.

The Chicago Convention initiated the establishment of the International Civil Aviation Organisation (ICAO). The ICAO is a specialised agency of the United Nations and is based in Montreal. Its function is primarily to supervise the application of air law, report any breaches of the Convention and conduct research into matters of air transport and navigation which are of international importance.

OUTER SPACE

The launching of the first artificial satellite round the Earth by the Soviet Union in 1957 heralded the beginning of outer space exploration, and the evolution of a legal regime regulating activities in outer space. Contrary to the position in respect of airspace, states have accepted that satellites may pass above their territory and no state has contended that such activity constitutes a violation of airspace sovereignty. The exploration of outer space has modified inevitably the view that airspace extends upwards to an indefinite limit. It is now recognised that national sovereignty must cease at some point.

The United Nations Committee on the Peaceful Uses of Outer Space established in 1958 has been responsible for the measures adopted regulating outer space activity, and all such measures recognise that outer space is (a) to be used for peaceful means; and (b) that it is the common heritage of all mankind.

The Treaty on Principles Governing the Activities of States in the Exploration and Use of Outer Space, including the Moon and Other Celestial Bodies (commonly referred to as the Outer Space Treaty)[33] affirms that:

" ... exploration and use of outer space including the Moon and other celestial bodies, shall be carried out for the benefit

[33] U.K.T.S. 10 (1968) Cmnd. 3519; 610 U.N.T.S. 205; Harris, p. 187.

and in the interests of all countries, irrespective of their degree of economic or scientific development, and shall be the province of all mankind."[34]

No area of outer space is to be appropriated by any state,[35] and the exploration is to be conducted "in accordance with international law, including the Charter of the United Nations . . ."[36] Article 4 is particularly important in that it prohibits the installation of nuclear weapons or any other weapons of mass destruction in outer space. The proposed United States "Star Wars" development has been justified on the grounds that they are designed to take defensive rather than offensive action. Jurisdiction over an object once launched into space remains with the state of registration.[37] Article 9 requires states to conduct exploration so as to avoid the harmful contamination of outer space and "also adverse changes in the environment of the Earth resulting from the introduction of extra terrestrial matter . . ."

The 1967 Treaty has been revised and clarified by the 1979 Moon Treaty (Agreement Concerning the Activities of States on the Moon and Other Celestial Bodies).[38] In particular, the Moon Treaty provides that the natural resources of the Moon and other celestial bodies should be exploited as the common heritage of mankind in accordance with an international legal regime. This Treaty entered into force on July 11, 1984. The 1967 Treaty has been supplemented by two further agreements:

(i) The Agreement on the Rescue of Astronauts, the Return of Astronauts and the Return of Objects Launched into Outer Space, 1968[39]; and

(ii) Convention on International Liability for Damages caused by Space Objects, 1972.[40]

The Rescue and Return Agreement is essentially concerned with securing co-operation between Contracting Parties for the rescue and return of astronauts, while the 1972 Convention establishes the strict liability of a launching state "for damage caused by its space object on the surface of the earth or to aircraft in flight,"[41] and fault

---

[34] Outer Space Treaty (*supra*), Article 1.
[35] *Ibid.* Article 2.
[36] *Ibid.* Article 3.
[37] *Ibid.* Article 8.
[38] 18 I.L.M. 1434 (1979).
[39] U.K.T.S. 56 (1969) Cmnd. 3997; 63 A.J.I.L. 382 (1969).
[40] 10 I.L.M. 965 (1971); U.K.T.S. 16 (1974) Cmnd. 5551.
[41] Liability Convention, Article II. Article VI establishes joint and several liability in the event of a joint launch.

liability "in the event of damage being caused elsewhere other than on the surface of the earth to a space object of one launching State or to persons or property on board such a space object . . ."[42]

Every launch and its intended purpose must be registered by the launching state on a public register maintained by the Secretary General of the United Nations. This is required by the 1975 Convention on Registration of Objects Launched into Outer Space,[43] introduced when the voluntary registration system initially envisaged proved unsatisfactory. The development of telecommunication networks has been an important by-product of space exploration and, today, the use of telecommunications in space is governed by a number of international agreements, such as the Agreement Relating to the International Communications Satellite Organisation (INTELSAT),[44] Convention Relating to the Distribution of Programme-Carrying Signals Transmitted by Satellite,[45] and the 1982 International Telecommunications Convention and Optional Protocol,[46] while the United Nations specialised agency, the International Telecommunications (ITU) in Geneva, promotes international co-operation in the use of telecommunications.

CONCLUSION

As has been said, states enjoy territorial sovereignty. However, that sovereignty is not unfettered. A state may, for instance, have to recognise that its territory has to be used for the benefit of another state, *e.g.* a right of passage, taking of water for irrigation purposes, or alternatively a state may have to refrain from taking certain action on its territory, *e.g.* the stationing of forces. Such rights (servitudes) attached to territory have to be recognised by successor states. Benefits may exist not for a single state, but for the international community, *e.g.* international waterways such as the Suez Canal.

In recent years there has been an increasing awareness and concern for environmental issues. The need for international regulation of the environment has been recognised.

---

[42] *Ibid.* Article III.
[43] 14 I.L.M. 43 (1975).
[44] U.K.T.S. 80 (1973) Cmnd. 5416.
[45] 13 I.L.M. 1444 (1974).
[46] This replaces the 1973 International Telecommunications Conventions and Optional Protocol, U.K.T.S. 104 (1975) Cmnd. 6219.

INTERNATIONAL PROTECTION OF THE ENVIRONMENT

Principle 21 of the Stockholm Declaration on the Human Environment,[47] adopted at a UN Conference on the subject, recognises that while "States have, in accordance with the Charter of the United Nations and the principles of international law, the sovereign right to exploit their own resources pursuant to their own environmental policies" they have a responsibility "to ensure that activities within their jurisdiction or control do not cause damage to the environment of other States or of areas beyond the limits of national jurisdiction."

Principle 21 is declaratory of customary international law. The extent and scope of a state's responsibility under customary international law and now under Principle 21, is illustrated in two cases involving the United States and Canada, the *Trail Smelter Arbitration*[48] and *Gut Dam Arbitration*.[49]

The *Trail Smelter Arbitration* related to damage caused in the State of Washington by sulphur dioxide emitted since 1925 from a smelter plant at Trail on the Columbian River and 10 miles from the United States/Canadian border on the Canadian side.

In the Tribunal's final decision in 1941 a general principle of international law was recognised, *viz.* that "a State owes at all times a duty to protect other States against injurious acts by individuals from within its jurisdiction."[50] The Tribunal concluded from decisions of the United States Supreme Court in controversies between Member States of the Union, that there existed as a principle of United States' law and of international law that:

"[N]o State has the right to use or permit the use of its territory in such a manner as to cause injury by fumes in or to the territory of another or the properties or persons therein, when the cause is of serious consequences and the injury is established by clear and convincing evidence."

The Gut Dam on the international boundary between the United States and Canada raised the water levels of Lake Ontario between 1947 and 1952 and resulted in considerable damage being sustained to properties on the lake shore. Following the re-establishment of an international arbitral tribunal, Canada agreed to pay compensation

[47] 11 I.L.M. 1416 (1972).
[48] 3 R.I.A.A. 1905.
[49] 8 I.L.M. 118 (1969).
[50] *Supra* n. 48 at 1963.

in respect of the damage caused to the property of United States citizens.

Principle 22 of the Stockholm Declaration requires states to co-operate in the further development of international law on liability and compensation for the victims of pollution and extra-territorial damage.

The International Law Commission has identified massive pollution of the atmosphere or the seas as an international crime,[51] while the parties to the 1979 Convention on Long-Range Trans-boundary Air Pollution agree to "endeavour to limit and, as far as possible, gradually reduce and prevent air pollution including long-range transboundary air pollution." The Convention defines transboundary air pollution as that which originates:

> "within the area under the national jurisdiction of one State and which has adverse effects in the area under the jurisdiction of another State at such a distance that it is not generally possible to distinguish the contribution of individual emission sources or groups of sources."

The Convention does not address itself to the issue of liability for pollution across state frontiers, but rather emphasises research and the exchange of information.[52]

Although not specifically mentioned in the Treaty of Rome, the European Economic Community has initiated three policy and action programmes on the environment.[53] The third, an action programme for 1982–86, was adopted late in 1981.[54] The Community's programme is ambitious. It envisages protecting not only human health and the environment, but the good management of natural resources which is to be achieved by introducing qualitative considerations into the planning and organisation of economic and social development. The Commission anticipates an environmental policy which is linked to and supportive of the Community's major objectives, especially that of economic recovery. The Commission emphasises that the socio-economic context of the 1980s means that environmental action must take account not only of the major problems confronting the Community (employment, inflation,

---

[51] Article 19(3). Draft Articles on State Responsibility 1976, Report on the I.L.C. 31. G.A.O.R., Supp. No. 10 (A/31/10) at 226 (1976).

[52] 18 I.L.M. 1442 (1979).

[53] The first Community environmental policy was adopted on November 22, 1973, O.J. No. C112, December 20, 1973 and was updated on May 17, 1977, O.J. No. C 139, June 13, 1977.

[54] O.J. No. C 305/2, November 25, 1981.

energy, balance of payments and growing regional disparities), but must also contribute to the efforts made in other ways to find solutions. Accordingly, the environmental policy is to be concerned with *inter alia* assisting in creating new jobs through the promotion and stimulation of the development of key industries with regard to products, equipment and processes that are either less polluting or use fewer non-renewable resources; reducing any form of pollution or nuisance, or of interference with spatial features, the environment or resources which creates waste or unacceptable cost for the Community; economising certain raw materials that are non-renewable, or of which supplies can be obtained only with difficulty, and to encourage the recycling of waste and the search for less polluting alternatives. The enlargement of the Community and its new Mediterranean dimension must also be recognised by any Community environmental protection policy.

The policy is to be effected, where appropriate, through local, regional, national, Community and international action.

Fears of radioactive fall-out prompted the 1963 Treaty Banning Nuclear Weapons Tests in Outer Space and Under Water.[55] Article 1(1)(*b*) of the Treaty forbids testing "in any . . . environment if such explosion causes radioactive debris to be present outside the territorial limits of the State under whose jurisdiction or control such explosion is conducted."[56]

Protection of the environment is a relatively new area for international regulation. Environmental international law is constantly developing and expanding as it attempts to grapple with and solve the problems presented by greater intercourse in a technologically advanced international community. The response of international law to environmental issues simultaneously demonstrates the youthfulness and topicality of the international legal system.

Having looked at territory, one of the principle attributes of territorial sovereignty shall now be considered, *viz.* the exercise of state jurisdiction.

---

[55] 480 U.N.T.S. 43; U.K.T.S. 3 (1964) Cmnd. 2245.
[56] Discussed further in Chapter 7 at pp. 131, 132.

FURTHER READING

Cases and Materials

D.J. Harris, *Cases and Materials on International Law* (1983), Chapter 5.
L. Henkin, R. Pugh, O, Schachter and H. Smit, *International Law: Cases and Materials* (1980), Chapter 5.
J. Sweeny, C. Oliver and N. Leech, *The International Legal System: Cases and Materials* (1981), Chapter 4.

Specialised Texts

J.E.S. Fawcett, *Outer Space: New Challenges to Law and Policy* (1985).
R.Y. Jennings, *The Acquisition of Territory in International Law* (1962).
A. Springer, *The International Law of Pollution in Protecting the Global Environment in a World of Sovereign States* (1983).

General Texts

M. Akehurst, *A Modern Introduction to International Law* (1982), Chapters 11 and 19.
I. Brownlie, *Principles of Public International Law* (1979), Chapters VI, VII, VIII, XII and XVII.
L. Green, *International Law: A Canadian Perspective* (1984), Part III, §§3, 4 and 8; Part IV, §1.
D.W. Greig, *International Law* (1976), Chapter 5.
J.G. Starke, *An Introduction to International Law* (1984), Chapters 7 and 14.

Chapter Six

JURISDICTION

Jurisdiction is an attribute of state sovereignty. A state's jurisdiction refers to the competence of the state to govern persons and property by its municipal law (criminal and civil). This competence embraces jurisdiction to prescribe (and proscribe), to adjudicate and enforce the law. Jurisdiction is primarily exercised on a territorial basis, but there are exceptions, *e.g.* there will be persons within the territory who will be immune from jurisdiction, whilst there will be occasions when a state may exercise jurisdiction outside its territory. The exercise and the non-exercise of jurisdiction is governed by a state's municipal law. In international law jurisdiction relating to the allocation of competences between states is an ill-defined concept. International law confines itself to criminal rather than civil jurisdiction. The civil law is the concern of private international law or, more correctly, the conflict of laws, though in the last resort civil jurisdiction may be backed by the sanctions of the criminal law. International law does not prescribe rules *requiring* (emphasis added) the exercise of jurisdiction. International law concerns itself principally with the propriety of the exercises of state jurisdiction. The exercise of jurisdiction remains, for the most part, a discretionary matter for the state concerned.

Bases on which jurisdiction may be exercised are:

Territorial Principle
Nationality Principle
Protective (or Security) Principle
Universality Principle
Passive Personality Principle

The first four principles, *territorial principle, nationality principle, protective (or security) principle* and *universality principle,* were accepted by the Harvard Research Draft Convention of 1935. The Convention was an unofficial work produced by a number of American international lawyers. Although not binding on any state, it remains of interest because of the extensive study of state practice which was undertaken. The *passive personality principle* was not adopted by the Convention.

The bases of jurisdiction are not listed in any hierarchy. No state can claim precedence simply on the principle on which it exercises jurisdiction. A state may legitimately possess jurisdiction concurrently with another state, the state which will exercise jurisdiction will be decided by other factors, *e.g.* physical presence of the alleged offender.

What international law today demands is the existence of a tangible link between the alleged offender and the state exercising jurisdiction.[1]

Territorial Principle

This is the favoured basis for the exercise of state jurisdiction. Events occurring within a state's territorial boundaries and persons within that territory, albeit their presence temporary, are as a rule subject to the application of local law.

An offence may not, however, be entirely committed within the territory of one state. A crime may be commenced in one state and consummated in another. If a person stands near to the border between two countries and fires a gun and thereby injures a person on the other side, which state has jurisdiction? The answer is both. The state from which the gun was fired has jurisdiction under the *subjective territorial principle*, whilst the state where the injury was sustained has jurisdiction under the *objective territorial principle*.

The *subjective territorial principle* allows the exercise of jurisdiction in the state where a crime is commenced.

The *objective territorial principle* gives jurisdiction to the state in which the crime has been completed and has effect—the forum of injury.

Both states may claim jurisdiction and both may do so legitimately. The one which will actually exercise jurisdiction will most probably be the one which has custody of the alleged offender. Nor is there any rule of international law which gives a state where a crime is completed exclusive jurisdiction. The right of the state in which the crime was initiated is, in other words, not restricted from exercising jurisdiction. Such a state may bring preparatory criminal acts within the ambit of its criminal law. There is:

> "no rule of comity to prevent Parliament from prohibiting under pain of punishment persons who are present in the United Kingdom, and so owe local obedience to our law, from

[1] See Harris, p. 212 for the judgment of the *Lotus Case*, P.C.I.J. Rep., ser. A, No. 10, p. 25 (1927) in which the Court emphasised the need for a prohibition to be evident under international law for a state's jurisdiction to be instituted. Otherwise the state enjoyed a wide measure of discretion in the exercise of its jurisdiction.

doing physical acts in England, notwithstanding that the consequences of those acts take effect outside the United Kingdom."[2]

More controversial has been the exercise of jurisdiction based on the effects principle so as to regulate the affairs of foreign nationals abroad, because such activities have an economic impact in the regulating state, *e.g.* United States and EEC anti-trust laws.

Nationality Principle

Jurisdiction exercised on this principle relates to the nationality of the offender. A state may exercise jurisdiction over any of its nationals wherever they may be and so in respect of offences committed abroad. Although universally acknowledged as a basis of jurisdiction, it is utilised more extensively by civil law countries than those with a common law system. The latter restrict jurisdiction exercised on the nationality principle to more serious crimes such as, in the case of the United Kingdom, offences committed under the 1911 and 1970 Official Secrets Acts, murder, manslaughter and bigamy.

The United States has similarly restricted prosecutions on the grounds of nationality to such crimes as treason, drug trafficking and crimes by or against the armed forces.

The fact that jurisdiction may be claimed on the *nationality principle* does not preclude the state in which the offence was committed from exercising jurisdiction on the *territorial principle*.

Protective (Security) Principle

On the basis of this principle, a state may exercise jurisdiction in respect of offences which, although occurring abroad and committed by non-nationals, are regarded as injurious to the state's security. Although acknowledged as a justification for the exercise of jurisdiction it remains ill-defined. It is undoubtedly open to abuse if "security" or "vital interests" are given a broad interpretation. However, the justification lies in the need to protect a state from the prejudicial activities of an alien when such activities are not, for instance, unlawful in the country in which they are being carried out.

Examples of when a state might claim jurisdiction on this

---

[2] Lord Diplock in *Treacy* v. *D.P.P.* [1971] A.C. 537 (H.L.) at 561. The case related to an attempted blackmail by letter mailed in England to a person in Germany. See also case of *R.* v. *Markus* [1974] 3 All E.R. 705.

principle would be in respect of plans to overthrow its government or counterfeit its currency. The principle was invoked by Israel along with the *universality principle* in the case against *Eichmann* (see below), while in the English courts it has been said "no principle of comity demands that a state should ignore the crime of treason committed against it outside its territory."[3] "Lord Haw Haw" was found guilty of treason because of his pro-Nazi propaganda radio broadcasts from Germany to Britain during the war. His duty of allegiance was founded on his having acquired a British passport, albeit fraudulently.

Universality Principle

One interpretation of this principle is that it gives jurisdiction to a state (any and every) over all crimes perpetrated by foreigners abroad. Such an interpretation is not regarded as being in conformity with international law. Where the principle may be acceptably invoked is in respect of international crimes, *i.e.* offences which are prohibited by international law and the international community as a whole.

The idea of a universal crime over which all states could exercise jurisdiction regardless of the alleged offender's nationality evolved with piracy. Under customary international law the crime of piracy has long been recognised as one over which all states could exercise jurisdiction provided that the alleged offender was apprehended either on the high seas or within the territory of the state exercising jurisdiction. The arresting state may also legitimately punish pirates. This rule of customary international law is reaffirmed in Article 19 of the 1958 Geneva Convention on the High Seas and Article 105 of the 1982 Convention on the Law of the Sea. Piracy in international law—*piracy jure gentium*—is strictly defined. This is in contrast to piracy in municipal law where the term is used somewhat loosely. Piracy, for the purposes of international law, is essentially any illegal act of violence or depredation which is committed for private ends either on the high seas or outwith the territorial control of any state.[4] Only acts which satisfy this definition of piracy are susceptible to the exercise of jurisdiction on the *universality principle*. Attempts to commit acts of piracy, even though unsuccessful, shall also constitute the offence of piracy.

War crimes and genocide are now widely accepted as being susceptible to universal jurisdiction. No state has exercised jurisdic-

---

[3] *Joyce* v. *D.P.P.* [1946] A.C. 347 (H.L.) at 372.
[4] Article 15 of the 1958 Convention on the High Seas; Article 101 of the 1982 Convention on the Law of the Sea; see pp. 133–134 below.

tion exclusively on such a basis. In the *Eichmann Case*[5] Israel successfully (at least in Israeli courts) claimed jurisdiction on two cumulative grounds:

> "a universal source (pertaining to the whole of mankind), which vests the right to prosecute and punish crimes of this order in every state within the family of nations; and a specific or national source, which gives the victim nation the right to try any who assault its existence."[6]

The Charter of the Nuremberg Military Tribunal, in particular Article 6 which referred to crimes against peace, violations of the laws and customs of war, and crimes against humanity and for which there was to be individual responsibility, and the judgment of the Tribunal are now accepted as international law. Genocide has been unanimously condemned by the General Assembly and the 1948 Convention on the Prevention and Punishment of the Crime of Genocide has been adhered to by some 90 states. The Convention provides for trial by either the territorial state or by an international penal tribunal (no such tribunal has been established), but a state which encourages, practices or fails to punish genocide would today be held guilty of having contravened customary international law.

Other crimes which are of international concern have been tackled by way of Conventions. The Hague Convention on the Suppression of Unlawful Seizure of Aircraft 1970[7] and the Montreal Convention for the Suppression of Unlawful Acts against the Safety of Civil Aviation 1971[8] were the response of the international community to the problem of hijacking which became acute in the 1960s. Both Conventions have been adhered to by a large number of states, and what they impose is an obligation on Contracting States to punish "by severe penalties" implemented by way of their domestic law offenders (or alternatively extradite) even in such circumstances as when the offence was neither committed in their territory nor committed by a national. Similar provisions are contained in the Convention on the Prevention and Punishment of Crimes against Internationally Protected Persons including Diplo-

---

[5] *Attorney-General of the Government of Israel* v. *Eichmann* (1961) 36 I.L.R. 5; Harris, p. 223.
[6] See Harris, p. 226. For Genocide Convention see U.K.T.S. 58 (1970) Cmnd. 4421; 78 U.N.T.S. 277; 4 A.J.I.L. Supp. 6 (1951); Harris, p. 561.
[7] 860 U.N.T.S. 105; U.K.T.S. 39 (1972) Cmnd. 4956; 10 I.L.M. 133 (1971); Harris, p. 236.
[8] U.K.T.S. 10 (1974) Cmnd. 5524; 10 I.L.M. 1151 (1971).

matic Agents.[9] Such agreements are effective only between contracting parties. States do not automatically possess competence
under customary international law to apprehend and punish alleged
offenders. What the Conventions spell out are the particular
situations in which states are required to exercise jurisdiction.

International crimes "proper" are susceptible to universal jurisdiction under customary international law regardless of whether a
state is party to any international agreement. There is nothing to
preclude offences currently regulated by Convention from crystal-
lising into customary international law. An issue of current
international concern and for which no satisfactory solution has yet
been found is that of terrorism. A principal problem has been that
of definition. International crimes are not clearly defined nor are
they a closed category, *e.g.* a United States tribunal in 1980 held, in
the case of *Filartiga* v. *Pena-Irala*,[10] that torture was a recognised
crime under international law and that every country could exercise
jurisdiction over the alleged offenders of such an offence. Torture is
prohibited by treaties, *e.g.* European and American Conventions on
Human Rights.[10a] Whether it is prohibited by customary international law remains uncertain.

Passive Personality Principle

The link between the state exercising jurisdiction and the offence is
the nationality of the victim. A state may exercise jurisdiction over
an alien in respect of an act which has taken place outwith its
boundaries, but against one of its nationals. It has not been widely
accepted as a basis of jurisdiction—see Judge Moore's objection in
the *Lotus Case*.[11] Civilian legal systems recognise it more readily
than common law systems. The vigorous opposition of countries of
the Anglo-American tradition was responsible for the principle not
being adopted by the Draft Convention.

EXTRADITION

If an alleged offender is in a territory other than the state seeking to
exercise jurisdiction, the lawful method of securing his return to
stand trial is to request his extradition. Extradition is the handing
over of an alleged offender (or convicted criminal who has escaped
before completing his prison term) by one state to another.

---

[9] 13 I.L.M. 41 (1974); U.K.T.S. 3 (1980) Cmnd. 7765.
[10] 630 F. 2d. 876 (1980).
[10a] See also United Nations Convention Against Torture and Cruel Inhuman or
Degrading Treatment and Punishment, (1985) 7 E.H.R.R. 339.
[11] P.C.I.J. Rep., ser. A, No. 10, pp. 141–148 (1927).

Extradition as a rule is effected by bilateral treaty. There is no duty to extradite in the absence of a treaty. Extradition treaties normally relate only to serious crimes and impose the same obligations on both the parties concerned, *e.g.* the offence must be designated a crime under the domestic law of both countries. A country's own nationals may be protected from extradition as may be persons who have committed offences of a "political" or "religious" character. The power of Governments to deport aliens has brought about a decline in the use of extradition.

ILLEGAL ARREST

A tribunal does not normally concern itself with the means by which the accused is brought before it. If the alleged offender has been procured by illegal means, *e.g.* kidnap or in violation of an extradition treaty, this will not preclude the tribunal from exercising jurisdiction. Unlawful arrest does not affect the court's jurisdiction to hear a case. However, this established rule was modified to some extent in the *Toscanino Case*[12] in which it was stated that a court was divested of jurisdiction when the accused had been brought before it through the illegal conduct of the law enforcement authorities. Forcible abduction involving brutality and like behaviour by a state's representatives could impair a state's exercise of jurisdiction. The norm, however, is that a state will, in the absence of protest from other states, try alleged offenders brought before the courts by irregular means.

The state whose sovereignty has been violated may initiate an international claim against the offending state. Argentina lodged a complaint with the United Nations Security Council in protest at the abduction of Eichmann to Israel, and called for the immediate return of Eichmann. The claim was dropped and in August 1960 Argentina and Israel announced in a joint decision that any violation of international law which had occurred had been "cured." States will only refrain from exercising jurisdiction over persons illegally brought before their courts from another state if the latter protests.

DOUBLE JEOPARDY

What of the person who is susceptible to the jurisdiction of more than one country? Does conviction or acquittal in one country constitute a bar to a subsequent prosecution elsewhere?

---

[12] *U.S.* v. *Toscanino* 500 F. 2d. 207 (1945) (United States Court of Appeals, 2nd Circuit).

International law does not provide an unequivocable answer, though Article 13 of the Harvard Draft Convention does provide that, at least in respect of exercising jurisdiction under the Draft Convention, no state should prosecute or punish an alien who "has been prosecuted in another state for a crime requiring proof of substantially the same acts or omissions and has been acquitted on the merits, or having been convicted, has been pardoned."

Article 13 refers only to aliens. It does not apply to nationals. Regarding the person who finds himself required to do in one state something which is prohibited in another, Article 14 of the Draft Convention provides that "... no State shall prosecute or punish an alien for an act which was required of that alien by the law of the place where the alien was at the time of the act or omission." Article 14 applies only to aliens and not to nationals.

IMMUNITY FROM JURISDICTION

Sovereign immunity and diplomatic immunity are the two principal exceptions to the exercise of territorial jurisdiction. Sovereign immunity refers to immunities enjoyed by foreign heads of state. Diplomatic immunity refers to the immunities enjoyed by their official representatives.

Sovereign Immunity

"*Par in parem non habat imperium*"—one cannot exercise authority over an equal. All states are equal. No state may exercise jurisdiction over another state without its consent. Historically, a sovereign and his state were regarded as synonymous. The ruler of a foreign state enjoys complete immunity—the principle that this extends to acts done in a private capacity was confirmed in *Mighell* v. *Sultan of Jahore*[13] and still applies today.

Traditionally, foreign states were likewise immune from the jurisdiction of the courts of other states. States in the twentieth century however became increasingly involved in commercial activities until eventually state enterprises enjoyed an immunity not enjoyed by non-state counterparts. Sovereign immunity placed state enterprises in a privileged position. Consequently, a number of states adopted a modified absolute immunity policy. A distinction was drawn between the public acts of a state (government acts) *jure imperii*, and private acts (trading and commercial acts) *jure gestionis*. Immunity was granted in respect of *jure imperii* acts, but not in

[13] [1894] 1 Q.B. 149.

respect of *jure gestionis*. Not all states abandoned the doctrine of absolute immunity. As a result some states were affording complete immunity to the commercial activities of foreign states whereas the same privileges were not being reciprocated.

The principle of absolute immunity was established in *The Parlement Belge* case,[14] in which it was held that *The Parlement Belge*, a mail packet vessel belonging to the Belgian King, was entitled to complete immunity. The principle was confirmed in subsequent cases, *e.g.* the *Porto Alexandre*,[15] *The Cristina*,[16] *Krajina* v. *Tass Agency*,[17] *Baccus SRL* v. *Servicio Nacional del Trigo*.[18]

Moves towards the modified sovereign immunity approach

The United States was the first country to declare that it was no longer prepared to accord immunity to foreign government agencies which were engaged in commercial activities. The so-called "Tate-letter" issued by the State Department in 1952 intimated the change in American policy " ... the immunity of the sovereign is recognised with regard to sovereign or public acts (*jus imperii*) of a State, but not with respect to private acts (*jus gestionis*)."[19] A state acting as a private individual was no longer to be placed in the advantageous position of receiving immunity and was to be liable in the same way and to the same extent as a private individual under similar circumstances. The American Foreign Sovereign Immunities Act of 1976[20] confirms restrictive immunity as American policy. The Act spells out the type of acts which are commercial and those which are private. A notable change of policy is provided for in the Act—the decision as to whether or not sovereign immunity is to be accorded is now the responsibility of the courts rather than the State Department.

An increasing number of states followed the United States and adopted a restrictive immunity policy. The number of states acceding to the 1926 Brussels Convention for the Unification of Certain Rules relating to the Immunity of State Owned Vessels,[21] under which government owned vessels engaged in commercial purposes are subjected to the same legal regime as private vessels, also increased.

[14] (1879) 4 P.D. 129.
[15] [1920] P. 30.
[16] [1938] A.C. 485.
[17] [1949] 2 All E.R. 274.
[18] [1957] 1 Q.B. 438.
[19] 6 Whiteman, 569–571.
[20] 90 Stat. 2891; P.L. 94–583 (1976); 15 I.L.M. 1388 (1976).
[21] U.K.T.S. 15 (1980) Cmnd. 7800.

The United Kingdom and Commonwealth countries, however, maintained a strict adherence to absolute immunity—at least until the 1970s. Britain in the 1970s adopted a restricted immunity policy. The common law was effected by decisions of the courts—*The Philippine Admiral*,[22] *Trendtex Trading Corp.* v. *Central Bank of Nigeria*,[23] and *I Congreso del Partido*.[24] The State Immunity Act was introduced in 1978 and came into effect on November 22 of that year. Some cases may still yet be decided on the basis of the common law, but sovereign immunity in Britain is now governed primarily by statutory law.[25] Canada adopted the restrictive doctrine in the State Immunity Act 1982. The State Immunity Act enabled the United Kingdom to become a party to both the 1926 Brussels Convention and the 1972 European Convention on State Immunity.[26] The 1972 Convention was initiated in an attempt to obtain amongst states a uniform approach to the issue of sovereign immunity. The Convention, for instance, specifies the circumstances in which sovereign immunity may and may not be claimed before the courts of Contracting States. Immunity may not be pleaded in proceedings with respect of contractual obligations to be carried out in the state exercising jurisdiction. States are also required, with certain exceptions, to give effect to judgments against them.

Today most countries have adopted a restrictive immunity approach in respect of state trading enterprises.

Diplomatic Immunity

"... the institution of diplomacy, with its concomitant privileges and immunities, has withstood the test of centuries and proved to be an instrument essential for effective co-operation in the international community, and for enabling States, irrespective of their differing constitutional and social systems, to achieve mutual understanding and to resolve their differences by peaceful means; ... [w]hile no State is under any obligation to maintain diplomatic or consular relations with another, yet it cannot fail to recognise the imperative obligations inherent therein now codified in the Vienna Conventions of 1961 and 1963 ... "

[22] [1977] A.C. 373 (J.C.).
[23] [1977] Q.B. 529 (C.A.).
[24] [1981] 3 W.L.R. 329 (H.L.).
[25] For details of the Act and the effect of its provisions, see Harris, pp. 247, *et seq.*
[26] U.K.T.S. 74 (1979) Cmnd. 7742; 66 A.J.I.L. 923; 11 I.L.M. 470 (1972). The United Kingdom is not a party to the Additional Protocol. 11 I.L.M. 485 (1972).

"The rules of diplomatic law... constitute a self-contained régime which, on the one hand, lays down the receiving State's obligations regarding the facilities, privileges and immunities to be accorded to diplomatic missions and, on the other, foresees their possible abuse by members of the mission and specifies the means at the disposal of the receiving State to counter any such abuse."[27]

The second principal exception to territorial jurisdiction is diplomatic immunity—representatives of a foreign state are immune from the application of the host state's municipal law. Diplomatic immunity was enjoyed by representatives from Greek city states. International diplomatic law was the earliest expression of international relations. Generally the privileges and immunities accorded by customary international law have not been controversial and have been adopted and respected by states. The customary law was codified in the 1961 Vienna Convention on Diplomatic Relations.[28] Diplomatic privileges and immunities have, as their *raison d'être*, a functional objective—the purpose of such privileges and immunities is not to benefit individuals, but to ensure the efficient performance of the functions of diplomatic missions as representing states.[29]

The Convention which came into force in 1964 deals with the immunities of foreign missions and foreign personnel in receiving states.

Diplomatic relations exist only by the mutual consent of states. There is no right to diplomatic relations. The consent, *agrément*, of the host state must be obtained for the proposed head of the mission.[30] Reasons for refusal of *agrément* need not be given. The receiving state may at any time and without providing reasons notify the sending state that the head of the mission or any member of the diplomatic staff of the mission is *persona non grata*, or that any other member of the staff of the mission is unacceptable. The sending state is required to either recall the person concerned or terminate his functions with the mission. Should the sending state refuse or fail to do this within a reasonable period, the receiving

---

[27] *Case concerning U.S. Diplomatic and Consular Staff in Tehran (Provisional Measures)* I.C.J. Rep. 1979, p. 7 at pp. 19–20 and *(Judgment)* I.C.J. Rep. 1980, p. 3 at p. 40.
[28] U.K.T.S. 19 (1965) Cmnd. 2565; 500 U.N.T.S. 95; 55 A.J.I.L. 1064 (1961). See Harris, p. 264.
[29] Preamble to Vienna Convention.
[30] Article 4.

state may refuse to recognise the person concerned as a member of the mission.[31]

Article 3 spells out the functions of a diplomatic mission as consisting, *inter alia*:

"(a) representing the sending State in the receiving State;
(b) protecting in the receiving State the interests of the sending State and of its nationals within the limits permitted by international law;
(c) negotiating with the government of the receiving State;
(d) ascertaining by all lawful means conditions and developments in the receiving State, and reporting thereon to the government of the sending State;
(e) promoting friendly relations between the sending state and the receiving state, and developing their economic, cultural and scientific relations."

Article 11 provides that in the absence of specific agreement the receiving state may require that the size of the mission be kept within reasonable limits.

The premises of a diplomatic mission are inviolable.[32] Agents of the receiving state may not enter there without the consent of the head of the mission and the receiving state must "take all appropriate steps to protect the premises of the mission against any intrusion or damage and to prevent any disturbance of the peace of the mission or impairment of its dignity."[33] Article 22 further provides that the premises of the mission, their furnishings and other property and the means of transport of the mission are immune from search, requisition, attachment or execution. The archives and documents of the mission are inviolable "at any time and wherever they may be."[34] The private residence of a diplomatic agent enjoys the same inviolability and protection as the premises of the mission.[35] The receiving state is thus under a duty to afford a high level of protection (higher than that afforded to "ordinary" aliens) and must accord "full facilities for the performance of the functions of the mission."[36]

Respect for the inviolability of a foreign mission precluded the British police from entering the Libyan "Peoples Bureau" in April

[31] Article 9.
[32] Article 22(1).
[33] Article 22(2).
[34] Article 24.
[35] Article 30.
[36] Article 25.

1984. On April 17, 1984 a demonstration against the Gaddafi regime occurred outside the Libyan "Peoples Bureau" in St. James Square, London. Shots were fired from inside the Bureau and a police constable on duty outside the premises, W.P.C. Yvonne Fletcher, was hit and died from the injuries which she sustained. The "Peoples Bureau's" inviolability was respected by Britain[37] and continued to be respected for a limited period after the diplomats had left for Libya, even though the mission premises had been used to endanger the host state's nationals.[38] The diplomats left on April 27, but the diplomatic status of the premises did not cease until midnight on April 29 and at six in the morning of April 30 the British police legally entered the "Peoples Bureau." The sanction invoked by Britain to resolve the situation was that of severing diplomatic relations with Libya and expelling the members of the mission. Inviolability is an absolute principle under the Vienna Convention and entry to mission premises is prohibited in all circumstances save with the consent or invitation of the head of the mission.[39]

The 1979 Iranian hostages incident is an illustration of a receiving state failing to afford due protection to a foreign embassy. On November 4, 1979 during a demonstration several hundred armed individuals overran the United States Embassy Compound in Tehran. Mission archives and documents were seized and 52 American nationals were taken as hostages. Iranian security personnel failed to counter the attack and in the subsequent case before the International Court of Justice, the lack of the protection afforded to the mission was held to be directly attributable to the Iranian government, even although the initial seizure was "executed by militants not having an official character."[40]

Inviolability does not mean extra territorial jurisdiction. The premises are not an extension of the sending state's territory. Acts committed on mission premises are within the territorial jurisdiction of the receiving state. Only in exceptional cases will a state grant asylum to an individual within an embassy. To do otherwise would be regarded as a grave violation of another state's sovereignty.

Diplomatic staff enjoy free movement and travel within the

---

[37] The exact legal nature status of a Peoples Bureau nevertheless remains obscure.

[38] Article 41(3) provides that "the premises of the mission must not be used in any manner incompatible with the functions of the mission."

[39] This is not to deny that although legally prohibited there may be occasions where it might be argued that entry might be justified because, *e.g.* a threat to the host state, the embassy in question is being used to store armaments, *e.g.* Pakistani raid of the Iraqi Embassy in 1973.

[40] *Case concerning U.S. Diplomatic and Consular Staff in Tehran* I.C.J. Rep. 1980, p. 3 at p. 30.

territory of the host state, subject to laws regulating entry into certain areas for reasons of national security. The receiving state must also allow and protect free communication by the mission for all official purposes and the diplomatic bag, which must be clearly marked as such, must be neither opened nor detained. The right of challenge in respect of the diplomatic bag which was accepted practice before 1961 is not included in the Convention. Whether a diplomatic bag should be subject to a degree of scrutiny remains controversial.

The person of a diplomatic agent is inviolable and is not liable to any form of arrest or detention and the receiving state must treat such a person with due respect and must take all appropriate steps to prevent any attack on his person, freedom or dignity.[41] A "diplomatic agent" is, for the purposes of the Convention, the head of the mission or a member of the diplomatic staff of the mission.[42]

A diplomatic agent enjoys absolute immunity from the criminal jurisdiction of the receiving state. He is also immune from the receiving state's civil and administrative jurisdiction, except in the case of:

> "(a) a real action relating to private immovable property situated in the territory of the receiving State, unless he holds it on behalf of the sending State for the purposes of the mission;
>
> (b) an action relating to succession in which the diplomatic agent is involved as executor, administrator, heir or legatee as a private person and not on behalf of the sending State;
>
> (c) an action relating to any professional or commercial activity exercised by the diplomatic agent in the receiving State outside his official functions."[43]

In such instances, immunity from jurisdiction is not available. A diplomatic agent is not obliged to give evidence as a witness.[44] The immunity enjoyed by a diplomatic agent is extended to the members of his family if they are not nationals of the host state.[45] The immunity of a national of the receiving state is limited to official acts performed in the exercise of his functions.[46] Immunity is

---

[41] Article 29.
[42] Article 1(3).
[43] Article 31(1).
[44] Article 31(2).
[45] Article 37.
[46] Article 38.

from jurisdiction and *not* from liability. The sending state may waiver the right to immunity.[47] Waiver must be express.[48] If a diplomatic agent or other person enjoying immunity initiates proceedings, they are then precluded from claiming immunity from jurisdiction in respect of any counter claim which is connected with the principal claim.[49] Waiver of immunity from jurisdiction in respect of civil or administrative proceedings does not imply waiver of immunity with regard to the execution of the judgment. A separate waiver is necessary.[50] A host state always reserves the right to declare a member of the diplomatic mission as a *persona non grata*.

Not all the staff of a foreign mission enjoy the same immunities. The Vienna Convention distinguishes between diplomatic agents, administrative and technical staff (*e.g.* archivists, clerical and secretarial staff) and service staff (*e.g.* kitchen staff). The administrative and technical staff, if non-nationals of the host state, enjoy complete immunity from criminal jurisdiction, but their immunity from civil and administrative jurisdiction extends only to acts performed in the fulfilment of their duties.[51] Non-national service staff likewise enjoy immunity only in respect of their official acts.[52] Distinguishing between mission staff and their respective immunities was an innovation in the Vienna Convention and represents a modification of the absolute immunity previously enjoyed under, for example, English law—see *Empson* v. *Smith*.[53] A diplomat who is either recalled or who is declared by the sending state a "*persona non grata*" is allowed a period of grace during which his immunity continues. Thereafter if he has not left the country he may be sued for private acts committed during his term in office. Immunity continues to subsist in respect of official acts.[54]

In addition to immunity from jurisdiction, diplomatic agents are, with certain exceptions such as purchase tax, exempt from taxes levied in the host state.[55] Mission premises are similarly exempt from local taxes except for those levied in respect of specific services rendered.[56] The right of immunity carries with it an obligation. It is the duty of all persons enjoying such privileges and immunities to respect the laws and the regulations of the receiving state. Such

[47] Article 32(1).
[48] Article 32(2).
[49] Article 32(3).
[50] Article 32(4).
[51] Article 37(2).
[52] Article 37(3).
[53] [1966] 1 Q.B. 426 (C.A.).
[54] Article 39(2).
[55] Article 34.
[56] Article 23.

persons are also required not to interfere in the internal affairs of the receiving state,[57] *e.g.* in the political affairs of the host state. This was the dilemma facing the United Kingdom in September 1984 when six South African nationals sought refuge in the United Kingdom Consulate in Durban. The United Kingdom was sympathetic to the plight of the six, but was acutely aware of their duty to respect internal laws. The same considerations would have applied had the premises in question been an embassy.

The Vienna Convention was made part of the United Kingdom law by the Diplomatic Privileges Act 1964 and part of United States municipal law by the Diplomatic Relations Act 1978. The American legislation applies the Convention's provisions to all states and not just to those who have become a party to the Convention.

Consular Relations

Consuls represent their state in another state with the consent of the latter. Consuls are concerned not with political affairs, but rather with administrative issues, *e.g.* the issue of visas. They also give various forms of assistance to nationals of the sending state when they are in the territory of the receiving state. They are posted in provincial towns as well as in capital cities.

Consular relations, unlike diplomatic relations between states, were largely governed by bilateral agreements. The Vienna Convention on Consular Relations[58] was adopted in 1963 to regulate on a universal basis the position and functions of consuls. The Convention entered into force in 1967. If two states have a bilateral agreement and both are parties to the Vienna Convention, the provisions which extend the greater immunities prevail. Consular immunities, unlike diplomatic immunities, may not be assumed, but must be shown to derive from either the Convention on Consular Relations, or from a bilateral agreement. The immunities and privileges enjoyed by consuls and consular premises resemble those accorded to diplomatic agents and diplomatic missions; however they are more limited in their scope.

The principal difference is that in the absence of special agreement, consuls are immune from arrest, detention and the criminal process only in respect of acts and omissions in the performance of their official functions. A consular officer must appear if summoned before the courts and later plead and prove immunity on the ground that the act or omission in question was in the performance of his official functions. Some states have by

[57] Article 41.
[58] 596 U.N.T.S. 261; U.K.T.S. 14 (1973) Cmnd. 5219.

special agreement and on a reciprocal basis extended full immunity from criminal jurisdiction to consular personnel, *e.g.* United States-Soviet Union Convention. A consular officer may only be arrested or detained in respect of a grave crime and pursuant to a decision by a competent judicial authority.[59] Proceedings against a consular officer should be conducted "with the respect due to him by reason of his official position" and save when charged with a grave crime, "in a manner which will hamper the exercise of consular functions as little as possible."[60] Members of a consul's family do not enjoy the same extensive jurisdictional immunities as the members of a diplomat's family, but they are exempt from such restrictions as immigration controls, customs duties and taxes, if they are not nationals of the receiving state.

Special Missions

Special *ad hoc* missions sent by a state to fulfil a specific purpose in another state are a recent innovation. There are no rules of customary international law on the subject. A Convention guaranteeing immunities to special missions was drawn up in 1969.[61] The Convention, which is not yet in force, is based essentially on the 1961 Vienna Convention on Diplomatic Relations. Under Article 8 of the 1969 Convention the sending state must inform the host state of both the size and composition of the mission, whilst Article 17 provides that the location of the mission must be mutually agreed by the states concerned, or must be in the Foreign Ministry of the receiving state.

International Organisations

International organisations enjoy those privileges and immunities from the jurisdiction of a member state as are necessary for the fulfilment of the organisation's purposes. Such immunities include immunity from legal process, financial controls, taxes and duties. The immunities and privileges to be enjoyed by the organisation and its personnel *vis-à-vis* member states are provided for in the constituent charter of the organisation and supplementary agreements adhered to by members of the organisation, *e.g.* the General Convention on the Privileges and Immunities of the United Nations 1946.[62] The General Convention gives immunity from the legal process to, *inter alia*, the property and the assets of the United Nations unless such immunity is waived as well as immunity from criminal jurisdiction for its representatives.

[59] Article 41(1).
[60] Article 41(3).
[61] 9 I.L.M. 127 (1970).
[62] 1 U.N.T.S. 15; U.K.T.S. 10 (1950) Cmd. 7891; 43 A.J.I.L. Supp. 1.

FURTHER READING

Cases and Materials

D.J. Harris, *Cases and Materials on International Law* (1983), Chapter 6.

L. Henkin, R. Pugh, O, Schachter and H. Smit, *International Law: Cases and Materials* (1980), Chapters 7 and 8.

J. Sweeny, C. Oliver and N. Leech, *The International Legal System: Cases and Materials* (1981), Chapters 2, 5, 6, 7 and 13.

Specialised Texts

G. Badar, *State Immunity. The Developments in International Law* (1984).

C. Lewis, *State and Diplomatic Immunity* (1980).

C. Olmstead (ed.), *Extra-Territorial Application of Laws and Responses Thereto* (1984).

General Texts

M. Akehurst, *A Modern Introduction to International Law* (1982), Chapters 8 and 9.

I. Brownlie, *Principles of Public International Law* (1979), Chapters XIII, XIV, XV and XVI.

L. Green, *International Law: A Canadian Perspective* (1984), Part III, §§1, 2 and 6; Part IV, §2.

D.W. Greig, *International Law* (1976), Chapters 6 and 8.

J.G. Starke, *An Introduction to International Law* (1984), Chapters 8 and 15.

Chapter Seven

THE LAW OF THE SEA

The law of the sea[1] is that law by which states, coastal and land-locked, and/or international organisations regulate their relations in respect of those areas subject to coastal state jurisdiction and in relation to those areas of the sea and the sea bed beyond national jurisdiction. The rules governing the sea are drawn from both custom and treaty.

In the 1950s, the profusion of claims, the advance of technology and the need for a protection of conventional sea uses were responsible for the Geneva Conventions on the Law of the Sea. The Conventions were the outcome of the initial work undertaken by the International Law Commission. The four Conventions adopted by the 1958 Conference were, the Convention on the Territorial Sea and Contiguous Zone,[2] the Convention on the High Seas,[3] the Convention on the Continental Shelf[4] and the Convention on Fishing and Conservation of Living Resources of the High Seas.[5] The Conventions have all entered into force, though by 1982 three-quarters of the nations of the world were not a party to them. The Conventions, which codified certain existing state practices and also articulated rules of progressive development, proved inadequate, particularly with regard to the continental shelf and the ocean bed which, with advancing technology, came within the potential acquisition of certain states.

The need to preserve the seas as the common heritage of all mankind and the danger of a "scramble for the seas" precipitated the calling of the Third United Nations Conference on the Law of the Sea. The 1982 Convention on the Law of the Sea,[6] adopted on April 30, 1982, was the culmination of nine years protracted negotiations. The Convention was opened for signature in December 1982, and has been signed by some 159 states but not, however,

[1] As distinct from admiralty law or maritime law which is essentially concerned principally with relations between private persons involved in the transport of passengers or goods.
[2] U.K.T.S. 3 (1965) Cmnd. 2511; 516 U.N.T.S. 205; 52 A.J.I.L. 834 (1958).
[3] U.K.T.S. 5 (1963) Cmnd. 1929; 450 U.N.T.S. 82; 52 A.J.I.L. 842 (1958).
[4] U.K.T.S. 39 (1964) Cmnd. 2422; 499 U.N.T.S. 311; 52 A.J.I.L. 858 (1958).
[5] U.K.T.S. 39 (1966) Cmnd. 3208; 599 U.N.T.S. 285; 52 A.J.I.L. 851 (1958).
[6] Misc. II (1983) Cmnd. 8941; 21 I.L.M. 1261 (1982).

by major countries such as Germany, the United Kingdom and the United States. Only 19 nations have ratified it (60 ratifications are required before the Convention will come into force). Opposition has been primarily with respect to the provisions regarding the exploitation of the deep sea bed, and as the Convention was designed as a "complete package" with the provision for reservation being limited,[7] it is unlikely that the Convention will enter into force within the foreseeable future.

Some of the provisions of the 1982 Convention simply re-state provisions of the Geneva Conventions—these probably represent customary international law. Other provisions, notably those on the exclusive economic zone, reflect what is now customary international law—they reflect state practice as it had become established before the 1982 Convention was completed. Other provisions represent a departure from established law and indicate the direction that the law is taking. The rules on the law of the sea are undergoing transition[8] and remain in a state of flux.

TERRITORIAL SEA

A coastal state enjoys sovereignty over "a belt of sea adjacent to its coast, described as the territorial sea"[9] which extends "to the air space over the territorial sea as well as to its bed and subsoil."[10] The consequence of being a coastal state is that it possesses a territorial sea:

> "To every State whose land territory is at any place washed by the sea, international law attaches a corresponding portion of maritime territory consisting of what the law calls territorial waters ... International law does not say to a State: 'You are entitled to claim territorial waters if you want them.' No maritime States can refuse them. International law imposes upon a maritime State certain obligations and confers upon it certain rights arising out of the sovereignty which it exercises over its maritime territory. The possession of this territory is not optional, not dependent upon the will of the State, but compulsory."[11]

---

[7] For reservations and their effect see Chapter 10.

[8] See Harris, pp. 284–287.

[9] Article 1, Geneva Convention on the Territorial Sea and the Contiguous Zone 1958; Article 1, 1982 Convention on the Territorial Sea and the Contiguous Zone.

[10] Article 2, 1958 Convention; Article 2, 1982 Convention.

[11] Judge McNair (dissenting opinion), *Anglo-Norwegian Fisheries Case*, I.C.J. Rep. 1951, p. 116 at p. 160.

Article 3 of the 1982 Convention establishes the breadth of the territorial sea at a limit "not exceeding 12 nautical miles."

Previously, agreement on the breadth of the territorial sea had eluded definition. State practice had been uncertain and varied. Some countries, for example, the United Kingdom and the United States, rigidly maintained the traditional three-mile territorial sea,[12] while certain Latin American countries made extensive claims to a maximum of 200 miles. The norm, however, was for states to claim a territorial sea of a width somewhere between three and 12 miles. The uncertainty of state practice was reflected in the 1958 and 1960 Geneva Conferences—neither Conference was successful in defining the breadth of the territorial sea. Various permutations were suggested, such as the United States formula of six-plus-six, *i.e.* a six mile territorial sea with a six mile fishing zone, an Asian/Latin American sponsored proposal calling for a 12 mile territorial sea, and a Soviet proposal whereby every state should enjoy the discretion to declare the width of its territorial sea between a distance of three and 12 miles. None of the proposals was successful. The 12 mile maximum has now been accepted.The advent and acceptance of a coastal state's exclusive economic zone (E.E.Z.—see below) has enabled the territorial sea question to be settled separately.

In the 1950s and 1960s increased fishing activity and advancing technology witnessed anxiety amongst coastal states in respect of fisheries. There was a need to control fishing, but at that time fisheries jurisdiction was very much an integral aspect of territorial jurisdiction. The failure of the 1958 and 1960 Conferences to reach agreement regarding the territorial sea and fishing zones prompted states to take matters into their own hands and unilaterally extend their fisheries jurisdiction beyond the territorial sea.

Measurement of the Territorial Sea

As a general rule, the baseline employed to determine the breadth of the territorial sea is the low-tide water line as marked on large-scale charts recognised by the coastal state.[13] The outer limit of the territorial sea is the line every point of which is at a distance from the nearest point of the baseline equal to the breadth of the territorial sea.[14] Geography can present problems and rules to resolve these have been evolved.

In respect of deeply indented coastlines, the 1958 and 1982

---

[12] A limit to which they continue to adhere.
[13] Article 3, 1958 Convention; Article 5, 1982 Convention.
[14] Article 6, 1958 Convention; Article 4, 1982 Convention.

Conventions reflect the International Court of Justice's judgment in the *Anglo-Norwegian Fisheries Case*.[15] This case came before the Court because Britain challenged the method employed by Norway to measure its territorial sea. Rather than use the low-water mark, Norway used the baseline system. As a result, waters which would otherwise have been high seas were characterised as territorial sea. The Court affirmed the legality of the straight baseline method and that in delimiting Norway's territorial sea cognisance had to be given to "geographical realities" and that the drawing of the baselines had to be adapted to the special conditions obtaining in different regions.[16]

As indicated, both the 1958 Convention and the 1982 Convention acknowledge the derogation from the low-water mark allowed by the Court. Straight baselines joining appropriate points may be employed where a coastline is deeply indented,[17] provided that the lines do:

> "not depart to any appreciable extent from the general direction of the coast, and the seas lying within the lines must be sufficiently closely linked to the land domain to be subject to the regime of internal waters."[18]

They may not normally be drawn "to and from low tide elevations" unless "lighthouses or similar installations which are permanently above sea level have been built on them"[19] or "where the drawing of baselines to and from such elevations has received general international recognition."[20]

Both the 1958 Convention and the 1982 Convention allow account to be taken of a further possible consideration which may be employed in the delimitation of the territorial sea and this was acknowledged by the International Court when it stated that:

> "... one consideration not to be overlooked, the scope of which extends beyond purely geographical factors: that of certain economic interests peculiar to a region, the reality and importance of which are closely evidenced by a long usage."[21]

[15] *Supra* n. 11.
[16] *Ibid.* p. 128.
[17] Article 4(1), 1958 Convention; Article 7(1), 1982 Convention.
[18] Article 4(2), 1958 Convention; Article 7(3), 1982 Convention.
[19] Article 4(3), 1958 Convention.
[20] Added by Article 7(4), 1982 Convention.
[21] *Anglo-Norwegian Fisheries Case, supra* n. 11 at p. 133.

Thus, the Court recognised that the special economic interests of a region could be taken into consideration. However, such a consideration is only supplementary (*i.e.* special economic interests in themselves cannot be grounds justifying the application of straight baselines) and is at all times optional rather than mandatory. Likewise, under the 1958 Convention and the 1982 Convention, special economic interests may be invoked to support an application of the straight baseline system, but only if their reality and importance is clearly evidenced by long usage.[22]

States are prohibited from applying straight baselines in order to cut off from high seas or an exclusive economic zone the territorial sea of another state, and a state using the straight baseline system must publicise by way of charts the lines being employed. The 1982 Convention requires the coastal state to deposit copies of charts and lists of geographical co-ordinates with the Secretary-General of the United Nations.[23]

The 1982 Convention alone provides that:

> "Where because of the presence of a delta and other natural conditions the coastline is highly unstable, the appropriate points may be selected along the furthest seaward extent of the low-water line and, notwithstanding subsequent regression of the low-water line, the straight baselines shall remain effective until changed by the coastal State in accordance with this Convention."[24]

Bays

A bay is defined under Article 7(2) of the 1958 Convention as a:

> "well-marked indentation whose penetration is in such proportion to the width of its mouth as to contain landlocked waters and constitute more than a mere curvature of the coast. An indentation shall not, however, be regarded as a bay unless its area is as large as, or larger than, that of the semi-circle whose diameter is a line drawn across the mouth of that indentation."

Article 10(2) of the 1982 Convention reiterates this definition.

A special formula has been evolved in respect of bays which belong to a single state and are more than mere curvatures of the

---

[22] Both Conventions are silent on what constitutes real and important.
[23] Articles 4(5) and (6), 1958 Convention; Article 7(6) and Article 16, 1982 Convention.
[24] Article 7(2).

coast. The salient feature of the formula is that straight baselines may be employed "If the distance between the low-water marks of the natural entrance points of a bay does not exceed twenty-four miles . . . "[25] In the event of twenty-four miles being exceeded, a straight baseline of twenty-four miles may be drawn within the bay in such a manner as to enclose the maximum area of water that is possible with a line of that length.[26]

Neither Conventions apply to historic bays—*i.e.* bays the waters of which have been treated as internal waters by the coastal state with the acceptance of other states, such as the Hudson Bay and the Gulf of Foncesca.[27]

Outermost permanent harbour works (which under the 1982 Convention do not include "offshore installations and artificial islands") forming an integral part of the harbour system are to be regarded as part of the coast for the purpose of delimiting the territorial sea.[28]

Islands

An island is defined in Article 10 of the 1958 Convention "as a naturally-formed area of land, surrounded by water, which is above water at high tide." The territorial sea of an island is decided in the same way as the territorial sea of mainland territories. The 1982 Convention retains the same definition of an island, but introduces a "regime of islands."[29] This provides that "the territorial sea, the contiguous zone, the exclusive economic zone and the continental shelf of an island are to be determined in accordance with the provisions . . . applicable to other land territory." However, rocks which cannot sustain human habitation or economic life of their own are denied both an exclusive economic zone and a continental shelf, though they may continue to have a territorial sea.[30] Low-tide

---

[25] Article 7(4), 1958 Convention; Article 10(4), 1982 Convention.

[26] Article 7(5), 1958 Convention; Article 10(5), 1982 Convention.

[27] Previous to the 1958 Convention it had been generally accepted under customary international law that straight baselines could be employed in respect of bays, but there was uncertainty as to beyond what width the closing line could not be employed. The International Court of Justice in the *Anglo-Norwegian Fisheries Case, supra,* n. 11, rejected, because of inconsistent state practice, the 10 mile rule (which the United Kingdom was claiming as the maximum width) and refuted that such a rule had ever acquired the character of international law.

[28] Article 8, 1958 Convention; Article 11, 1982 Convention.

[29] Part VIII, Article 121.

[30] Article 121(3). This provision would deny an E.E.Z. and continental shelf, *e.g.* to the Island of Rockall, currently the subject of a territorial dispute between principally the United Kingdom and Ireland—Denmark and Iceland have, however, also advanced claims.

elevations, on the other hand, do not have a territorial sea of their own, though the low-water mark on such an elevation, if it is within the territorial sea of a coastal state, may be utilised as a baseline.[31]

De-limitation of Territorial Seas between Opposite or Adjacent States

The territorial sea between opposite or adjacent states is determined in one of three ways: by agreement between the states; by the median line every point of which is equidistant from the nearest points on the baselines from which the breadth of the territorial seas of each of the two states is measured; or by another line required by historic title or other special circumstances.[32] The 1982 Convention envisages that a coastal state "may determine baselines . . . by any of the methods provided for . . . to suit different conditions."[33]

Archipelagic States

States such as Indonesia and the Philippines which are made up of a number of islands have, in the absence of international agreement, drawn straight baselines round the outer limits of their islands. The effect has been to turn what were formerly "high seas" into territorial waters.

International law has side-stepped the problems raised by archipelagic states and the Geneva Convention makes no provision for special treatment of mid-ocean archipelagos. The 1982 Convention, however, does deal separately with such states.[34] An archipelagic state is, for the purposes of the Convention, constituted wholly of one or more archipelagos and may include other islands; "archipelago" means a group of islands, including parts of islands, interconnecting waters and other natural features which are so closely interrelated that such islands, water and other natural features form an intrinsic geographical, economic and political entity, or which historically have been regarded as such.[35] The 1982 Convention recognises archipelago baselines joining the outermost points of the outermost islands. Such baselines may "not exceed 100 nautical miles, except that up to three per cent. of the total number of baselines enclosing any archipelago may exceed that length, up to a maximum length of 125 nautical miles" and must "not depart to any appreciable extent from the general configuration of the archipelago."[36] The territorial sea, the contiguous zone, the exclu-

[31] Article 11, 1958 Convention; Article 13, 1982 Convention.
[32] Article 12, 1958 Convention; Article 15, 1982 Convention.
[33] Article 14, 1982 Convention.
[34] Part IV, Articles 46–54.
[35] Article 46.
[36] Article 47.

sive economic zone and the continental shelf are drawn from the archipelagic baselines.[37] Archipelagic waters enclosed by the archipelago baselines fall within the territorial sovereignty of the archipelagic state,[38] subject to the right of all states to enjoy the right of innocent passage[39] similar to that enjoyed in territorial waters (see below). An archipelagic state may designate archipelagic sea lanes passage and prescribe traffic separation schemes[40] comparable to the right of passage through straits.

The 1982 Convention does not provide for the use of straight baselines by continental states with archipelagos. Nevertheless, Canada in September 1985 announced its intention to establish baselines round the entire Arctic archipelago from latitude 60°E to the Beauford Sea in the west, and the designation of all waters enclosed within the baselines as Canadian as from January 1, 1986.

Innocent Passage

The Geneva Convention recognises what had become established under customary international law, *viz.* that a coastal state's sovereignty over its territorial sea is subject to the obligation to allow a right of innocent passage to all foreign ships.[41] Innocent passage is defined in a very general way as that which "is not prejudicial to the peace, good order or security of the coastal State."[42] Fishing vessels are required to observe the laws and regulations of the coastal state[43] and submarines are required to navigate on the surface and to show their flag,[44] otherwise their passage will not be regarded as innocent. The 1982 Convention is more specific in its definition of "innocent" and enunciates a list of activities which, if occurring in the coastal state's territorial waters, would not be characterised as "innocent." Such activities include: any threat or use of force against the sovereignty, territorial integrity or political independence of the coastal state; any exercise or practice with weapons of any kind; any act aimed at collecting information to the prejudice of the defence or security of the coastal state; any act of

---

[37] Article 48.
[38] Article 49.
[39] Article 52.
[40] Article 53.
[41] Article 5, 1958 Convention and Article 8, 1982 Convention provide that where the straight baseline is employed, because of an indented coastline and this has led to territorial waters or high seas being designated internal waters, a right of innocent passage shall exist in those waters.
[42] Article 14(4).
[43] Article 14(5).
[44] Article 14(6).

propaganda aimed at affecting the defence or security of the coastal state; any fishing activities and the carrying out of research or survey activities.[45] The coastal state is under a duty not to hamper innocent passage.[46] The 1982 Convention again is more precise and stipulates that the coastal state shall not:

"(a) impose requirements on foreign ships which have the practical effect of denying or impairing the right of innocent passage; or

(b) discriminate in form or in fact against the ships of any State or against ships carrying cargoes to, from or on behalf of any State."[47]

Under both Conventions, coastal states are required to give appropriate publicity of any dangers to navigation of which it has knowledge within its territorial sea.[48]

Article 17 of the 1958 Convention simply provides that foreign ships engaging in innocent passage must comply with the coastal state's laws and regulations. Again, the 1982 Convention articulates to a greater extent the laws and regulations which a coastal state may adopt. These may, for instance, include measures on the safety of navigation and the regulation of maritime traffic, the protection of navigational aids and facilities and other facilities or installations, the protection of cables and pipelines, the conservation of the living resources of the sea, and the preservation of the environment of the coastal state and the prevention, reduction and control of pollution thereof.[49]

Two new provisions are included in the 1982 Convention: Article 22 provides that a coastal state may require foreign ships to use such sea lanes and traffic separation schemes as it (*i.e.* the coastal state) may designate or prescribe for vessels, in particular tankers, nuclear-powered ships and ships carrying nuclear or other inherently dangerous or noxious substances, or materials, engaged in innocent passage. Article 23 provides that foreign nuclear-powered ships and ships carrying nuclear or like material shall be required to carry documents and observe special precautionary measures established for such ships by international agreements.

A coastal state may take the steps necessary to prevent passage

---

[45] Article 19, 1982 Convention.
[46] Article 16, 1958 Convention.
[47] Article 24.
[48] Article 15(2), 1958 Convention; Article 24(2), 1982 Convention.
[49] Article 21.

which is not innocent,[50] and may without discrimination amongst foreign ships suspend innocent passage temporarily in specified areas of its territorial sea if that is required in the interest of its security.[51] If a vessel is proceeding to internal waters the coastal state may take the steps necessary to prevent any breach of the conditions to which the admission of the ships to internal waters is subject.[52]

Foreign vessels engaged in innocent passage are only subject to the coastal state's criminal and civil jurisdiction in limited defined circumstances. A coastal state may only exercise jurisdiction:

(a) if the consequences of the crime extend to the coastal state; or

(b) if the crime is of a kind to disturb the peace of the country or the good order of the territorial sea; or

(c) if the assistance of the local authorities has been requested by the captain of the ship or by the consul of the country whose flag the ship flies; or

(d) if it is necessary for the suppression of illicit traffic in narcotic drugs (or psychotropic substances—1982 Convention only).[53]

Civil jurisdiction may not be exercised against either a person on board or against the ship save in respect of obligations and liabilities assumed by the ship itself in the course of, or for the purpose of, its voyage through the waters of the coastal state, or if the vessel is passing through the territorial sea after having left internal waters.[54] Government vessels operated for commercial purposes come within the ambit of the foregoing provisions. In respect of warships and government vessels operated for non-commercial purposes, the Convention does not affect the immunities from jurisdiction to which they are entitled.

A foreign warship which does not comply with the coastal state's regulations may be required to leave the territorial sea ("immediately" has been added by the 1982 Convention).[55] Although mention is made of warships, neither the 1958 nor the 1982 Convention expressly grants or denies foreign warships a right of innocent passage. The 1982 Convention does provide, however, that the flag state of a vessel shall incur international liability for "any loss or damage to the coastal State resulting from the non-compliance by a warship or other government ship operated for

---

[50] Article 16, 1958 Convention; Article 25, 1982 Convention.
[51] Article 16(3), 1958 Convention; Article 25(3), 1982 Convention.
[52] Article 16(2), 1958 Convention; Article 25(2), 1982 Convention.
[53] Article 19, 1958 Convention; Article 27, 1982 Convention.
[54] Article 20, 1958 Convention; Article 28, 1982 Convention.
[55] Article 23, 1958 Convention; Article 30, 1982 Convention.

non-commercial purposes with the laws and regulations of the coastal State . . . "[56]

Passage through Straits

What is a coastal state's jurisdiction in international straits bordering its coast?

Article 16(4) of the Geneva Convention on the Territorial Sea prohibits a coastal state from suspending innocent passage in territorial sea straits which are used for international navigation between one part of the high seas and another part of the high seas, or the territorial sea of a foreign state.

The right of innocent passage similar to that provided by Article 16(2) is retained by the 1982 Convention for straits which are formed by an island of a state bordering the strait and its mainland and where there exists seaward of the island a high seas route or an exclusive economic zone (E.E.Z.—see below),[57] and secondly where the strait is between a part of the high seas or an exclusive economic zone and the territorial sea of a foreign state, *viz.* where there is only territorial sea at one end of a strait.[58] The coastal state may not suspend such innocent passage.[59] However, for straits which are used for international navigation between one part of the high seas or an exclusive economic zone and another part of the high seas or an exclusive economic zone,[60] the 1982 Convention dispenses with the right of innocent passage and provides rather for a right of transit. In other words, the right of transit will only apply in straits which have high seas or an exclusive economic zone at both ends.

Article 38(2) defines transit passage as "the freedom of navigation and overflight solely for the purpose of continuous and expeditious transit of the strait." Ships and aircraft are charged with certain duties when travelling through and over the strait, *e.g.* proceeding without delay and refraining from any threat or use of force against the sovereignty, territorial integrity or political independence of states bordering the strait.[61] The strait state may, in the interest of safe passage, prescribe sea lanes and traffic separation schemes, but only after its proposals have been referred to and adopted by the "competent international organisation"[62]: the authority of the strait state is thus more restricted than under the 1958 Convention. The

[56] Article 31.
[57] Article 38.
[58] Article 45(1)(b).
[59] Article 45(2).
[60] Article 37.
[61] Article 39.
[62] Article 41.

strait state may also adopt laws and regulations designed to prevent, reduce or control pollution. The strait state is, however, under a duty not to hamper transit passage and is required "to give appropriate publicity to any danger to navigation or overflight within or over the strait of which they have knowledge."[63] There may be no suspension of transit passage.[64]

Why are international straits subject to a special regime under the 1982 Convention?[65] The effect of extended territorial seas has been to bring straits, through which there was previously high seas, exclusively within territorial waters. Consequently, maritime powers sought definite guarantees for shipping as a condition to their accepting a 12 mile territorial sea. The Geneva Convention is also deficient in that it grants no right of passage to aircraft (under the 1982 Convention all aircraft would enjoy the right of transit) and that submarines have to navigate on the surface and show their flag, whereas the 1982 Convention allows underwater passage by submarines. The 1982 Convention would appear, with respect to warships in time of peace, to support the I.C.J.'s pronouncement in the *Corfu Channel Case (Merits)*[66] that it was generally accepted international custom:

> "that States in time of peace have a right to send their warships through straits used for international navigation between two parts of the high seas without the previous authorisation of a coastal State, provided that the passage is *innocent.*"[67]

Contiguous Zone

A coastal state, under the 1958 Geneva Convention, may claim a zone of the high seas, not exceeding 12 miles from the territorial sea baselines, contiguous to its territorial sea. A contiguous zone need not be claimed, but if it is it must be done so specifically. Although the status of the contiguous zone remains that of high seas, the coastal state may exercise control to prevent or punish infringement of its customs, fiscal, immigration or sanitary regulations within *its territory or territorial sea* (emphasis added). The maximum breadth of the contiguous zone is extended under the 1982 Convention to 24 miles from the territorial baselines.[68]

---

[63] Article 44.
[64] *Ibid.*
[65] The regime does not apply to straits regulated by treaty, *e.g.* the 1936 Treaty of Montreux in respect of the Straits of the Bosphorus and Dardanelles.
[66] I.C.J. Rep. 1949, p. 4.
[67] *Ibid.* at p. 28.
[68] Article 33.

HIGH SEAS

The high seas constitutes "all parts of the sea that are not included in the territorial sea or in the internal waters of a State."[69] This definition has had to be modified with the advent of the exclusive economic zone and the recognition of archipelagic waters. Waters not included in the E.E.Z, the archipelagic waters of a archipelagic state, the territorial waters or internal waters of a state constitute the high seas.[70]

According to classical doctrine, the high seas are free and may not be apportioned by any one nation. The freedom of the high seas, with qualified jurisdiction over adjacent waters by the coastal state, was articulated by Hugo Grotius in *Mare Liberum* (1609). The freedom principle was initially articulated with a view to breaking the monopoly of the Spanish and Portuguese over the seas and was accepted by the major maritime states, such as the United Kingdom, the United States, the Netherlands and Japan, which all sought to keep the territorial waters narrow and the high seas as broad as possible.

The freedoms of the high seas, which may be exercised by both coastal and non-coastal states, are the freedom of navigation, of fishing, to lay submarine cables and pipelines and the freedom of overflight.[71] These freedoms are not exhaustive, and others which are recognised by the general principles of international law and which may be "exercised by all States with reasonable regard to the interests of other States in their exercise of their freedom of the high seas"[72] may also exist.

The 1982 Convention reaffirms the four freedoms[73] (though the freedom of fishing is now subject to the rules governing the exclusive economic zone) and acknowledges two additional freedoms: the freedom to construct artificial islands and other installations permitted by international law, and the freedom of scientific research. As under the 1958 Convention, consideration must be given to the rights of other states on the high seas and must be "with respect to activities in the area"[74] (*i.e.* the area of the deep sea bed and ocean floor and subsoil—see below).

Nuclear Testing

The testing of conventional weapons and nuclear weapons may limit other states from exercising the freedom of navigation. The

---

[69] Article 1, Geneva Convention on the High Seas 1984.
[70] Article 86, 1982 Convention.
[71] *Ibid.* Article 2.
[72] *Ibid.*
[73] Article 87.
[74] Article 87(2), 1982 Convention.

International Court of Justice in the *Nuclear Tests Cases*,[75] brought by Australia and New Zealand against France, did not address itself to the legality under international law of nuclear testing.[76] Judge Petrén,[77] however, highlighted the fact that in spite of the 1963 Nuclear Test Ban Treaty[78] the prohibition on nuclear testing had not evolved into a rule of customary international law. Indeed, he asserted that the signatories to the 1963 Treaty by mutually banning themselves from carrying out further atmospheric nuclear tests had shown that "they were still of the opinion that customary international law did not prohibit atmospheric nuclear tests." China and France are the two major powers which have not become parties to the Nuclear Test Ban Treaty. France has, with interruptions, continued testing in the South Pacific.

Nationality of Ships

Ships must fly the flag of a state; their nationality is that of the state whose flag they fly. A state may establish its own conditions for the granting of nationality to a ship, but there:

> "must exist a genuine link between the State and the ship; in particular, the State must effectively exercise its jurisdiction and control in administrative, technical and social matters over ships flying its flag."[79]

A ship may sail under the flag of one state only and a ship:

> "which sails under the flags of two or more States, using them according to convenience, may not claim any of the nationalities in question with respect to any other State, and may be assimilated to a ship without nationality."[80]

A ship is not prohibited from sailing without a flag, but if it does it cannot invoke diplomatic protection for any international wrong it may have allegedly suffered: *Naim Molvan* v. *Att.-Gen. for Palestine*.[81] A ship may not normally change its flag during a voyage.

---

[75] I.C.J. Rep. 1974, p. 253 (*Australia* v. *France*); I.C.J. Rep. 1974, p. 457 (*New Zealand* v. *France*).
[76] The cases were withdrawn following assurances by France in a number of statements that the tests would cease.
[77] I.C.J. Rep. 1975, p. 305.
[78] 480 U.N.T.S. 43; U.K.T.S. 3 (1964) Cmnd. 2245; 14 U.S.T. 1313.
[79] Article 5, 1958 Convention; Article 91, 1982 Convention.
[80] Article 6, 1958 Convention; Article 92, 1982 Convention.
[81] [1948] A.C. 351; see 369–370.

The importance of the genuine link requirement was prompted by the increase in the use of "flags of convenience"—*i.e.* where ship owners register in a particular state because of less onerous municipal taxation and labour laws.

Jurisdiction on the High Seas

Jurisdiction over ships on the high seas lies with the flag state. The flag state is, for instance, responsible for the manning of ships and the labour conditions of the crew.[82] The 1982 Convention's counterpart Article [83] spells out in greater detail the measures which a flag state is required to take to ensure safety at sea.

In respect of a collision on the high seas, neither penal nor disciplinary proceedings may be initiated against either the master or a crew member except before the judicial or administrative authorities of the flag state or the state of which such person is a national. The ship itself may only be arrested or detained, even for investigation purposes, by the authority of the flag state.[84] Warships and government ships used for other than commercial purposes are accorded sovereign immunity and are subject only to the jurisdiction of their flag state.

Exceptions to the Freedom of Navigation—Interference with Ships on the High Seas

The most important limitation to the freedom of navigation is that:

"every State may seize a pirate ship or aircraft, or a ship taken by piracy and under the control of pirates, and arrest the persons and seize the property on board."[85]

Piracy is strictly defined in international law as:

"(1) Any illegal acts of violence, detention or any act of depredation committed for private ends by the crew or the passengers of a private ship or a private aircraft, and directed:
(a) On the high seas, against another ship or aircraft, or against persons or property on board such ship or aircraft;

---

[82] Article 10, 1958 Convention.
[83] Article 94.
[84] Article 11, 1958 Convention; Article 97, 1982 Convention; *cf.* decision in the *Lotus Case*, P.C.I.J. Rep., ser. A, No. 10 (1927).
[85] Article 19, 1958 Convention; Article 105, 1982 Convention.

       (b) Against a ship, aircraft, persons, or property in a place outside the jurisdiction of any State;

(2) Any act of voluntary participation in the operation of a ship or of an aircraft with knowledge of facts making it a pirate ship or aircraft;

(3) Any act of inciting or of intentionally facilitating an act described in sub-paragraph 1 or sub-paragraph 2 of this article."[86]

The courts of the seizing state are competent to decide the penalties which may be imposed.[87] If the suspicion for the seizure proves groundless the state making the seizure is liable for any loss or damage it has caused as a consequence.[88] Only warships or military aircraft or other authorised vessels may carry out such a seizure.

Unless provided for by treaty, a foreign merchant ship may only be boarded by a warship if it has reasonable ground for suspecting:

"(a) that the ship is engaged in piracy; or

(b) that the ship is engaged in the slave trade; or

(c) that, though flying a foreign flag or refusing to show its flag, the ship is, in reality, of the same nationality as the warship."[89]

Again, if the suspicions prove unfounded the boarded ship shall be entitled to receive compensation.

The 1982 Convention requires states to co-operate in the suppression of illicit traffic in narcotic drugs and psychotropic substances engaged in by ships on the high seas contrary to international conventions, and provides that a state:

"which has reasonable grounds for believing that a ship flying its flag is engaged in illicit traffic in narcotic drugs or psychotropic substances may request the co-operation of other States to suppress such traffic."[90]

---

[86] Article 15, 1958 Convention; Article 101, 1982 Convention. The hijacking of the Italian liner *Achille Lauro* by four Palestinians in October 1985 did not constitute an act of piracy under international law.

[87] *Ibid.*

[88] Article 20, 1958 Convention; Article 106, 1982 Convention.

[89] Article 22, 1958 Convention; Article 110, 1982 Convention—the latter also includes the right of visit in respect of ships suspected of engaging in unauthorised broadcasting—see below.

The 1982 Convention also tackles the problem of high seas broadcasting (pirate radio), particularly in Article 109(3) which provides that a person:

> "engaged in unauthorised broadcasting may be prosecuted before the Court of:
> (a) the flag State of the ship;
> (b) the State of registry of the installations;
> (c) the State of which the person is a national;
> (d) any State where the transmissions can be received; or
> (e) any State where authorised radio communication is suffering interference."

Article 109(4) confirms the right of visit to ships suspected of engaging in unauthorised broadcasting and provides that any person or ship engaged in unauthorised broadcasting may be arrested and the broadcasting apparatus seized by any state which has jurisdiction under Article 109(3).

Fishing Activities on the High Seas

The 1982 Convention[91] provides for a management and conservation scheme for the living resources of the high seas. These provisions, which consolidate and elaborate on those imposed upon states by the 1958 Geneva Convention on the Fishing and Conservation of Living Resources, are, of course, independent of those provisions in respect of the coastal state's rights in the exclusive economic zone.

Hot Pursuit

The warships, law enforcement vessels or aircraft (the 1982 Convention requires that such vessels and aircraft should be clearly marked) of a coastal state may pursue a vessel leaving its territorial waters when it suspects it of having violated its laws and regulations.[92] The 1982 Convention extends pursuit to violations of the coastal state's regulations applicable to the exclusive economic zone and continental shelf.[93] Pursuit must be continuous and must cease immediately the pursued vessel reaches the territorial waters of another state, be it the vessel's national state or a third state. If pursuit is initiated in contiguous waters, it must only be because of a

---

[90] Article 108.
[91] Articles 116–120.
[92] Article 23, 1958 Convention; Article 111, 1982 Convention.
[93] Article 111(2).

violation of the rights for which the contiguous zone was established (see above). Pursuit may only be initiated after the offending vessel has received a visual or auditory signal to stop. Failure to stop may lead to force being used.[94]

Pollution on the High Seas

The 1958 Geneva Convention on the High Seas requires every state to draw up regulations to prevent pollution of the seas by the discharge of oil from ships or pipelines or resulting from the exploitation and exploration of the sea bed and its subsoil, taking account of existing treaty provisions on the subject.[95]

In spite of growing concern of the dangers of oil pollution on the marine environment, it was not until 1954 that an international convention was agreed upon, *viz.* the International Convention for the Prevention of the Pollution of the Sea by Oil (OILPOL).[96] Essentially, the Convention prohibited the discharge of oil or any oily mixture by vessels and made any such violation subject to the jurisdiction of the state of registration. The 1954 Convention as amended in 1962, 1969 and 1971 has been replaced for parties to both Conventions by the 1973 Convention for the Prevention of Pollution from Ships (MARPOL)[97] which covers not only oil discharges from ships, but discharges such as sewage and garbage and other noxious harmful substances.[98]

The *Torrey Canyon* incident of 1967, when the United Kingdom bombed a Liberian tanker stranded off the Cornish coast so as to avoid further damage through the spillage of oil, precipitated the 1969 International Convention Relating to Intervention on the High Seas in Cases of Oil Pollution Casualties.[99] The Convention allows parties to:

> "take such measures on the high seas as may be necessary to prevent, mitigate or eliminate grave and imminent danger to their coastline or related interests from pollution or threat of pollution of the sea by oil, following upon a maritime casualty

---

[94] *The I'm Alone Case*, 3 R.I.A.A. 1609; 29 A.J.I.L. 326 (1935).
[95] Article 24.
[96] 327 U.N.T.S. 3; U.K.T.S. 56 (1958) Cmnd. 595; 12 U.S.T. 2989.
[97] Misc. 26 (1974) Cmnd. 5748; 12 I.L.M. 1319 (1973).
[98] Technical difficulties in respect of the provisions dealing with noxious liquid substances acted as an obstacle to the ratification of the 1973 Convention. A Protocol was adopted in 1978 (Misc. 26 (1974) Cmnd. 5748) to facilitate the entry into force of the regulations concerning oil discharge.
[99] U.K.T.S. 77 (1975) Cmnd. 6056; 26 U.S.T. 765; 9 I.L.M. 25 (1969); Harris, p. 341.

or acts related to such a casualty, which may reasonably be expected to result in major harmful consequences."[1]

The measures taken must be "reasonably necessary" and proportionate to the damage actual or threatened.[2]

A 1973 Protocol to the Convention[3] authorises intervention with respect to threats of pollution from substances other than oil. The Intervention Convention is supplemented by the Convention on Civil Liability for Oil Pollution Damage.[4] The Convention imposes a regime of strict liability (save in certain circumstances) on the owners of vessels and provides for the payment of compensation in respect of damage caused by oil spillage. The Liability Convention is supplemented by the 1971 Convention on the Establishment of an International Fund for Compensation for Oil Pollution Damage,[5] which established a fund for the payment of compensation in circumstances where the Liability Convention proves deficient. Tanker owners have also established their own compensation schemes, namely, the Tanker Owners' Voluntary Agreement concerning Liability for Oil Pollution 1969 (TOVALOP)[6]; and the Contract Regarding an Interim Supplement to Tanker Liability for Oil Pollution 1971 (CRISTAL).[7]

Article 25 of the Geneva Convention further required states to take measures to prevent pollution of the seas from the dumping of radioactive waste as well as co-operating with competent international organisations, while Article 5(7) of the Convention on the Continental Shelf required coastal states "to undertake, in the safety zones all appropriate measures for the protection of the living resources of the sea from harmful agents." These provisions have been reinforced by international conventions on dumping, pollution from land-based sources, such as the Oslo Convention for the Prevention of Marine Pollution by Dumping from Ships and Aircraft 1972,[8] the London Convention on the Prevention of Marine Pollution by Dumping of Wastes and Other Material 1972,[9] the Paris Convention for the Prevention of Marine Pollution from

---

[1] Article 1.
[2] Article 5.
[3] U.K.T.S. 27 (1983) Cmnd. 8924; 13 I.L.M. 605 (1974).
[4] U.K.T.S. 106 (1975) Cmnd. 6183; 9 I.L.M. 45 (1970); Harris, p. 343. Amending Protocol 1976, U.K.T.S. 26 (1981) Cmnd. 8238; 16 I.L.M. 617.
[5] U.K.T.S. 95 (1978) Cmnd. 7383; 11 I.L.M. 284 (1972). Amending Protocol Misc. 27 (1977) Cmnd. 7029; 16 I.L.M. 621 (1979).
[6] 8 I.L.M. 497 (1969).
[7] 10 I.L.M. 137 (1971).
[8] U.K.T.S. 119 (1975) Cmnd. 6228; 11 I.L.M. 262 (1972).
[9] U.K.T.S. 43 (1976) Cmnd. 6486; 26 U.S.T. 2403; 11 I.L.M. 1294 (1972).

Land-based Sources 1974,[10] and regional arrangements such as the Barcelona Convention for the Protection of the Mediterranean against Pollution 1976.[11] The United Nations Environment Programme (UNEP) operates a Regional Seas Programme.

The most important international organisation engaged in vessel pollution issues is the International Maritime Organisation (IMO) which is responsible for convening conferences and the drafting and revision of conventions.

The 1982 Convention envisages a comprehensive regime (provided for in 46 articles)[12] for the protection and preservation of the marine environment. Article 192 places states under a general obligation to protect and preserve the marine environment, and to this end parties will be required to adopt national and international measures. The Convention further provides, *inter alia*, for global and regional co-operation, contingency plans against pollution, studies, research programmes and exchange of information and data, and scientific and technical assistance to developing states. States are required to adopt laws and regulations with regard to pollution from land-based sources, sea bed activities, dumping, pollution from vessels and pollution from or through the atmosphere. Enforcement is envisaged by flag states, port states and coastal states. Non-fulfilment of international obligations by a party will give rise to international responsibility.

EXCLUSIVE ECONOMIC ZONE

The 1982 Convention acknowledges the exclusive economic zone as "an area beyond and adjacent to the territorial sea..."[13] which "shall not extend beyond 200 nautical miles from the baselines from which the breadth of the territorial sea is measured."[14]

The concept of the exclusive economic zone evolved with the realisation that fishery resources are not inexhaustible and that thus it was imperative to adopt conservation measures.

It was only with the failure of both the 1958 and 1960 Conferences to establish the width of the territorial sea and fisheries zone that the two jurisdictional areas became independent of each other. Fisheries jurisdiction, until then, was an integral part of territorial waters jurisdiction. The failure to reach international

[10] U.K.T.S. 64 (1978) Cmnd. 7251; 13 I.L.M. 352 (1974).
[11] 15 I.L.M. 290 (1976).
[12] Articles 192–238.
[13] Article 55.
[14] Article 57.

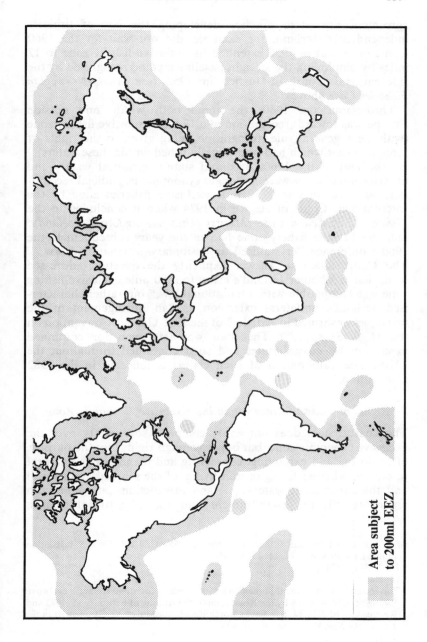

Area subject
to 200ml EEZ

agreement saw state practice developing the law of fisheries independently. Iceland, for example, did not wait for the 1960 Conference, but in 1958 extended its exclusive fishery zone to 12 miles by employing the straight baseline method recognised by the International Court of Justice in 1952 (see *Anglo-Norwegian Fisheries Case* above).

Throughout the 1960s the trend both within and outside Europe was towards recognition of a 12 mile exclusive fishery zone (with, as a general rule, recognition being given to the rights of foreign vessels which had traditionally fished within these waters).[15] By the end of the 1960s a coastal state's territorial waters and fisheries jurisdiction were no longer synonymous. Judicial recognition was accorded to a 12 mile exclusive fisheries zone by the International Court of Justice in 1974 when it concluded in the *Fisheries Jurisdiction Case (Merits) (United Kingdom* v. *Iceland)*[16] that the 12 mile fishery zone had in the years subsequent to the 1960 Conference "crystallised as customary international law."[17] The Court failed to answer explicitly the question addressed to it, that is whether Iceland's claim to a 50 mile exclusive fishing zone was compatible with international law,[18] but rather characterised Iceland's unilateral extension as "an infringement of the principles enshrined in Article 2 of the 1958 Geneva Convention on the High Seas...."[19] The door was left open for continued expansion by coastal states and so it continued throughout the 1970s. The culmination of such claims is reflected in the 1982 Convention.

Rights of Coastal States within the Exclusive Economic Zone

The coastal state does not enjoy complete sovereignty over the exclusive economic zone, but only sovereign rights "for the purpose of exploring and exploiting, conserving and managing the natural resources, whether living or non-living, of the sea bed and subsoil and the superjacent waters..." and jurisdiction, *inter alia*, with regard to "(i) the establishment and use of artificial islands,

---

[15] See, *e.g.* 1964 European Fisheries Convention, 581 U.N.T.S. 57; U.S. legislation Public Law 89–658, 5 I.L.M. 1103 (1966).

[16] I.C.J. Rep. 1974, p. 3.

[17] *Ibid.* at p. 23.

[18] The Icelandic Government implemented its intention to extend Iceland's exclusive fishing zone to 50 miles by the Resolution of the Althing of February 15, 1972 and Regulations of July 14. See Lay, Churchill and Nordquist, *New Directions in the Law of the Sea*, Vol. 1, pp. 89 and 90.

[19] *Supra*, n. 16 at p. 29.

installations and structures; (ii) marine scientific research; (iii) the protection and preservation of the marine environment."[20]

The coastal state is responsible for determining both "the allowable catch of the living resources in its exclusive economic zone"[21] and "its capacity to harvest the living resources of the exclusive economic zone."[22] The coastal state's task is to conserve resources within the E.E.Z. and to this end is charged with adopting measures which shall:

> "maintain or restore populations of harvested species at levels which can produce the maximum sustainable yield, as qualified by relevant environmental and economic needs of coastal fishing communities and the special requirement of developing States ... "[23]

Account must be taken of "the best scientific evidence available" with the coastal state co-operating where appropriate with the "competent international organisations, whether sub-regional, regional or global."[24]

The coastal state's most important task as far as foreign states are concerned is to decide, in respect of the exclusive economic zone's living resources, the surplus available over its own harvesting capacity.[25] That surplus, the Convention provides, is to be made available to other states either through agreements or other arrangements according to certain criteria which the coastal state is, especially with regard to developing states, to take into account. Such criteria include the "significance of the living resources of the area to the economy of the coastal state and its other national interests," the interests of land-locked states and those states "with special geographical characteristics" and the interests of those states "whose nationals have habitually fished in the zone."[26] The say remains, however, with the coastal state.

The coastal state is responsible for regulating fishing by foreign vessels within the exclusive economic zone,[27] and is required to give

[20] Article 56.
[21] Article 61(1).
[22] Article 62(2).
[23] Article 61(3).
[24] Article 61(2).
[25] Article 62(2).
[26] See Article 62(2); Article 69; Article 70; Articles 69 and 70 do not apply to coastal states whose economy is overwhelmingly dependent on the exploitation of the living resources of its exclusive economic zone.
[27] Article 62(4) gives a list of the measures which the coastal state may take, *e.g.* licensing of fishermen.

due notice of conservation and management regulations[28] and to exercise control over foreign vessels granted access.[29] The Convention provides for co-operation in the event of stocks occurring within the exclusive economic zone of two or more coastal states.[30] The coastal state enjoys rights within the exclusive economic zone, but it is also charged with obligations. The coastal state is not the owner, but rather the guardian of the natural resources within its exclusive economic zone.

Rights and Duties of Other States

Other states enjoy the right of free navigation, overflight and the laying of submarine cables and pipelines in the exclusive economic zone, provided they respect the rights and duties of the coastal state and comply with the laws and regulations of the latter.[31] The rights of foreign states are reinforced by the obligation on the coastal state to pay "due regard to the rights and duties of other States ... "[32]

Delimitation of the Exclusive Economic Zone between States with Opposite or Adjacent Coasts

Article 74 of the 1982 Convention provides that the delimitation of the exclusive economic zone between states with opposite or adjacent coasts is to be effected "by agreement on the basis of international law as referred to in Article 38 of the Statute of the International Court of Justice, in order to achieve an equitable solution."

In the *Delimitation of the Maritime Boundary in the Gulf of Maine Area*[33] the Chamber established to decide the delimitation of both the continental shelf and the fishery zone submitted that the criteria to be employed should be those which, by their neutral character, were best suited for employment in a multi-purpose delimitation. In the case before it, the Chamber utilised criteria especially derived from geography. Likewise, the practical methods to be employed to give effect to the criteria should, the Chamber held, be "basically founded upon geography and be as suitable for the delimitation of the sea-bed and subsoil as to that of the superjacent waters and their living resources" and, accordingly, the Chamber concluded that

---

[28] Article 62(5).
[29] Article 73.
[30] Article 63(1); Article 63(2); Article 64.
[31] Article 58(1) and (3).
[32] Article 56(2).
[33] I.C.J. Rep. 1984, p. 246.

"only geometrical methods" would be utilised. The Chamber denied that the parties' respective scale of fishing or petroleum exploitation could serve as an equitable criterion unless:

> "... unexpectedly, the overall result should appear radically inequitable as entailing disastrous repercussions on the subsistence and economic development of the population concerned."[34]

CONTINENTAL SHELF

Continental shelf is the geographical term used to describe the gently sloping ledge covered by shallow water projecting from the shoreline of many land masses before a steep descent to the ocean waters. Continental shelves vary considerably in width: off the west coast of the United States the shelf is less than five miles, whereas the entire area under water of the North Sea is continental shelf.

The freedom of the high seas meant that all states equally enjoyed the right to explore the sea bed. Continental shelves are rich in oil reserves and by the 1940s states possessed the technology to exploit such resources. Furthermore, economically, exploration had become a viable proposition.

President Truman's Proclamation of September 28, 1945, whereby the United States regarded:

> "... the natural resources of the subsoil and sea bed of the continental shelf beneath the high seas but contiguous to the coasts of the United States as appertaining to the United States, subject to its jurisdiction and control,"

but that "the character as high seas of the waters above the continental shelf and the right to their free and unimpeded navigation are in no way affected,"[35] precipitated numerous assertions of coastal states' rights over the continental shelf and marked the beginning of the change in the legal status of the continental shelf.

The claims which followed in the wake of the Truman Proclamation differed in nature. Some were restrained, some asserted exclusive sovereignty by the coastal state, whilst Argentina and El Salvador claimed not only the continental shelf, but also the superjacent waters and the airspace above, whereas Chile and Peru

---

[34] *Ibid.* at p. 342.
[35] 4 Whiteman 756; Harris, p. 354.

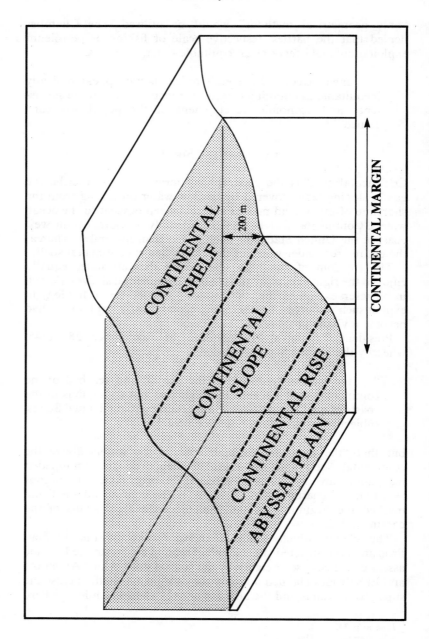

claimed sovereignty over the sea bed, subsoil and water around their coasts to a limit of 200 miles.[36] It was against the background of such claims that the International Law Commission addressed itself to the issue of the continental shelf.

Article 1 of the Geneva Convention defines the continental shelf as referring:

"(a) to the sea bed and subsoil of the submarine areas adjacent to the coast but outside the area of the territorial sea, to a depth of 200 metres or, beyond that limit, to where the depth of the superjacent waters admits of the exploitation of the natural resources of the said areas; (b) to the sea bed and subsoil of similar submarine areas adjacent to the coasts of islands."

The 1958 definition emphasises exploitability, whereas the 1982 Convention does not. Article 76 of the 1982 Convention defines the continental shelf as:

"the sea-bed and subsoil of the submarine areas that extend beyond its territorial sea throughout the natural prolongation of its land territory to the outer edge of the continental margin,[37] or to a distance of 200 nautical miles from the baselines from which the breadth of the territorial sea is measured where the outer edge of the continental margin does not extend up to that distance."

The continental shelf extends to 200 nautical miles for all states, but retains an advantage for the geographically favoured. However, Article 76(6) provides that the continental shelf shall not exceed 350 nautical miles from territorial baselines. Article 76(7) provides the method of delimitation to be employed where the continental shelf exceeds 200 nautical miles.

Regarding a coastal state's rights over the continental shelf, the 1982 Convention essentially reproduces the provisions of the 1958 Convention. A coastal state's rights are not territorial sovereign rights but are, rather, functional rights for the purpose of exploring and exploiting the natural resources of the continental shelf.[38] The coastal state's rights are exclusive, and exploration and exploitation activities may not be undertaken without the consent of the coastal

[36] Chile and Peru possess no geographical continental shelf.
[37] *i.e.* the continental margin consists of the continental shelf, slope and rise that separates the land mass from the deep ocean floor (abyssal plain).
[38] Article 2, 1958 Convention; Article 77(1), 1982 Convention.

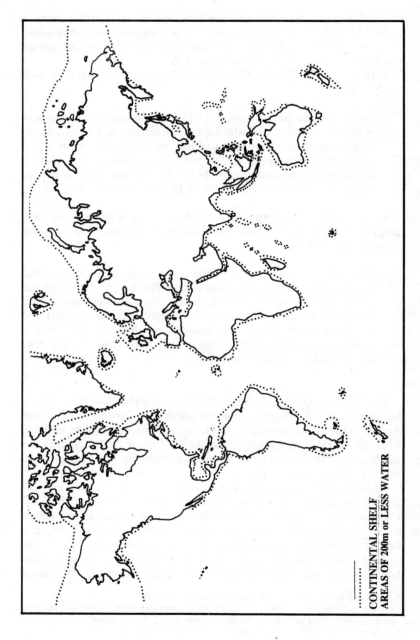

CONTINENTAL SHELF
AREAS OF 200m or LESS WATER

state. Natural resources are defined as the mineral and other non-living resources of the sea bed and subsoil, together with living organisms belonging to sedentary species. The 1982 Convention provides that the coastal state has the exclusive right to authorise and regulate drilling on the continental shelf for all purposes.

The coastal state's rights in the continental shelf do not affect the status of the superjacent waters, and states, in exercising their rights on the continental shelf, must not impede the laying or maintenance of submarine cables or pipelines and must not result in:

> "any unjustifiable interference with navigation, fishing or the conservation of the living resources of the sea, nor result in any interference with fundamental oceanographic or other scientific research carried out with the intention of open publication."[39]

A coastal state may construct artificial installations on the continental shelf and may establish safety zones around such installations to a maximum of 5,000 metres. Article 82 of the 1982 Convention further restricts the maximum limit of the continental shelf (see above) by providing for the payment of contributions in kind by coastal states in respect of the exploitation of the non-living resources when their continental shelf exceeds 200 nautical miles from the territorial baselines. Payments and contributions are to be made five years after production. Developing states which are net importers of a mineral resource produced from its continental shelf will be exempt from making such payments or contributions. The payments or contributions shall be made through the Authority (see below) which shall distribute to states who are parties to the Convention "on the basis of equitable sharing criteria, taking into account the interests and needs of developing States, particularly the least developed and land-locked among them."[40]

Delimitation of the Continental Shelf between States with Opposite or Adjacent Coasts

Article 6(1) and (2) of the 1958 Convention on the Continental Shelf provide formulae for delimiting the outer limit of the continental shelf between opposite and adjacent states. In both instances, the boundary should be determined by agreement between the states concerned, in the absence of which the boundary

---

[39] Article 5(1), 1958 Convention; Article 246, 1982 Convention applies to research on the continental shelf and the exclusive economic zone.
[40] Article 82.

for opposite coasts "is the median line, every point of which is equidistant from the nearest point of the baselines from which the breadth of the territorial sea of each State is measured" and for adjacent coasts "the boundary shall be determined by application of the principle of equidistance from the nearest point of the baselines from which the breadth of the territorial sea of each State is measured." Both rules show a recognised exception, namely, that neither the median line nor the principle of equidistance will apply if "another boundary is justified by special circumstances."

The Geneva Convention failed to provide any indication of what would constitute "special circumstances." The International Court of Justice in the *North Sea Continental Shelf Cases*[41] provided that delimitation was to be "effected by agreement in accordance with equitable principles, and taking account of all the relevant circumstances."[42] Relevant circumstances identified by the Court were, *inter alia*, the general configuration of the coasts of the parties; so far as known or readily ascertainable, the physical and geological structure and the natural resources, of the continental shelf areas involved; the element of a reasonable degree of proportionality, which a delimitation carried out in accordance with equitable principles ought to bring about between the extent of the continental shelf areas appertaining to the coastal state and the length of its coast measured in the general direction of the coastline, account being taken for this purpose of the effects, actual or prospective, of any other continental shelf delimitations between adjacent states in the same region.[43]

In the *Continental Shelf (Libyan Arab Jamahiriya v. Malta) Case*, the International Court refuted that the respective economic positions of the parties concerned could be taken into account, but did acknowledge that possibly security and defence interests might be given cognisance.[44] The International Court of Justice, when confronted with delimitation disputes, has emphasised that parties "are under an obligation to enter into negotiations with a view to arriving at an agreement" and that parties "are under an obligation so as to conduct themselves that the negotiations are meaningful...."[45] In the *North Sea Continental Shelf Cases*, the Court maintained that the equidistance principle was not, in light of the special circumstances exception, a principle of international law, but merely an application in appropriate situations of a more

[41] I.C.J. Rep. 1969, p. 3.
[42] *Ibid.* at p. 46.
[43] *Ibid.* at pp. 50–52.
[44] I.C.J. Rep. 1985, p. 13 at pp. 41–42.
[45] *Supra* n. 41 at p. 47.

general rule. In the *English Channel Arbitration*,[46] the arbitrators held that Article 6 did not formulate the equidistance principle and "special circumstances" as two separate rules, but rather as a combined equidistance-special circumstances rule. Similarly, in the *Continental Shelf (Tunisia* v. *Libya) Case*, the Court maintained that "each continental shelf case in dispute should be considered and judged on its own merits, having regard to its peculiar circumstances."[47]

The International Court has, in other words, minimised the equidistance principle.[48] This is reflected in the 1982 Convention, which has abandoned the Article 6 formulae and provides that delimitation is to be "effected by agreement on the basis of international law, as referred to in Article 38 of the Statute of the International Court of Justice, in order to achieve an equitable solution."[49]

Provision for the establishment of a Commission on the Continental Shelf is made under Article 76(8) in an effort to obtain international objectivity in the national delimitation of the continental shelf, the limits of which are to be established by a coastal state on the basis of Commission recommendations, which are to be final and binding. Article 298 of the 1982 Convention provides that states may opt to exclude delimitation disputes from procedures involving a binding decision and may refer them instead to "compulsory" conciliation.

DEEP SEA BED

The deep sea bed and its subsoil is rich in mineral resources, particularly in manganese nodules. The extraction of these resources is close to becoming a reality (albeit still an expensive process).

To whom should the resources belong? Should they belong to those relatively few states which, because of a technological and capital advantage, are able to finance deep sea mining, or should the resources of the ocean bed belong to all states and should the benefits derived be distributed amongst the international

---

[46] 18 I.L.M. 397 (1979).

[47] I.C.J. Rep. 1982, p. 18 at p. 92; see also *Delimitation of the Maritime Boundary in the Gulf of Maine (Canada* v. *United States of America), supra,* n.33 at p. 292"... any agreement or other equivalent solution should involve the application of equitable criteria."

[48] The equidistance principle has been used in treaties between states.

[49] Article 83(1); Article 74 articulates a similar formula for the delimitation of the exclusive economic zone between states with opposite or adjacent coasts.

community generally? If the answer is the latter then what conditions should apply?

The United States, for example, regards deep sea mining as a freedom of the high seas, whereas developing and technologically disadvantaged states in particular have adopted the view that the deep sea bed should be designated an "area" which is the "common heritage of mankind" and whose natural resources should not be liable to appropriation by any state. The years preceding the sessions of UNCLOS witnessed the emergence of two groups, one representing developing states, calling for an international body to conduct all exploitation in the deep sea bed and, secondly, that of the developed states, maintaining that deep sea activity should be undertaken by states and/or national companies subject to a registration and licensing system. Both groups did, however, agree on the need to avoid a "free for all." Accordingly, the General Assembly Declaration of Principles Concerning the Sea Bed and the Ocean Floor and the Subsoil Thereof, Beyond the Limits of National Jurisdiction 1970[50] provided that the area and its resources thereof "are the common heritage of mankind" and that no state or person, natural or juridical could "claim, exercise or acquire rights with respect to the area or its resources incompatible with the international regime to be established . . . ."[51]

The regime articulated in the 1982 Convention represents a compromise between the demands of the developed and the developing states. A very detailed regime is provided by the Convention, but its viability is tenuous in spite of the inclusion during the final session of the Preparatory Investment Protection (P.I.P.). Dissatisfaction with the Convention's provisions on the deep sea bed has been and remains responsible for the non-signature of the Convention by major powers such as West Germany, the United Kingdom and the United States of America.

Under the 1982 Convention all deep sea bed exploration and exploitation is to be carried out and controlled by an International Sea Bed Authority.[52] However, the Convention does provide for "parallel access." Activities in the deep sea bed are to be carried out either by the Authority (through its organ, the Enterprise—see below) or by way of contracts entered into by the Authority with a state, private company or consortium. A company or consortium must have a nationality so that it can have a sponsoring state, which must have ratified the Convention.

---

[50] G.A. Resolution 2749 (XXV), December 17, 1970. 10 I.L.M. 230 (1970); Harris, p. 363.
[51] *Ibid.* Articles 1 and 3.
[52] Article 153.

Work plans must be submitted for the Authority's approval. Each sea bed tract for which a work plan is tendered must be capable of including two mining operations so that when the plan receives approval, the tract is split into two halves of equal commercial value. The "reserved site" is to be retained by the Authority for exploitation by either the Enterprise or a developing country, while the applicant is to be granted exclusive rights in the other half[53] against payment of an annual fee determined by production value less costs, but not less than $1 million. A set fee of $500,000 is to be charged by the Authority for processing each application.[54] The Convention provides for a five year review of a deep sea regime[55] and for a review conference 15 years after commercial production has begun.[56] The advantage of "parallel access" for the International Authority is that the Enterprise is saved the cost of prospecting and exploration. Otherwise, it is on an equal footing with a state or consortium which makes application to the Authority. Thus, it must submit to the same approval procedures plans of work that are both technologically and financially sound. Production levels are to be regulated by the Authority so that production by producers of land-based minerals will be safeguarded.

A problem that beset UNCLOS, which was not settled until the final session, was that of pre-Convention investment. What was adopted was an interim arrangement, transitory in character, designed to bring pioneer preparatory investments within the framework of the Convention. A Pioneer Investor (registration as one was dependent on certain conditions being satisfied) will be able to operate in a pioneer area within which the Pioneer Investor will enjoy only exclusive rights of exploration. Exploration may not go beyond the pioneer area until the Authority has approved a plan of work. Approval will be forthcoming provided the states or consortium members have signed the Convention. Pioneer Investors will also enjoy priority exploitation rights (though not over the Enterprise) once the Convention's regime comes into effect. Four states were identified as being eligible to register as pioneer investors: France, India, Japan and the Soviet Union. Consortium entities with the nationality of or controlled by one or more of the following countries: Belgium, Canada, Federal German Republic, Italy, Japan, Netherlands, United Kingdom and the United States were identified as eligible for pioneer investor status, provided the

[53] Annex III, Article 8 and Article 9.
[54] Should the processing cost be less than $500,000 the difference will be repaid to the applicant.
[55] Article 154.
[56] Article 155.

entity concerned had attained a certain level of expenditure in pioneer activities (U.S. $30 million) before January 1983 and the sponsoring state had signed the Convention by December 10, 1984.

Currently, it appears that the first generation of deep sea mining may be a system of state reciprocity—co-existing possibly with that of the international regime. The United States was the first country to pass legislation adopting an interim programme for the regulation of the exploration and commercial exploitation of the deep sea bed by United States' nationals pending the entry into force of an international treaty on the subject. The United States' Deep Sea Bed Hard Mineral Resources Act 1980[57] authorised the issue of exploration licences after July 1981, but delayed the issue of commercial recovery licences until January 1, 1988. The United States Act, so as to prevent conflicts between licences and permits issued by the United States and those issued by other states, initiated the concept of reciprocating states. Each state is to regulate the issue of sea bed licences and permits in a way compatible with the United States Act and is to establish similar procedures for recognising licences/permits issued by the United States and other reciprocating states. The United States Act has served as a blueprint for other states' domestic legislation on the subject, *e.g.* the United Kingdom's Deep Sea Mining (Temporary Provisions) Act 1981.[58] The reciprocity system is born from the assumption that mining is a legitimate freedom of the high seas. To date no reciprocating treaties have been concluded, but preliminary agreements between the United States, the United Kingdom, the Federal Republic of Germany and France have been reached on interim arrangements for resolving overlapping claims with respect to mining areas for polymetallic nodules of the deep sea bed.[59]

International Sea Bed Authority[60]

The organs of the International Sea Bed Authority are the Assembly, the Council and the Enterprise. The Assembly, with a representative from each Member State, is the supreme policy-making organ, adopting decisions by a two-thirds majority. The Council is made up of 36 Member States elected by the Assembly, representing various special interest groups, such as the largest

[57] 30 U.S.C §1401; 19 I.L.M. 1003 (1980).
[58] 20 I.L.M. 1217 (1981); Harris, p. 369; France, the Federal Republic of Germany, Japan and Italy have all passed similar legislation—see 21 I.L.M. 808 (1982); 20 I.L.M. 393 (1981) and 21 I.L.M. 832 (1982); 22 I.L.M. 102 (1983); 24 I.L.M. 983 (1985).
[59] 21 I.L.M. 950 (1982).
[60] Articles 156–188.

investors in sea mining, land-locked nations and potential producers. The Council, which will take decisions, depending on the
subject by two-thirds, three-quarters or consensus, is to be the
executive organ of the Authority. The Enterprise is the body which
will be responsible for conducting the activities of the Authority.

The Authority is to be financed by Member States on the scale of
their contributions to the United Nations and from the activities of
the Enterprise.

The Convention also provides for the compulsory settlement of
deep sea bed disputes, either by judicial settlement (by reference to
the International Tribunal for the Law of the Sea) or by commercial
arbitration.

FURTHER READING

Cases and Materials

D.J. Harris, *Cases and Materials on International Law* (1983), Chapter 7.

L. Henkin, R. Pugh, O. Schachter and H. Smit, *International Law: Cases and Materials* (1980), Chapter 6.

J. Sweeny, C. Oliver and N. Leech, *The International Legal System: Cases and Materials* (1981), Chapter 3.

Specialised Texts

R. Churchill and A.V. Lowe, *The Law of the Sea* (1983).

D.P. O'Connell (Shearer ed.), *The International Law of the Sea* (1984) Vols. I and II.

General Texts

M. Akehurst, *A Modern Introduction to International Law* (1982), Chapter 18.

I. Brownlie, *Principles of Public International Law* (1979), Chapters IX, X and XI.

L. Green, *International Law: A Canadian Perspective* (1984), Part IV, § 2.

D.W. Greig, *International Law* (1976), Chapter 7, pp. 284–348.

J.G. Starke, *An Introduction to International Law* (1984), Chapter 9.

Chapter Eight

STATE RESPONSIBILITY

State responsibility in international law refers to liability—that of one state to another for the non-observance of the obligations imposed by the international legal systems. A state may incur liability for injury to the defendant state itself. This may be, for example, for breach of a treaty obligation, or for injury to the defendant state's nationals or their property.

State responsibility is a complex issue. The International Law Commission initiated a study of state responsibility in 1949. The Commission's early efforts to produce a draft Convention linking questions of responsibility generally with responsibility for the treatment of aliens in particular proved inconclusive. The Commission reconvened in 1969 and this time confined itself to considering the general issues of responsibility. Thirty five draft articles indicating when responsibility may be incurred have been adopted by the Commission. The draft articles are concerned with the content, forms and degrees of state responsibility.[1]

All states are equally responsible under international law for their illegal acts. This rule is absolute. A state cannot, for example, plead lack of capacity. "New" states do not enjoy a period of grace before they assume responsibility for the discharge of their obligations.

A state cannot relieve itself of responsibility by invoking either provisions or omissions of its domestic legislation.[2] In a federal state, such as Canada or the United States, the Federal Government is responsible on the international plane and will incur international liability for any actions or omissions of its member states which result in international injury. A federal government may not exonerate itself of responsibility by submitting that individual member states are independent or autonomous.

Recognised defence pleas which may be utilised by a state to deny responsibility are consent, reprisal, *force majeure*, distress, necessity and self-defence.

---

[1] I.L.C. Draft Articles on State Responsibility, Y.B.I.L.C., 1979, II (Pt. II), p. 90; Y.B.I.L.C., 1980, II (Pt. II), pp. 14, 70; Articles 1–32, 18 I.L.M. 1568 (1979); Articles 33–35, 74 A.J.I.L. 962 (1980).

[2] *Free Zones of Upper Savoy and the District of Gex*, P.C.I.J. Rep., ser. A/B, No. 46 at 167 (1932).

NATURE OF LIABILITY

Liability may be civil or criminal.

An international delict is simply defined as any internationally wrongful act "which is not an international crime.... "[3] Breach of a treaty obligation is, for example, an international delict.

An international crime is defined as:

> "[A]n internationally wrongful act which results from the breach by a State of an international obligation so essential for the protection of fundamental interests of the international community that its breach is recognised as a crime by that community as a whole ... "[4]

An international crime may arise from:

> "(a) a serious breach of an international law of essential importance for maintenance of international peace and security ...;
>
> (b) a serious breach of an international obligation of essential importance for safeguarding the right of self-determination of peoples ...;
>
> (c) a serious breach on a widespread scale of an international obligation of essential importance for safeguarding the human being, such as those prohibiting slavery, genocide, apartheid;
>
> (d) a serious breach of an international obligation of essential importance for the safeguarding and preservation of the human environment, such as those prohibiting mass pollution of the atmosphere or of the seas."[5]

The examples in the draft article are only illustrative—the list is not exhaustive.

Having recognised the possibility of international criminal responsibility, the International Law Commission has reserved for a later date any consideration of the principles and sanctions applicable to criminal responsibility. International criminal responsibility remains, as a consequence, undeveloped. International law has concentrated primarily on the responsibility of a state for its treatment of aliens in respect of both their person and their property.

[3] Draft Article 19(4).
[4] Draft Article 19(2).
[5] Draft Article 19(3).

The origin of an internationally unlawful act is irrelevant. The origin neither affects the characterisation of the act as unlawful nor does it affect the international responsibility of the state concerned.[6] "Every internationally wrongful act of a State entails the international responsibility of that State."[7] Article 1 of the International Law Commission's Draft Articles spells out a rule of customary international law. This rule was acknowledged in the *Chorzów Factory Case (Indemnity) (Merits)*[8] when the Court maintained that "... any breach of an engagement involves an obligation to make reparation."[9]

Is state responsibility absolute or must there be fault? In other words, is liability strict or must there be a degree of blameworthiness which can be attributed to the state? Must there be intention or negligence?

The customary international law rule on these questions is not clear. While evidence in the form of arbitral and judicial decisions can be found in support of both standpoints, conclusive evidence in support of either theory is absent. Fault liability appears to have received support in the *Home Missionary Society Claim*[10] and the *Corfu Channel Case (Merits)*,[11] while the Claims Commission in the *Caire Claim*[12] supported absolute liability. State practice throws little light on the issue which is, anyway, essentially theoretical and one of largely academic interest. The proliferation of state organs and agencies has seen an increased application of strict liability. Fault liability has, because of the extension of state activities, become too complicated to apply in practice.

Imputability

"Imputability" in the context of state responsibility means "attributable." A state is only responsible for acts or omissions which can be attributed to it as its own. What, for the purposes of state responsibility, constitutes the state?

In international law, a state is responsible for the actions of:
(a) the government;
(b) any political sub-division of the state;
(c) any organ, agency official employee or other agent of its government or of any sub-division acting within the scope of their employment.

[6] Draft Article 17.
[7] Draft Article 1.
[8] P.C.I.J. Rep., ser. A, No. 17 (1928).
[9] *Ibid.* at 29.
[10] 6 R.I.A.A. 42 (1920).
[11] I.C.J. Rep. 1949, p. 4.
[12] 5 R.I.A.A. 516 (1929).

Imputability is a legal fiction assimilating the acts of those identified above to the state as if they were its own.

A state is not responsible for acts committed by one of its nationals (provided, that is, he is a private individual and is not, for example, a policeman) against a foreigner. The individual may, of course, be liable to prosecution in the domestic courts and indeed the government concerned may be held internationally liable if it fails to discharge its duty "of diligently prosecuting and properly punishing."[13] Acts of private persons performed on their own initiative in an emergency, *e.g.* a natural disaster, are attributable to the state.[14]

A state cannot deny responsibility for an international wrong on the grounds that the act is under its domestic law *ultra vires*. A state can be held liable for the conduct of an official even when official competence has been exceeded, provided that is, the officials acted with apparent authority as competent officials or organs and the powers or methods used were appropriate to this official authority.[15]

In the *Youmans Claim*,[16] Mexico was held liable for the conduct of certain members of its militia who acted in defiance of orders and instead of affording protection to a group of Americans, opened fire on the house where the latter were seeking refuge. The United States-Mexican General Claims Commission maintained that the Mexican Government was liable for the soldiers' unlawful acts even though the soldiers had exceeded their powers.

A state is responsible for the acts of all its officials irrespective of their rank.[17] It is not responsible for the conduct of either foreign states or international organisations within its territory.[18] A state is not held liable for the activities of insurrectionaries,[19] but should the insurrectionaries be successful in their objective and become the subsequent government they (as the legitimate government) will be held liable for any wrongful act committed during their struggle for power.[20]

---

[13] *Noyes Claim*, 6 R.I.A.A. 308 at 311 (1933); see also the *Zafiro Case*, 6 R.I.A.A. 160 (1925).
[14] Draft Article 8(b).
[15] Draft Article 10; *Caire Claim*, *supra*, n. 12.
[16] 4 R.I.A.A. 110 (1926).
[17] Draft Article 6; see also *Massey Case (U.S. v. Mexico)*, 4 R.I.A.A. 155 at 157 (1927).
[18] Draft Articles 12 and 13.
[19] Draft Article 14; see also *Sambaggio Case (Italy v. Venezuela)*, 10 R.I.A.A. 499 at 513 (1903).
[20] Draft Article 15.

Reparation

Diplomatic negotiation may produce an apology or an assurance that the offending breach of international law will not recur. If, however, material loss has been sustained by a state or one of its nationals the question of reparation frequently has to be determined.

The object of reparation should be to wipe out, as far as possible "all the consequences of the illegal act and re-establish the situation which would in all probability have existed if the act had not been committed."[21] Reparation is designed to restore previous conditions and if this is not possible to compensate for the injury itself.

Reparation may be awarded through restitution in kind and if restitution is not possible, through:

> "payment of a sum corresponding to the value which a restitution in kind would bear; the award, if need be, of damages for loss sustained which would not be covered by restitution in kind or payment in place of it—such are the principles which should serve to determine the amount of compensation due for an act contrary to international law."[22]

Restitution in kind is infrequent.[23] More frequently, monetary compensation is awarded to cover the cost of the injury suffered. In the *Chorzów Factory Case (Indemnity)*[24] the Permanent Court of International Justice held that the rules of law governing reparation should be:

> "the rules of international law in force between the two States concerned, and not the law governing relations between the State which has committed a wrongful act and the individual who has suffered damage. Rights or interests of an individual the violation of which rights causes damage are always in a different plane to rights belonging to a State, which rights may also be infringed by the same act. The damage suffered by an individual is never therefore identical in kind with that which will be suffered by a State; it can only afford a convenient scale for the calculation of the reparation due to the State."[25]

---

[21] *Chorzów Factory Case (Indemnity) (Merits)*, P.C.I.J. Rep., ser. A, No. 17 at p. 47 (1928).

[22] *Ibid.*

[23] Restitution in kind was ordered in the *Martini Case (Italy v. Venezuela)*, 2 R.I.A.A. 975, 1002 (1930) and in the *Temple Case*, I.C.J. Rep. 1962, p. 6.

[24] *Supra*, n. 21.

[25] *Ibid.* at 28.

Compensation is normally a matter of negotiation. There are no established principles for calculating the sum to be paid. In respect of material loss, the sum awarded is generally commensurate with the loss sustained and will take account of "loss of profits . . . as compared with other owners of similar property."[26]

Damages have been awarded for non-material loss, but international tribunals have been reluctant to grant exemplary or punitive damages:

> " . . . Counsel has failed to point us to any money award by an international arbitral tribunal where exemplary, punitive, or vindictive damages have been assessed against one sovereign nation in favour of another presenting a claim on behalf of its nationals."[27]

In the *Lusitania Case* the United States Germany Mixed Claims Commission refused to award punitive damages. The Commission did not impose a penalty and only awarded reparation in respect of the injury suffered. However, in the *I'm Alone Case*,[28] $25,000 was awarded against the United States as a "material amount in respect of the wrong suffered by Canada."

A state will be liable to another state if it *inter alia* breaches a treaty obligation, violates its territorial integrity, injures its diplomatic representatives or mistreats one of its nationals or causes injury to the property of one of its nationals.

It is in the context of the treatment of aliens and aliens' property that the issue of state responsibility will be examined.

TREATMENT OF ALIENS—THE TREATMENT OF NATIONALS OF OTHER STATES

If an individual allegedly sustains injury while in another state, redress may only be sought through the individual's state of nationality. (See nationality of claims rule below). An individual cannot force a state to espouse a claim on his behalf. It is a matter of state discretion whether a claim is taken up and if a state does pursue a claim on behalf of an individual it is not required to hand over any damages which may be received.[29] Nor can an individual

---

[26] *Norwegian Shipowners Claim (Norway v. U.S.)*, 1 R.I.A.A. 307 at 338 (1922).

[27] *Lusitania Case (United States v. Germany)*, 7 R.I.A.A. 32, 38–44 (1956), Judge Parker.

[28] *(Canada v. United States)*, 3 R.I.A.A. 1609 (1933/35); 29 A.J.I.L. 326 (1935).

[29] *Civilian War Claimants Association v. The King* [1932] A.C. 14.

prevent a state from exercising its rights of diplomatic protection if it (the state) feels its right to have its nationals treated properly has been violated:

> "... an alien ... cannot deprive the government of his nation of its undoubted right of applying international remedies to violations of international law committed to his damage. Such government frequently has a larger interest in maintaining the principles of international law than in recovering damage for one of its citizens in a particular case, and manifestly such citizen cannot by contract in this respect, tie the hands of his Government."[30]

In other words, in espousing a claim on behalf of an individual a state is protecting one of its own rights, which must be respected, *viz* that its nationals be treated in a particular manner. Once a state has taken up a claim on behalf of an individual it enjoys exclusive control over the handling and presentation of a claim[31] and the claim becomes one between two states:

> "it is true that the dispute was at first between a private person and a State ... Subsequently, the Greek Government took up the case. The dispute then entered upon a new plane; it entered the domain of International Law, and became a dispute between two States ... Once a State has taken up a case on behalf of one of its subjects before an international tribunal in the eyes of the latter the State is the sole claimant."[32]

Standard of Treatment

A state is not required to admit foreign nationals. Immigration control is a matter of national law. Once aliens are admitted, however, if a state should then fail to treat foreign nationals in a required way it may be held guilty of having breached an international obligation.

By what standard is the treatment to be gauged? There are two views, one representing that of developing "new" states and the other representing that of developed states.

The National Treatment Standard

Originally supported by the Latin American countries during the

---

[30] *North American Dredging Co. Case (U.S./Mexican)*, 4 R.I.A.A. 26 at 29 (1926).
[31] See, *e.g. Administrative Decision No. V (U.S. v. Germany)*, 7 R.I.A.A. 119 (1924).
[32] *Mavrommatis Palestine Concessions Case*, P.C.I.J. Rep., ser. A, No. 2, p. 12 (1924).

nineteenth and early twentieth centuries, this view is favoured today by Eastern European socialist states and some developing states. According to the national treatment standard aliens are to be treated in the same way as nationals of the state concerned. Obviously, if applied consistently this would be to the advantage of aliens. However, international law does not regulate a state's treatment of aliens in all activities, *e.g.*, aliens in the United Kingdom may not vote nor may they be admitted to public office. The disadvantage of the national treatment standard is obvious. A state could subject an alien to inhuman treatment and justify such treatment on the grounds that nationals could be similarly treated. Thus, international arbitration tribunals and developed western states have denied that a state can exonerate itself by pleading that nationals are treated likewise if the treatment of aliens falls short of the international minimum standard.[33]

International Minimum Standard

The international minimum standard is difficult to define. International law has not provided a definition, although an attempt to do so was made in 1957 when the International Law Commission debated the Second Report on State Responsibility of its Special Rapporteur.[34] In the Report an article which embraced both the national minimum standard and the international minimum standard was proposed. States were to afford to aliens the same treatment as that enjoyed by nationals, but in no circumstances was such treatment "to be less than the 'fundamental human rights' recognised and defined in the contemporary international instruments." However, the proposal was too far-reaching and since then the International Law Commission has concentrated its attention on the codification of general principles of responsibility.

To violate the international minimum standard, a state's treatment of foreign nationals must fall so short of established civilised behaviour "that every reasonable and impartial man would readily recognise its insufficiency."[35]

A state may incur responsibility if an alien is physically ill-treated,[36] or if an alien's property is damaged.[37] A state may also

---

[33] *Roberts Claim*, 4 R.I.A.A. 77 (1926).

[34] Y.B.I.L.C., 1957, II, p. 104; Harris, p. 403.

[35] *Neer Claim*, 4 R.I.A.A. 60 at 62 (1926).

[36] *Roberts Claim*, *supra*, n. 33; *Quintanilla Claim (Mexico v. U.S.)*, 4 R.I.A.A. 101 (1926).

[37] *Zafiro Case*, *supra*, n. 13. Article 9, Harvard Draft Convention on the International Responsibility of States for Injuries to Aliens 1961, 55 A.J.I.L. 548 (1961).

incur responsibility if an alien suffers a maladministration of justice, *e.g.* is denied assistance of counsel,[38] or denied adequate protection. Liability will only be incurred if the lack of protection has been either wilful or due to neglect.[39]

States, as already mentioned (see diplomatic immunity p.110) are required to afford a higher degree of protection to internationally protected persons[40] than to "ordinary" aliens.

Although international law is against the arbitrary and unjustified expulsion of aliens,[41] states do enjoy a discretion to deport aliens if the presence of such aliens is a threat to the public interest. Article 7 of the Treaty of Rome prohibits discrimination between the nationals of Member States on the grounds of nationality and Articles 48–51 of the Treaty provide for the free movement of workers. Member States can deny the exercise of that right on the grounds of public health, public security and public order.[42] However, when deported, the individuals concerned should be advised of the reasons for their deportation, save where to do so would be contrary to national security.[43]

Nationals

If nationals of a state are expelled from another state the state of nationality is obliged to receive them unless they are willing to go to another state and that state is willing to admit them. It was in acknowledgment of this obligation imposed by international law that the United Kingdom in 1972 admitted all East African Asians who were not Ugandan nationals.

Refugees

International law does not require states to admit refugees, but under the 1951 Convention Relating to the Status of Refugees[44] and

---

[38] *Pope Case*, 8 Whiteman 709.

[39] *Noyes Claim (U.S.* v. *Panama), supra*, n. 13; *Janes Claim (U.S.* v. *Mexico)*, 4 R.I.A.A. 82 (1926).

[40] See, The Convention on the Prevention and Punishment of Crimes against Internationally Protected Persons including Diplomatic Agents 1973, 13 I.L.M. 42 (1974); Misc. 19 (1975) Cmnd. 6176.

[41] See Article 3, 1955 European Convention on Establishment, 529 U.N.T.S. 141; U.K.T.S. 1 (1971) Cmnd. 4573; Fourth Protocol of the European Convention of Human Rights 1963, Misc. 6 (1964) Cmnd. 2309; 58 A.J.I.L. 334 (1964).

[42] Article 48(3).

[43] Regulation No. 72/194 EEC Council Directive of May 18, 1972, O.J. May 26, 1972 L. 121/32.

[44] 189 U.N.T.S. 150; U.K.T.S. 39 (1954) Cmd. 9171.

the 1967 Protocol Relating to the Status of Refugees,[45] Contracting Parties undertake to accord refugees treatment no less favourable than that accorded to aliens generally and no refugee may be expelled to territory "where his life or freedom would be questioned."[46]

Expropriation of the Property of Aliens

Expropriation is the compulsory taking of private property by the state. Expropriation, particularly in the post-colonial period, became an important issue in international law. Possibly more than any other issue, expropriation has highlighted the opposing views of the capitalist developed countries and socialist states and the "new" developing states. Capitalist developed countries seek a guarantee of protection and security before investing abroad, whilst the latter (*i.e.* socialist and developing states) are reluctant to allow too much foreign investment and wish to retain control over their own resources. Both developed and developing states recognise that every state has a legitimate right to expropriate property, but, while the developed states of the Western tradition maintain that expropriation is only legitimate if it complies with an international minimum standard and if, in particular, it is accompanied by effective compensation, the developing "new" states deny this.

The position of the capitalist developed states is represented in General Assembly Resolution 1803 on Permanent Sovereignty over Natural Resources.[47] The Resolution recognises the right of peoples and nations "to permanent sovereignty over their natural wealth and resources . . . "[48]

Article 4 of the Resolution which is regarded as reinforcing customary international law provides that:

> "[N]ationalisation, expropriation or requisitioning shall be based on grounds or reasons of public utility, security or the national interest which are recognised as overriding purely individual or private interests, both domestic and foreign. In such cases the owner shall be paid appropriate compensation in accordance with the rules in force in the State taking such measures and in accordance with international law."

[45] 606 U.N.T.S. 267; U.K.T.S. 15 (1969) Cmnd. 3906; 6 I.L.M. 78 (1967). 63 A.J.I.L. 385 (1969).
[46] *Supra*, n. 43, Article 32(1). Article 32(1) will not apply if the "individual is reasonably suspected of being a security risk or having been finally convicted of a particular serious crime, constitutes a danger to the Community"—Article 33(2).
[47] (1962), G.A.O.R., 17th Session, Supp. 17, p. 15—reprinted in Harris, p. 423.
[48] Article 1.

In other words, expropriation, in order to be valid, should be for public purposes, should not be discriminatory (not specified but implied in Article 4) and should be accompanied by compensation assessed in accordance with the rules in force in the appropriate state *and* international law.

Public Purpose

The requirement that nationalisation should be for a public purpose for it to be valid under international law was identified in the *Certain German Interests in Polish Upper Silesia Case*[49] and in the *BP Case* (1974),[50] in which the British challenged the Libyan nationalisation measures on the grounds *inter alia* that they were not motivated by considerations of a political nature related to the international well-being of the taking state. In that case, the arbitrator confirmed that the measures in question violated international law as they were made for purely extraneous political reasons.[51] However, three years later in the *Liamco Case*[52] the arbitrator dismissed the independent public purpose requirement, on the grounds that "it is the general opinion in international law that the public utility principle is not a necessary requisite for the legality of a nationalisation."[53] In practice, public purpose has not been predominant in international claims and where it has featured it has been of secondary importance. Public purpose is a broad concept which is not readily susceptible to objective examination by states.

Discrimination

Nationalisation which discriminates against foreigners, or foreigners of a particular nationality, or particular foreigners, has been regarded by developed states as being contrary to international law.[54] Discrimination is difficult to prove. There may, for example, be no comparable enterprises owned either by local nationals or nationals of other countries. Like public purpose, arguments inferring discrimination have not predominated when expropriation has been challenged.

---

[49] P.C.I.J. Rep., ser. A, No. 7, p. 22 (1929).
[50] 53 I.L.R. 297.
[51] *Ibid.* at 329.
[52] 20 I.L.M. 1 (1981).
[53] *Ibid.* 58–59.
[54] See United Kingdom's objections in the *Anglo-Iranian Oil Co. Case*, I.C.J. Rep. (Pleadings) 1951, p. 81; also in the *BP Case*, *supra*, n. 50; United States' argument in the *Liamco Case*, *supra*, n. 52, also arbitrator's findings in that case. See Harris, p. 427(5).

Compensation

What has been decisive has been whether or not compensation has been paid and whether, if paid, it complies to the standard prescribed by international law. To comply with international law as represented by Western developed states, compensation must be "prompt, adequate and effective."[55] These terms have been used in many bilateral commercial treaties. Generally, provision should be made for the payment of compensation either before or at the time of the takeover. Payment may be deferred if the full amount to be paid is fixed promptly and if provision is made for the payment of interest.

Adequate compensation which may also be defined as "full," "fair" and "just" is compensation which acknowledges the fair market value of the enterprise in question.

Effective compensation is that which is in readily convertible currency. The recipient should be in a position to use and to benefit from the compensation.

These traditional rules have been challenged and to some extent rejected by socialist/communist/developing countries. The position of these states is reflected particularly in Article 2(c) of the 1974 Charter of Economic Rights and Duties.[56] In respect of compensation, the Charter provides that "appropriate compensation should be paid by the State adopting such measures, taking into account its relevant laws and all circumstances, that the State considers pertinent." Article 2(c) further provides that in the event of a dispute arising over compensation it should be decided, unless otherwise mutually agreed, by the domestic law of the nationalising state. This is in contrast to Resolution 1803 which emphasised that disputes be settled by international arbitration. The traditional requirement that compensation should conform to international standards has been challenged by those states which favour the final say on the issue of compensation being made by the expropriating state. The 1974 Charter has, at least as yet, been denied the status of current international law.[57]

---

[55] See, *e.g.* Statement of U.S. Secretary of State, Hull, in letter to Mexican Government, Harris, p. 428(6) and *Anglo-Iranian Oil Co. Case, supra,* n. 54 at p. 105.

[56] G.A. Resolution 3281 (XXIV), 14 I.L.M. 251 (1975), printed in Harris, p. 429; see also G.A. Resolution 3171 (XXVIII) 1973, 68 A.J.I.L. 381 (1974); G.A. Resolution 3201 (S-VI) Declaration on the Establishment of a New International Economic Order 1974, 13 I.L.M. 765 (1974); Harris, p. 431.

[57] See Arbitrator's finding in the *Texaco Case,* 53 I.L.R. 389; 17 I.L.M. 1 (1978).

"Creeping Expropriation"

Creeping expropriation is where the same effect as formal expropriation is achieved by applying taxation and regulatory measures to a foreign enterprise so that the operation of the enterprise is eventually abandoned as uneconomical.

Expropriation in violation of a treaty obligation naturally incurs responsibility.

The increasing uncertainty regarding the customary international laws of expropriation has prompted bilateral treaties between developed and developing states guaranteeing, for example, provision of compensation in the event of expropriation. The United States and other developed Western capital exporting countries also operate insurance schemes for nationals engaged in foreign investment.

Settlement of Disputes

Very often disputes will be resolved by a compromise settlement whether settlement is by straightforward negotiation between the parties or by a lump sum settlement. Lump sum settlements have found increasing favour during the last 40 years. Under lump sum settlements the expropriating state agrees to pay the investor state a lump sum in respect of all subsisting claims by nationals of the investor state. The investor state is then responsible, normally via a national claims commission (*e.g.* in the United Kingdom the Foreign Compensation Commission and in the United States the Foreign Claims Settlement Commission of the United States) for adjudicating upon and settling in accordance with international law, individual claims.

In 1981 an international tribunal was established at The Hague to settle the claims of United States nationals against Iran and the claims of Iranian nationals against the United States.[58]

In 1965 the Convention on the Settlement of Investment Disputes between States and Nationals of Other States[59] established the International Centre for the Settlement of Investment Disputes in Washington D.C. The Convention through the Centre provides, for parties who agree, procedures for the settlement of disputes between contracting parties and companies of the nationality of a contracting party.

---

[58] The Tribunal was set up under the Claims Settlement Declaration made on January 19, 1981 by the Governments of Iran and the United States—see 20 I.L.M. 230 (1981).

[59] U.K.T.S. 25 (1967) Cmnd. 3255; 575 U.N.T.S. 159; 4 I.L.M. 532 (1965).

Breach of Contract

Contracts between a state and an alien as a rule are governed by the national law of the former and consequently seldom involve international law. A state will only therefore incur liability if it denies the foreigner concerned access to an effective domestic forum for adjudication of the alleged dispute.

A contract between a state and an alien, however, can be "internationalised." A contract may be "internationalised" if a state legislates to abolish or repudiate its contractual obligations. The state can by its unilateral action place itself on a different level than the other party to the contract. In the *Norwegian Loans Case*[60] such was the alleged effect of Norwegian legislation on the contract between Norway and French bondholders.[61] Others maintain that the insertion of a clause that a concession agreement is to be governed not by the law of the state party to the agreement, but, for example, by "general principles of the law of nations" or "principles of the law of the concessionary State not inconsistent with international law" removes the contract from the municipal plane and "internationalises" it. One view, for example, is that such a clause transforms the agreement into an international agreement and breaches of contract into breaches of international law.[62] Developing states, in particular, refute such arguments and do not accept such clauses as valid as they deny a state its sovereign right to control its natural resources. Accordingly, the norm is that a contract between a state and a foreigner will be governed by the domestic law of the state concerned.

The "Calvo" Clause

The Calvo Clause, which was named after its originator, an Argentinian jurist and statesman, was frequently included in agreements between Latin American states and foreigners. Under the Calvo Clause foreigners accepted in advance that in the event of a dispute they would not attempt to invoke the assistance of their national state. The Calvo Clause purported to deny a state of its right to exercise diplomatic protection on behalf of one of its nationals. The validity of the Calvo Clause has been refuted by international tribunals which have maintained that an individual is not competent to fetter its state in such a way and that the right of

---

[60] I.C.J. Rep. 1957, p. 9.

[61] The Court did not decide on the merits of the case, but individual judges considered the internationalisation of the contract; Judge Read at 87–88; Judge Lauterpacht at 38.

[62] See, *e.g.* Arbitrator in *Texaco Case, supra*, n. 57 and Harris, pp. 438–439.

diplomatic protection and of its exercise belong exclusively to the state of nationality.[63]

Nationality of Claims Rule

Nationality is important in the context of state responsibility. A state may only espouse a claim against another state on behalf of one of its nationals. International law lays down no definition of nationality, as the granting of nationality is exclusively a matter of domestic law.[64] A state is free to determine for itself who are to be deemed its nationals.[65] In spite of this *prima facie* unfettered discretion, a state may have its grant of nationality challenged when it attempts to raise a claim against another state. A state's right to afford diplomatic protection may be challenged on the grounds that the link between it and its alleged national is only tenuous and not genuine. In the absence of such a link a claimant state will be prohibited from proceeding with an international claim. The need for there to be an obvious genuine link between the claimant state and the individual concerned was emphasised in the *Nottebohm Case*. In that case, Liechtenstein attempted to exercise diplomatic protection on behalf of Nottebohm against Guatemala. Nottebohm had become a naturalised Liechtenstein citizen after only a few weeks residence in that state and Guatemala challenged Liechtenstein right to espouse a claim on his behalf. The International Court maintained:

> " . . . a State cannot claim that the rules it has thus laid down are entitled to recognition by another State unless it has acted in conformity with this general aim of making the legal bond of nationality accord with the individual's genuine connection with the State . . . "[66]

The Court characterised nationality as:

> "a legal bond having as its basis a social fact of attachment, a genuine connection of existence, interests and sentiments,

---

[63] *North American Dredging Co. Claim* (1926), *supra*, n. 30 at 29.

[64] Nationality may be acquired in a variety of ways but the two most common ways of attaining nationality are (i) by descent from parents (*jus sanguinis*), or (ii) by birth in the territory of the state (*jus soli*). British nationality is now governed by the British Nationality Act 1982.

[65] Article 1, 1930 Hague Convention on Certain Questions Relating to the Conflict of Nationality Laws, 179 L.N.T.S. 89; U.K.T.S. 33 (1937) Cmd. 5553; Harris, p. 441; *Nationality Decrees in Tunis and Morocco Case*, P.C.I.J. Rep., ser. B, No. 4 (1923); 2 A.D. 349; *Nottebohm Case*, I.C.J. Rep. 1955, p. 4 at p. 20.

[66] *Nottebohm Case*, at p. 23.

together with the existence of reciprocal rights and duties. It may be said to constitute the juridical expression of the fact that the individual upon whom it is conferred, either directly by the law or as the result of an act of the authorities, is in fact more closely connected with the population of the State conferring nationality than with that of any other State."[67]

From the *Nottebohm Case* it emerges that not only must an individual possess the claimant state's nationality, but that the nationality must be effective. The *Nottebohm* judgment extended the concept of "genuine connection," which previously had been utilised to resolve problems of dual nationality,[68] to the issue of diplomatic protection generally.

The general rule is that a state will only espouse a claim on behalf of an individual if the latter is a national at the time when the injury occurs and at the time when the claim is presented.

In respect of an individual possessing dual nationality, the traditional view has been that a claim by one national state against another national state would not be entertained. The United Kingdom has conceded, however, that it may take up a claim against the state of nationality if the latter has treated the claimant as a United Kingdom national.[69]

In respect of claims against a third state on behalf of an individual with dual nationality, it is not altogether clear which of the national states has the right to espouse the claim. In the *Mergé Claim*[70] it was suggested that only the state with which the individual had the closest connection could espouse a claim on his behalf whereas in the *Salem Case*[71] it was suggested that both states could do so. The British attitude is that although the government of the day may take up a claim on behalf of an individual possessing dual nationality, it prefers to do so jointly with the other national state.[72]

The absence of nationality, *i.e.* statelessness, means that a state which inflicts injury against a stateless person cannot be held internationally responsible nor is any state competent to intervene on such a person's behalf.

---

[67] *Ibid.*

[68] See *Canevaro Case (Italy v. Peru)*, 11 R.I.A.A. 397 (1912); 6 A.J.I.L. 746 (1912) Translation.

[69] Rule III of the Rules regarding International Claims issued by the British Foreign and Commonwealth Office 1971, reprinted in Harris, p. 453.

[70] 22 I.L.R. 443.

[71] (*Egypt* v. *U.S.*), 2 R.I.A.A. 1161 (1932).

[72] Rule III, *supra*, n. 69.

"Genuine link" is not limited to individuals. Accordingly, "ships have the nationality of the State whose flag they are entitled to fly. There must exist a genuine link between the State and the ship."[73]

Companies and Shareholders

Which state may espouse a claim on behalf of a corporation? A company has traditionally been regarded as having the nationality of "the State under the laws of which it is incorporated and in whose territory it has its registered office."[74] However, these are not the only two criteria whereby a link between a company and a state may be evidenced. For example:

> "it has been the practice of some States to give a company incorporated under their law diplomatic protection solely when it has its seat (*siège social*) or management or centre of control in their territory, or when a majority or a substantial proportion of the shares has been owned by nationals of the State concerned."[75]

The Court concluded in the *Barcelona Traction Case* that with respect to "the diplomatic protection of corporate entities, no absolute test of the 'genuine connection' has found general acceptance."[76] In the *Barcelona Traction Case* the International Court was confronted with the question of whether Belgium could intervene on behalf of Belgian nationals and shareholders in a company, the Barcelona Traction, which was incorporated in Canada and where it maintained its registered office. The losses sustained had been as a result of measures taken by Spain, the country in which the company operated. Canada initially intervened, but subsequently withdrew and did not proceed with a claim. The Court upheld Spain's objection to Belgian intervention on the grounds that Canada's failure to act did not increase Belgium's right. According to the Court's judgment the state whose nationality a company possesses, even if it operates in a foreign country and is controlled by foreign shareholders, has the right to make the claim on its behalf. It was the company which had suffered the injury, but the company was not defunct and, therefore, whether or not to espouse a claim on behalf of the company

---

[73] Article 5, Geneva Convention on the High Seas 1958—see above, p. 132. See also Chicago Convention 1944, Articles 12 and 18.
[74] *Barcelona Traction, Light and Power Co. Case*, I.C.J. Rep. 1970, p. 3. at p. 42.
[75] *Ibid.*
[76] *Ibid.*

remained within Canada's discretion. Regarding shareholders, the general rule is that a state may not pursue a claim on behalf of nationals who suffer injury as a consequence of a measure taken against foreign companies in which they own shares. The International Court in the *Barcelona Traction Case* concluded that to recognise diplomatic protection on behalf of shareholders would result in confusion as the shares of international companies are "widely scattered and frequently change hands."[77] The Court did admit one exception to the general rule, *viz.* if the company ceased to exist. In such circumstances, the Court recognised that the national state of the shareholders could initiate a claim on behalf of the shareholders in respect of losses sustained by them as a result of the injury to the company.[78] The Court's judgment failed to acknowledge that a state in which a company is incorporated may have little interest in pursuing a claim on its behalf. A company may be incorporated in a particular state as a matter of convenience. In that event, the state whose nationals are shareholders may indeed have considerable interest in espousing a claim.

The United Kingdom Rules Regarding International Claims[79] provide that where a United Kingdom national has an interest as a shareholder or otherwise in a company incorporated in another state and the company is injured by a third state, a claim will normally only be espoused by Britain in conjunction with the state in which the company is incorporated. Independent intervention will only take place exceptionally—when the company concerned has ceased to exist.[80] If a state in which a company is incorporated injures the company and a United Kingdom national is a shareholder, the British Government may intervene to protect the interests of the United Kingdom national.[81] There are, therefore, two exceptions in United Kingdom practice to the Court's denial of any right to intervene on behalf of shareholders. In instances where capital in a foreign company is owned in various proportions by shareholders of several nationalities including British nationals, Britain will seldom intervene unless those states whose nationals hold most of the capital support its representations.

Exhaustion of Local Remedies

It is an established rule of customary international law that before diplomatic protection is afforded, or before recourse may be made

[77] *Ibid.* at p. 49.
[78] *Ibid.* at p. 41.
[79] *Supra*, n. 69.
[80] *Ibid.* Article V.
[81] *Ibid.* Article IV.

to international arbitral or judicial processes, local remedies must be exhausted. The *raison d'être* of the rule is:
  (i) to allow the state concerned the opportunity to afford redress within its own legal system for the alleged wrong;
  (ii) to reduce the number of possible international claims;
  (iii) respect for the sovereignty of states.
Local remedies means:

> "not only reference to the courts and tribunals, but also the use of the procedural facilities which municipal law makes available to litigants before such courts and tribunals. It is the whole system of legal protection, as provided by municipal law . . . "[82]

An individual must, therefore, employ "all administrative, arbitral, or judicial remedies."[83] Only effective remedies which could affect the final outcome of the case need be exhausted.[84] The exhaustion of local remedies has been strictly applied, but local remedies need not be exhausted if it is evident that there is no justice to exhaust, or where it is apparent that any attempt to seek redress would be thwarted.[85] The exhaustion of local remedies is not required when the alleged wrong is a direct injury by one state against another state.

---

[82] *Ambatielos Arbitration (Greece v. U.K.)*, 12 R.I.A.A. 83 (1956); 23 I.L.R. 306 (1956).
[83] See Draft Article 19, 1961 Harvard Draft Convention on International Responsibility of States for Injuries to Aliens, see Harris, p. 376.
[84] *Finnish Ships Arbitration*, 3 R.I.A.A. 1479 (1934); *cf. El Oro Mining and Railway Co. Case (Great Britain v. Mexico)*, 5 R.I.A.A. 191 (1931) and *Interhandel Case (Preliminary Objections)*, I.C.J. Rep. 1959, p. 6 at pp. 26–29. See also Harris, p. 468.
[85] *Robert E. Brown Case*, 6 R.I.A.A. 120, 129 (1923).

FURTHER READING

Cases and Materials

D.J. Harris, *Cases and Materials on International Law* (1983), Chapter 8.

L. Henkin, R. Pugh, O. Schachter and H. Smit, *International Law: Cases and Materials* (1980), Chapters 9 and 11.

J. Sweeny, C. Oliver and N. Leech, *The International Legal System: Cases and Materials* (1981), Chapter 9, section A.

Specialised Texts

I. Brownlie, *State Responsibility* (1984).

R. Lillich (ed.), *International Law of State Responsibility for Injuries to Aliens* (1983).

General Texts

M. Akehurst, *A Modern Introduction to International Law* (1982), Chapter 7.

I. Brownlie, *Principles of Public International Law* (1979), Chapters XX, XXI and XXIII.

L. Green, *International Law: A Canadian Perspective* (1984), Part III, §7; Part IV, §3; Part V, §2.

D.W. Greig, *International Law* (1976), Chapter 10.

J.G. Starke, *An Introduction to International Law* (1984), Chapter 10 and Chapter 12, pp. 335–349.

Chapter Nine

HUMAN RIGHTS

WHAT ARE HUMAN RIGHTS?

Human rights are difficult to define. Generally speaking, they are regarded as those fundamental and inalienable rights which are essential for life as a human being. There is, however, no consensus as to what these rights should be. What human rights may be interpreted as being differs according to the particular economic, social and cultural society in which they are being defined. Human rights have therefore escaped a universally acceptable definition. This presents a problem to international regulation. It is not the only obstacle. A major contributing difficulty has been that many states regard human rights as falling within domestic jurisdiction and not a matter to be tackled by international law. In other words, treatment of one's own nationals should not according to those states be the focus of external review.

Human rights is a subject of contemporary international law and the efforts to regulate human rights at an international level only gained momentum after World War II.

Rights of the Individual Recognised by International Law

Pre-1945

Minority groups, *i.e.* those people of a different race, religion or language from the majority group within a state, came to be guaranteed certain rights, such as equality of treatment, by way of Minority treaties such as those concluded in Albania, Finland and Poland. Minority treaties were not renewed after World War II. Freedom from slavery has been recognised under customary international law since 1815 and was reaffirmed in international Conventions, such as the 1926 Slavery Convention[1] and the 1956 Supplementary Convention on the Abolition of Slavery, the Slave Trade and Institutions and Practices similar to Slavery.[2] Trafficking

---

[1] 60 L.N.T.S. 253; U.K.T.S. 16 (1927) Cmd. 2910.
[2] 266 U.N.T.S. 3; U.K.T.S. 59 (1957) Cmnd. 257.

in women and children was similarly prohibited by Convention,[3] but with the exception of such isolated *ad hoc* intervention there was no attempt to regulate human rights at an international level until after 1945. Prior to the Second World War, minority groups and foreign nationals were in a privileged position *vis-à-vis* majority groups and nationals of the host state. They were recognised as deserving at least a minimum standard of treatment.

Post 1945

The signing of the United Nations Charter marked the formal realisation that human rights is a matter for international concern. One of the purposes for which the United Nations was founded was "to achieve international co-operation . . . in promoting and encouraging respect for human rights and for fundamental freedoms for all without distinction as to race, sex, language or religion,"[4] whilst Articles 55 and 56 charge the United Nations and Member States with achieving *inter alia*, "universal respect for, and observance of, human rights and fundamental freedoms for all without distinction as to race, sex, language and religion." The language of the Charter is vague and although Members pledged themselves to the realisation of human rights they were not required to do so within a particular time period. The United Nations Charter acknowledges certain benefits which individuals should enjoy. It does not confer rights upon them.[5] In 1975 the Helsinki Conference on Security and Co-operation in Europe adopted a Final Act[6] containing statements of intent on human rights. Representatives from 35 states signed the Act. It is not a treaty and therefore is not legally binding on parties.

The protection of human rights in contemporary international law including the conferring of rights and the provision of the machinery whereby rights, if infringed, may be enforced, has been tackled at both a regional and universal level.

REGIONAL LEVEL

The European Convention on Human Rights

The Council of Europe is an inter-governmental organisation which was born in the chaotic aftermath of the Second World War. The

[3] *e.g.* International Convention for the Suppression of Traffic in Women and Children, 60 U.N.T.S. 416; U.K.T.S. 26 (1923) Cmd. 1986; and the 1947 Protocol 53 U.N.T.S. 13.
[4] Article 1(3) UN Charter.
[5] See *Sei Fujii* v. *California* (1952) 19 I.L.R. 312; see also *Filartiga* v. *Pena-Irala* 630 F. 2d. 876 (1980); 19 I.L.M. 966 (1980).
[6] 14 I.L.M. 1292 (1975).

aim of those establishing the Council of Europe was to achieve through the Council a greater unity between Member States, to safeguard and realise ideals and principles of common heritage and to facilitate economic and social progress.[7] How were such goals to be realised? Through the:

> "discussion of questions of common concern and by agreements and common action in economic, social, cultural, scientific, legal and administrative matters and in the maintenance and further realisation of human rights and fundamental freedoms."[8]

The Council was initially seen as a potential vehicle for promoting European integration. History has decided otherwise and the Council of Europe has become known almost exclusively for the promotion and protection within Member States of the rights articulated in the European Convention.

The European Convention for the Protection of Human Rights and Fundamental Rights was signed on November 4, 1950[9] and entered into force in September 1953. The Convention was the first attempt to articulate, at a regional level, substantive human rights. Any member of the Council of Europe may accede to the Convention. All 21 Members of the Council have ratified the Convention.

Article 3 of the Council's Statute emphasises the importance of human rights and provides that:

> "Every Member . . . must accept the principles of the rule of law and of the enjoyment by all persons within its jurisdiction of human rights and fundamental freedoms, and collaborate sincerely and effectively in the realisation of the aim of the Council . . ."

The aim of the Council is:

> "to achieve a greater unity between its Members for the purpose of safeguarding and realising the ideals and principles

---

[7] There were 10 original members. There are now 21.
[8] Article 1(b) Statute of the Council of Europe, U.K.T.S. 51 (1949) Cmd. 7778; 87 U.N.T.S. 105.
[9] 213 U.N.T.S. 221; U.K.T.S. 71 (1953) Cmd. 8969; 45 A.J.I.L. Supp. 24; Harris, p. 472.

which are their common heritage and facilitating their economic and social progress."[10]

The Rights and Freedoms Guaranteed

The rights and freedoms spelt out in the Convention are those which generally may be called civil and political rights. More specifically, the Convention guarantees the right to life; freedom from torture, inhuman or degrading treatment and punishment; freedom from slavery and forced labour; the right to liberty and security of persons and freedom from detention save when in accordance with procedures prescribed by law; the right to a fair administration of justice; respect for privacy and family life, home and correspondence; the right to freedom of thought, conscience and religion; the right to freedom of expression and opinion, peaceful assembly and association; the right to marry and found a family; the right to an effective remedy when a right or freedom has been violated and the right to enjoy all such rights and freedoms without discrimination on any ground "such as sex, race, colour, language, religion, political or other opinion, national or social origin, association with a national minority, property or other status." Subsequent protocols have added further substantive rights to the Convention, *viz.* protection for property; right to education in accordance with parents' wishes and religious beliefs; right to free elections; no deprivation of liberty because of an inability to fulfil contractual obligations; freedom of movement and choice of residence; freedom to leave a country; non expulsion from the country of one's nationality; the right to enter the territory of the state of which one is a national; prohibition on the collective expulsion of aliens and the right of residence of aliens. The Protocols have not been acceded to by all Members, *e.g.* the United Kingdom has not acceded to Protocol Four and its acceptance of Protocol One contains a reservation. Protocol Six which calls on Members to abolish the death penalty in peace time is not yet in force. The rights and freedoms guaranteed by the Convention are not enjoyed absolutely. The majority are subject to limitations provided such restrictions can be justifiably invoked on grounds such as public order, public security and the need to protect the rights and freedoms of others. Limitations on the exercise of rights and freedoms are legitimate provided the limitations are prescribed by law.

The guarantee of rights and freedoms is meaningless if no redress

---

[10] Article 1(a) Statute of the Council of Europe, *supra*, n. 8.

can be sought when a violation allegedly occurs. There must be an effective enforcement procedure.

The Convention's Enforcement Machinery

Three organs[11] are involved in the overseeing of the Convention's application, *viz*.:

the European Commission on Human Rights,
the European Court of Human Rights,
the Committee of Ministers.

Two of the organs, the Commission and the Court, were set up by the Convention specifically to ensure the observance of the Convention.[12]

The Commission. All parties to the Convention have a representative in the Commission. No two members of the Commission may be nationals of the same state.[13] Commissioners hold office for six years—it is a part-time position and Commissioners hold other appointments such as university lecturers and legal advisers. Members of the Commission sit in an individual capacity.[14] A proposal for the Commission to sit in Chambers of seven Commissioners in respect of certain applications submitted under Article 25 (see below) is contained in Protocol Eight to the Convention. The Protocol was opened for signature on March 19, 1985.[14a]

The Court. The Court consists of a number of judges equal to that of Member States of the *Council* (emphasis added). No two judges of the same nationality may be appointed.[15] Judges who are elected by a majority vote of the Consultative Assembly, are appointed for nine years and they may be re-elected. The office of judge is part-time, the Court not being in permanent session. A judge may not hold government office or hold a post or exercise a profession which is likely to affect his judicial function. The Court was founded in 1959.

Committee of Ministers. The Committee of Ministers is the executive organ of the Council of Europe and is composed of one representative from each Member State, normally a member of the government.

---

[11] The Council's Consultative Assembly is essentially a deliberate organ and is not actively involved in the Commission's application.
[12] Article 19.
[13] Article 20.
[14] Article 23.
[14a] 7 E.H.R.R. 339.
[15] Article 38.

The organ initially concerned with the implementation of the Convention is the Commission, be the application initiated by a state or by an individual. Any contracting state may petition the Commission regarding any alleged breach of the Convention's provisions by another contracting state.[16] The alleged breach need not be against nationals of the objecting state, but may be in respect of nationals of another Member State, *e.g.* as was the Greek complaint against British treatment of Cypriots in 1957 and the Irish complaint against the United Kingdom in respect of treatment of prisoners (all of whom happened to have British nationality) in Northern Ireland in 1971. The Commission is also competent to receive petitions from "any person, non-governmental organisation or group of individuals claiming to be the victim of a violation by one of the High Contracting Parties of the rights set forth in this Convention . . . "[17] Such petitions can only be received if the state against which the complaint has been lodged has recognised the Commission's competence to receive such petitions.

Recognition of individual petition is a matter of state discretion. States which do accept the right of individual petition are under an obligation not "to hinder in any way the effective exercise of this right."[18] Declarations under Article 25 may be made for a specific period, *e.g.* the United Kingdom's declaration is for five years.[19] Eighteen Contracting States have made declarations under Article 25. The three which have not are Cyprus, Malta and Turkey.

No application will be entertained by the Commission unless domestic remedies have been fully exhausted and the complaint is lodged within six months of the final domestic decision having been taken.[20] Nor will the Commission deal with any matter which is anonymous, or is substantially the same as one already examined by the Commission or which has been submitted to another form of international settlement.[21] An application under either Article 24 or Article 25 must be in writing, identify the state against which the complaint is being made and the provisions of the Convention which have allegedly been contravened.

On receipt, each application is examined to consider whether or not it is admissible. Admissibility is considered by the Commission

---

[16] Article 24.
[17] Article 25.
[18] *Ibid.*
[19] The United Kingdom's initial declaration was made on January 14, 1966. Its current declaration is as of January 14, 1986 and now excludes issues arising in respect of the Isle of Man and the British Virgin Islands.
[20] Article 26.
[21] Article 27.

in accordance with its Rules of Procedure. The decision on admissibility is final. No appeal lies against a Commission decision declaring an application inadmissible. A new application may be submitted if the applicant can provide new facts. Once an application is accepted the Commission examines it in greater depth. The facts of the case will, with the assistance of the parties concerned, be established and, if appropriate, an investigation may be held—if so, the respondent Government must provide the necessary facilities for the effective conduct of the investigation. The Commission is, under the Convention, charged to act as a conciliator.[22] The Commission must place itself at the disposal of the parties involved with a view to securing, on the basis of respect for human rights as defined in the Convention, a friendly settlement. The overriding aim is to achieve conciliation between the parties. Why? Intervention in human rights, particularly involving claims by nationals against their own government, is a delicate issue. The Commission's function is therefore not to characterise a state as "guilty" but rather, as far as possible, to correct unobtrusively any violation of human rights. All proceedings before the Commission are held in camera. However, if a friendly settlement is reached, a brief report is published setting out the terms of the settlement.

In the absence of a settlement, the Commission makes a report which it submits to the Committee of Ministers and the Government concerned. The applicant does not receive a copy of the report, which must include the legal opinion of the Commission as to whether, on the facts presented, a breach of the Convention has occurred. If the Commission is not unanimous in its opinion, the report may include the separate opinion(s) of the minority Commissioner(s).

The Commission may also make any proposals which it considers appropriate. The Report remains confidential until the Committee of Ministers reaches its decision on whether there has been a violation of the Convention. The Committee of Ministers makes its decision on the basis of the Report—it does not rehear the case or take fresh evidence from either the Commission or any individual applicant. A state, defendant or applicant, may explain its case through its representative on the Committee. The Committee's decision is taken by a majority of two thirds of the members entitled to sit. The Committee, on deciding that there has been a violation, will prescribe a period of time during which the defaulting state must take steps to amend the situation. If on expiry of the time limit

[22] Article 31.

no action has been taken, the Committee must decide what effect is to be given to its decision.

What enforcement measures can the Committee adopt? Very few. The Committee can bring pressure to bear on a state's representatives, publish the Commission's report (done in the majority of cases) or, as a last resort, a state's membership of the Council of Europe could be suspended.

The Committee of Ministers is not the only body competent to decide whether the Convention has been breached. Within three months of the Commission's report being submitted to the Committee of Ministers a case may be referred by the Commission and/or the Government concerned[23] to the Court for a decision on whether the Convention has been violated. An individual may not refer a case to the Court. A case can only be referred to the Court if the state concerned has recognised the jurisdiction of the Court. Nineteen States, *i.e.* all the Members of the Council of Europe with the exception of Malta and Turkey, have done so. In the absence of an acceptance of the Court's jurisdiction, the final decision lies with the Committee of Ministers. If the Court's jurisdiction is accepted, how is it decided which organ will be responsible for taking the final decision?

There are no rules. No guidance is given either in the Convention or the Commission's Rules of Procedure. States themselves probably favour the forum of the Committee of Ministers. Fourteen of the Members of the Committee of Ministers must decide there has been a violation of the Convention, whereas a simple majority of judges (possibly as few as four) is sufficient. The trend has been that if the Commission is either unanimous or feels by a large majority that the Convention has not been violated, the case is referred to the Committee of Ministers. However, the issues involved may be so complex or important that even in the absence of a conviction that the Convention has been breached, the case will be referred to the Court, *e.g. Schmidt and Dahlström Case.*[24] The Court is more likely to be chosen if the Commission is narrowly divided on whether there has been a violation of the Convention.

If a case is referred to the Court, it may be heard by a Chamber of seven judges (Protocol Eight proposes raising this to nine judges) including, as *ex officio* members, the President or the Vice President and the judge who is a national of any State Party concerned.[25] If the "national" judge is unable to sit or withdraws, or if there is

---

[23] *i.e.* A state whose national is a victim of the alleged breach; the state which referred the case to the Commission; the state against which the complaint has been made.
[24] Eur. Court H.R., Series A, Vol. 21 Judgment of February 6, 1976.
[25] Article 43.

none, the state in question is entitled to appoint a member of the Court (an elected judge of a different nationality) or a person from outside the Court (an *ad hoc* judge). The Chamber thus constituted may, or must, under certain conditions, relinquish jurisdiction in favour of the plenary Court. It may, for instance, do so when the case "raises one or more serious questions affecting the interpretation of the Convention" and it must when the case might lead to a decision which would be inconsistent with a previous ruling by the Court.[26] The Court has exercised plenary jurisdiction in about a third of cases, *e.g.* the *Golder Case*,[27] *National Union of Belgian Police Case*,[28] *Ireland* v. *United Kingdom*[29] and the *Marckx Case*.[30]

The state or states concerned are parties to the case before the Court. The Commission takes part and one or more of its members is appointed as a delegate for this purpose, but the Commission does not appear as a party. The Commission's principal task in the case at this stage, is to assist the Court. The Commission's function is essentially that of defender of the public interest. Under the Convention, individual applicants may neither refer a case to the Court nor appear before it as parties. Delegates could, however, have the assistance of any person of their choice, *e.g.* lawyer, former lawyer of an individual applicant or the applicant himself. This was confirmed by the Court in the *Vagrancy Cases*.[31] Such provision is included in the New Rules of Court with the important innovation that once a case has been referred to the Court by either a government or the Commission, the applicant may participate in proceedings before the Court and may plead his own case. If he does, he has in principle to be represented by an advocate. The Court gives its final judgment by a majority vote. The judgment is final and is binding on the states concerned.[32] Supervision of the execution of the judgment is the responsibility of the Committee of Ministers. In the event of a breach of the Convention being established by the Court and the internal law of the "offending" party offers only partial reparation, the Court may "afford just satisfaction to the injured party."[33] This may simply be a declaratory

---

[26] Plenary jurisdiction is not provided for by the Convention, but in its revised Rules of Court (Rule 50).
[27] Eur. Court H.R., Series A, Vol. 18 Judgment of February 21, 1975; 1 E.H.R.R. 524.
[28] Eur. Court H.R., Series A, Vol. 19 Judgment of October 27, 1975; 1 E.H.R.R. 578.
[29] Eur. Court H.R., Series A, Vol. 25 Judgment of January 18, 1978; 2 E.H.R.R. 25.
[30] Eur. Court H.R., Series A, Vol. 31 Judgment of June 13, 1979; 2 E.H.R.R. 330.
[31] Eur. Court H.R., Series A, Judgment of November 18, 1970 (Question of Procedure).
[32] Interpretation of a judgment may be sought within three years of the date of judgment.
[33] Article 50.

judgment. When just satisfaction has been awarded it has always taken the form of monetary compensation, *e.g.* £22,000 in the *Sunday Times Case*[34] to cover the costs of taking the case to Strasbourg and £130,000 in the *Young, James and Webster Case*.[35] The Court is required to give reasons for its judgment. If the judgment does not represent in whole or in part the unanimous opinion of the judges involved, each judge is entitled to deliver a separate opinion, be it concurring or dissenting.

Impact of the Convention

The Convention has served to focus a spotlight on deficiencies in Member States' municipal legal systems rather than serve as a weapon against the flagrant disregard of human rights. The Convention has provided for external judicial review of legislation especially, though not exclusively, with respect to the administration of the criminal law. Issues raised have included, *inter alia*, a prisoner's right of access to the English Courts,[36] criminal trials conducted in the absence of the accused,[37] the status of Belgian linguistic legislation regarding education,[38] compulsory sex education in state primary schools in Denmark[39] and the use of corporal punishment in Scottish schools.[40] The Convention was innovatory in that it provided the possibility for individuals to pursue claims against their own governments for alleged violations of the Convention. In spite of this, state applications, although they shall always be fewer in number, are potentially of greater importance —a victim is not required and state applications may refer to any Convention provision not just one protecting a right.

Member States are not required to incorporate the Convention

[34] Eur. Court H.R., Series A, Vol. 38 Judgment of November 6, 1980; 3 E.H.R.R. 317; for judgment on facts of the case see Eur. Court H.R., Series A, Vol. 30 Judgment of April 26, 1979; 2 E.H.R.R. 245.

[35] Eur. Court H.R., Series A, Vol. 55 Judgment of October 18, 1982; 5 E.H.R.R. 201; for judgment on facts of the case see Eur. Court H.R., Series A, Vol. 44 Judgment of August 13, 1981; 4 E.H.R.R. 38.

[36] *Golder*, Eur. Court H.R., Series A, Vol. 18 Judgment of February 21, 1975; 1 E.H.R.R. 524; *Campbell and Fell* Eur. Court H.R., Series A, Vol. 80 Judgment of June 28, 1984; 7 E.H.R.R. 165.

[37] *Colozza and Rubinat*, Eur. Court H.R., Series A, Vol. 89 Judgment of February 12, 1985.

[38] *Belgian Linguistic (Merits) Case* Eur. Court H.R., Series A, Vol. 16 Judgment of July 23, 1968; 1 E.H.R.R. 252.

[39] *Kjeldsen, Busk Medsen and Pedersen Case* Eur. Court H.R., Series A, Vol. 23 Judgment of December 7, 1976; 1 E.H.R.R. 711.

[40] *Campbell and Cosans* Eur. Court H.R., Series A, Vol. 48 Judgment of February 25, 1982; 4 E.H.R.R. 293; see Harris, pp. 470–532 for a resumé of most of the applications.

into their municipal law. It is, though to a greater or lesser extent, directly enforceable in the municipal courts of most Member States.[41]

The Convention is not part of British domestic law, but it is a presumption of statutory interpretation that domestic legislation will be construed to conform with the Convention rather than against it.

The European Court of Justice (*i.e.* the Court of the European Communities) has recognised:

" ... fundamental rights form an integral part of the general principles of law which it enforces. In assuring the protection of such rights, this Court is required to base itself on the constitutional traditions common to the member-States and therefore should not allow measures which are incompatible with the fundamental rights recognised and guaranteed by the constitutions of such States. The international treaties on the protection of human rights in which the member-States have co-operated or to which they have adhered can also supply indications which may be taken into account within the framework of Community law."[42]

Other Conventions and Charters Concerned with Human Rights

The European Convention is concerned with political and civil rights. The Council of Europe has also turned its attention to the protection of economic and social rights. The European Social Charter[43] was adopted in 1961 and entered into force in 1965. The rights articulated in the Charter include the right to work, the right to a fair remuneration, the right to bargain collectively and the right to social security. The Social Charter puts claims rather than restrictions on states. The enforcement scheme of the Charter is very different from that of the Convention. The Charter's mechanism is much more general. Seven articles are characterised as fundamental and parties to the Charter undertake to be bound by at least five—implementing them fully and promptly. In addition, a party must select from the 12 further articles a certain number of full articles or separate paragraphs, so that it is bound by not less than 10 articles or 45 numbered paragraphs.

The Council of Europe was the first institution to attempt to

---

[41] See *Drzemczewski,* "The European Human Rights Convention in Domestic Law" (1983) L.I.E.I. 1979/1.

[42] Case 4/73 *Nold* v. *The Commission of the European Communities* [1974] E.C.R. 491 at 505; [1974] 2 C.M.L.R. 338 at 354.

[43] 529 U.N.T.S. 89; U.K.T.S. 38 (1965) Cmnd. 2643.

tackle human rights at a regional level. Today, it is no longer the only one to address itself to the problem of protecting human rights. The American Convention on Human Rights[44] entered into force in 1976. It is open to all O.A.S. members.[45] The Convention protects essentially civil and political rights and seeks to promote the progressive realisation of economic, social, scientific and cultural rights. The Convention provided for the creation of the Inter-American Commission on Human Rights[46] and the Inter-American Court of Human Rights. Implementation may be by individual application with a decision on whether the Convention has been breached being taken by the Commission, or by the Court should the defendant state recognise the jurisdiction of the Court. The Commission may hear inter-state applications, but this is optional.

The African Charter on Human and Peoples' Rights[47] was adopted in June 1981, but it is not yet in force. The Convention protects civil, political, economic, social and cultural rights. It also imposes duties on individuals. A Commission is responsible for the Charter's implementation and a compulsory system of state and individual petition is envisaged.

INTERNATIONAL REGULATION

United Nations

One of the initial resolutions adopted by the United Nations General Assembly was the Universal Declaration of Human Rights.[48] The Declaration spells out a series of political, civil, economic, social and cultural rights. As a resolution it is not, of course, legally binding. It was never intended to be, but rather, in the words of the United States representative to the General Assembly and Chairman of the United Nations Committee on Human Rights during the drafting of the Declaration, Mrs. Eleanor Roosevelt, was to act as a "common standard of achievement for all peoples of all nations." The Declaration has been tacitly accepted by all Member States and has served as the blueprint for the constitutions of many newly independent states. It is arguable today that some, if not all, the rights and freedoms enunciated in the

[44] 9 I.L.M. 673 (1970); 1969 Y.B.H.R. 390; 65 A.J.I.L. 679 (1971); for the Court see 76 A.J.I.L. 231 (1982).
[45] Currently it has been accepted by 18 of the 31 OAS States (Organisation of American States)—the United States is not a party.
[46] The Commission since 1970 has enjoyed the status of a full organ of the OAS.
[47] 21 I.L.M. 59 (1982).
[48] G.A. Resolution 217 (III), G.A.O.R., 3rd Session, Part I, Resolutions, p. 71; Harris, p. 534.

Charter have become accepted as customary international law. The rights spelt out in the Universal Declaration are diverse and include, *inter alia*, the right to life, liberty and security of the person from slavery or servitude; freedom from torture or cruel, inhuman or degrading treatment or punishment; recognition as a person before the law; the right to nationality; the right to own property; freedom of thought, conscience and religion; the right to participate in government; the right to social security; the right to work and the right to education. The rights and freedoms are to be enjoyed without "distinction of any kind, such as race, colour, sex, language, religion, political or other opinion or social origin, property, birth or other status"[49] and are only to be curtailed by:

> "such limitations as are determined by law solely for the purposes of securing due recognition and respect for the rights and freedoms of others and of meeting the just requirements of morality, public order and the general welfare in a democratic society."[50]

The rights and freedoms set out in the Universal Declaration have been articulated more precisely in two separate international Covenants: the Covenant on Civil and Political Rights 1966,[51] which entered into force in March 1976; and the Covenant on Economic, Social and Cultural Rights 1966,[52] which entered into force in January 1976.

Under the Covenant on Civil and Political Rights, Contracting Parties undertake "to respect and to ensure to all individuals within its territory and subject to its jurisdiction the rights recognised in the present Covenant,"[53] whereas the Covenant on Economic, Social and Cultural Rights requires a Contracting Party "to take steps . . . to the maximum of its available resources, with a view to achieving progressively the full realisation of the rights recognised in the present Covenant."[54]

An initial difference between the two Covenants is that the obligations assumed by a state under the Covenant on Civil and Political Rights are required to be implemented immediately upon ratification of the Covenant by a state, while the Covenant on Economic, Social and Cultural Rights provides that the realisation

[49] Article 2.
[50] Article 29(2).
[51] U.K.T.S. 6 (1977) Cmnd. 6702; 6 I.L.M. 368 (1967).
[52] U.K.T.S. 6 (1977) Cmnd. 6702; 6 I.L.M. 360 (1967).
[53] Article 2(1).
[54] Article 2(1).

of the rights it recognises may be achieved progressively. The fulfilment of economic, social and cultural rights depend upon a state's economic development, whereas the right to recognition as a person before the law can be put into effect upon implementation of the appropriate legal measures.

Rights Protected

The rights guaranteed by the Civil and Political Covenant closely resemble those protected by the European Convention. The Covenant, it should be remembered, however, when being compared with the European Convention, is geared towards universal application. In other words, it is designed not to apply to a homogeneous grouping of states, but rather to states of a diverse social, economic, ideological and political background, *e.g.* there is no equivalent in the Convention to Article 26 of the Covenant which deals with racial discrimination. Certain Articles in the Covenant tend to be more detailed than those in the Convention, the Covenant having been refined over a longer period of time, *e.g.* see Article 6 of the Convention and Article 14 of the Covenant. The Covenant provides that the exercise of a right may be subject to restriction, but these limitations must be provided by law and must be necessary to protect national security, public order, public health or morals, or the rights and freedoms of others, *e.g.* Article 12(3) which concerns limitations on freedom of movement and residence within a country, and the right to leave a country. Derogation is allowed in times of public emergency.

The Covenant on Economic, Social and Cultural Rights guarantees those rights originally spelt out in Articles 22 to 27 of the Universal Declaration, *e.g.* the right to work, to just and favourable conditions of work and the right to medical and social services and social security. Article 4 of the Covenant provides that these rights are subject "only to such limitations as are determined by law only in so far as this may be compatible with the nature of these rights and solely for the purpose of promoting the general welfare in a democratic society."

Both Covenants recognise the right of all peoples to self-determination and the right to "freely dispose of their natural wealth and resources." These provisions do not appear in the Universal Declaration.

Implementation Machinery

Reporting system—common to both Covenants.
Inter-State complaint—Article 41 of the Covenant on Civil and Political Rights.

> *Individual communication to the Committee of Human Rights*
> —Optional Protocol to the Covenant on Civil and Political
> Rights.

Reporting System. A reporting system as a medium for enforcing
the rights guaranteed is common to both Covenants and states are
required to submit periodic reports. In the case of the Covenant on
Civil and Political Rights, states are required "to submit reports on
the measures they have adopted which give effect to the rights
recognised herein and on the progress made in the enjoyment of
those rights: (a) within one year of the entry into force of the present
Covenant for the States Parties concerned."[55]

The Human Rights Committee is a body of 18 elected by the
Contracting Parties, but who sit as individuals, *i.e.* not as
government representatives. The Committee's task is to study the
reports received and transmit a report and "such general comments
as it may consider appropriate to the States Parties." Additional
information may be requested from the state by the Committee and
will be provided either by a state representative who will be present
at the Committee's discussions, or at a later date by the government
concerned. The reporting system is essentially a means of providing
information. Westerners admittedly do favour more penetrating
questions than those from the Eastern bloc countries, but nonetheless the reporting system as articulated in Article 40 is not a
monitoring system. Those wishing to make it more than the
Covenant drafters intended must tread cautiously as Article 40 is
the only compulsory supervisory system to which states submit on
ratifying the Covenant. States submit subsequent reports whenever
required to do so by the Commission—currently every five years.

States Parties to the Covenant on Economic, Social and Cultural
Rights are also required to submit reports:

> "in stages, in accordance with a programme to be established
> by the Economic and Social Council within one year of the
> entry into force of the present Covenant after consultation with
> the States Parties and the specialised agencies concerned."[56]

Reports are submitted not to the independent Human Rights
Committee, but to the Economic and Social Council, an organ of
the United Nations. The reports may indicate factors and difficulties affecting the fulfilment of the obligations. The reports submitted by states are examined by a Working Group established by

[55] Article 40.
[56] Article 17.

ECOSOC for this purpose and subsequently may be transmitted to the Commission on Human Rights for study and general recommendation, or where appropriate for information.[57] The Economic and Social Council may submit to the General Assembly reports of a general nature with a summary of information received from states.[58] The reporting system is the only machinery of supervision provided for by the Covenant.

Inter-State Complaint—Article 41, Covenant on Civil and Political Rights. Article 41 is not compulsory for states. Acceptance of Article 41 by a state is independent to its ratification of the Covenant. Article 41 provides for optional inter-state petitions. A state may accept the right of other states to bring before the Human Rights Committee a claim alleging its violation of the Convention. The initiation of the Article 41 procedure is dependent upon:

(a) the condition of reciprocity—both states, the one alleging the violation and the alleged offender, must have accepted Article 41; and
(b) the exhaustion of local remedies.

The Committee makes its good offices available to the states and within 12 months submits a report indicating the facts and solution reached. If no solution is achieved the report will be confined to the facts along with the submission of the two parties. In the absence of a solution, the Committee may with the prior consent of the states concerned, appoint an *ad hoc* Conciliation Commission.[59] If the Commission is used, but a solution is not achieved, the Commission produces a report which is not binding, but in which the Commission may indicate "its views of the possibilities of an amicable settlement."[60] When compared to its counterpart, Article 24 in the European Convention, Article 41 lacks teeth. It makes no provision for reference to a judicial body or for the taking of a decision in accordance with judicial procedures. Conciliation remains the primary aim. Article 41 entered into force on March 28, 1979 on receipt of the tenth signature. The countries which have accepted Article 41 are all of the western tradition. The Article 41 procedure has yet to be utilised.

Individual communications to the Committee of Human Rights —Optional Protocol to the Covenant on Civil and Political Rights.[61]

[57] Article 19.
[58] Article 21.
[59] Article 42.
[60] Article 42(7)(c).
[61] U.K.T.S. 6 (1977) Cmnd. 6702; 6 I.L.M. 383 (1967); 61 A.J.I.L. 870 (1967).

Under the Optional Protocol to the Covenant on Civil and Political Rights, the Committee is competent to receive and consider communications from individuals who claim to be victims of a violation by a state party to the Covenant, provided that the latter is a party to the Optional Protocol. A communication must:

—not be anonymous;
—concern an alleged violation of one of the rights provided for in the Covenant;
—not relate to a matter which is under consideration in any other international forum. This provision is designed to prevent the simultaneous consideration of petitions by the Human Rights Committee and, for instance, the European Commission of the Council of Europe.

Unlike the European Convention, the Optional Protocol makes no provision for reference to a Court, nor does the Committee perform a conciliatory role. The Committee's function is simply to receive applications, examine them and subsequently "forward its views to the State Party concerned and the individual" on whether the Covenant has been breached. The Committee considers applications in private. There are no oral hearings. The Committee's views, which are not binding, are published as annexes to its annual report. A majority of the applications considered by the Committee have been against Uruguay (*e.g. The Weinberger Case*)[62] but the Committee has also confirmed alleged breaches by Canada and Mauritius. In the *Lovelace Case*[63] a provision of Canada's Indian Act, denying an Indian woman from returning to her native Indian reserve on the break up of her marriage to a non-Indian, was held to be in violation of Article 27 of the Covenant. In the *Mauritian Women Case*[64] Mauritian legislation placing Mauritian women married to foreign husbands, but not Mauritian men married to foreign women, at risk of deportation was found to be contrary to Articles 2(1), 3 and 26 in relation to Articles 17(1) and 23(1) of the Covenant.

The Optional Protocol entered into force in March 1976 and currently there are some 35 parties. Neither the United Kingdom nor the United States have accepted the Optional Protocol.

The Optional Protocol is not the only provision within the United Nations system which provides for individual application. In 1970

---

[62] 1981 Report of the Human Rights Committee, G.A.O.R., 36th Session, Supp. 40, p. 114; Harris, p. 550.
[63] 1981 Report of the Human Rights Committee, p. 166
[64] *Ibid.* p. 134.

the Economic and Social Council, under Resolution 1503 (XXVIII), authorised the Human Rights Commission's Sub-Commission on the Prevention of Discrimination and Protection of Minorities to appoint a working group to examine in private individual petitions received and to report to the Sub-Commission on those which appear to reveal a "consistent pattern of gross and reliably attested violations of human rights." Resolution 1503 has proved essentially ineffective as, although several situations have been referred to the Commission, they have only been considered in private by the Commission with no further action having been taken.

Do the Optional Protocol and Resolution 1503 overlap? Although *prima facie* there may appear to be a potential overlap there does remain a fundamental difference between the two procedures. The Optional Protocol is concerned primarily with individual identifiable violations of human rights, whilst Resolution 1503 is concerned with an examination of situations. Also the latter is applicable to all states and concerns violations of all human rights embodied in the Universal Declaration of Human Rights, whereas the former applies only to States Parties to the Optional Protocol and only to those civil and political rights mentioned in the Covenant on Civil and Political Rights. An *ad hoc* working group may be appointed by the Commission to examine, on a state's initiative, a situation of alleged human rights violations. Such groups have no mandatory authority to enter a territory or examine witnesses and their recommendations are simply that, *viz.* recommendations.

An optional system of individual petition is provided for in the 1966 Convention on the Elimination of All Forms of Racial Discrimination[65] which entered into force in 1969. An individual, or group of individuals, can lodge a complaint with the Committee on the Elimination of All Forms of Racial Discrimination alleging that their rights guaranteed by the Convention have been violated. This can only occur if the alleged offending state has accepted the optional individual complaint procedure. There is a compulsory inter-state complaint procedure, but this has never been utilised. The Committee on the Elimination of All Forms of Racial Discrimination is central to the enforcement of the Convention. It receives reports from Contracting Parties and forwards to the General Assembly suggestions and general recommendations as it sees fit. Article 22 of the Convention provides for compulsory reference to the International Court of Justice—this is an interesting

---

[65] 60 U.N.T.S. 195; U.K.T.S. 77 (1969) Cmnd. 4108.

attempt at strengthening international enforcement even though a number of states have made reservations to Article 22.

Other United Nations Conventions relating to human rights, *e.g.* the 1973 Convention on the Suppression and Punishment of the Crime of Apartheid[66] and the 1979 Convention on the Elimination of All Forms of Discrimination Against Women[67] require the submission of periodic reports by Contracting Parties.

The possibility of states having to submit a number of reports by virtue of their being a party to two or more instruments on human rights has prompted the suggestion that there should be a standardisation of reports, to the effect that such states could refer to documents already supplied, thereby preventing a duplication of information in the preparation of reports. Human rights are more successfully regulated at a regional level rather than at an international level, but this does mean that the United Nations system should be maligned and dismissed as ineffective. The United Nations system is of necessity founded on compromise. The United Nations system does not contain the potential for a more effective enforcement machinery. Essentially what is deficient is nothing inherent in the system itself *per se*, but rather a lack of willingness on the part of states which comprise that system to submit to more "searching" procedures.

HUMAN RIGHTS AND INTERNATIONAL CRIMINAL LAW

There is an absence on the international plane of either a criminal code or a criminal court. Attempts have been made to establish both, but none to date have been successful. The League of Nations in 1937, for instance, initiated a Convention for the Prevention and Punishment of Terrorism[68] and a Convention for the Creation of an International Criminal Court,[69] but the former received only one ratification, while the latter received none. The United Nations has drawn upon the principles enunciated by the Nuremberg Tribunal[70] to prepare a draft code of offences against peace and the security of mankind and more recently the International Law Commission has considered the issue of criminal responsibility of states. However, although the Commission has decided in the affirmative that a state may be held criminally liable and has identified offences which

[66] 13 I.L.M. 50 (1974).
[67] 19 I.L.M. 33 (1980).
[68] 7 Hudson 862.
[69] 7 Hudson 878.
[70] See Harris, pp. 555–561.

give rise to such liability, the Commission has reserved for a later date any further examination of criminal responsibility.[71]

---

[71] On criminal responsibility in international law, see above. p. 156; on individual responsibility for war crimes and genocide, see above pp. 65–66 and 105; See also section on *universality principle*, p. 104.

FURTHER READING

Cases and Materials

D.J. Harris, *Cases and Materials on International Law* (1983), Chapter 9.
L. Henkin, R. Pugh, O. Schachter and H. Smit, *International Law: Cases and Materials* (1980), Chapter 12.
J. Sweeny, C. Oliver and N. Leech, *The International Legal System: Cases and Materials* (1981), Chapter 9, sections B, C, D and E.

Specialised Texts

R. Beddard, *Human Rights in Europe* (1980).
F.G. Jacobs, *The European Convention on Human Rights* (1975).

General Texts

M. Akehurst, *A Modern Introduction to International Law* (1982), Chapter 6, pp. 74–86 and Chapter 17.
I. Brownlie, *Principles of Public International Law* (1979), Chapter XXIV.
L. Green, *International Law: A Canadian Perspective* (1984), Part III, §7.
D.W. Greig, *International Law* (1976), Chapter 14, pp. 799–816.
J.G. Starke, *An Introduction to International Law* (1984), Chapter 12, pp. 349–358.

Chapter Ten

THE LAW OF TREATIES

The importance of treaties has already been acknowledged. Treaties are increasingly utilised to regulate relations between international persons and the expansion in the subject-matter of international law is reflected in the diversity of subject-matter regulated by treaty.

Treaty law is for the most part non-controversial. As the international law of contract it is essentially lawyer's law. What is a treaty? How is a treaty concluded? How is a treaty to be interpreted?

The law relating to these questions is best considered against the backcloth of the 1969 Vienna Convention on the Law of Treaties.[1] The Convention, which entered into force in January 1980, was the product of 20 years work by the International Law Commission. The Convention is regarded as essentially codifying customary international law (hence its importance as the Convention has only been ratified by about one third of the international community) though some of the provisions are seen as representing progressive development, *e.g.* Article 53.

The Convention, as a Convention, does not have retroactive effect, but because it spells out established rules the Convention may be applied to agreements pre-dating the Convention, *e.g.* the Convention's rules on "material breach" were applied to the 1920 League of Nations Mandate in the *Namibia (South West Africa) Case*,[2] and similarly in the *Beagle Channel Arbitration*[3] the Convention's rules were applied to the 1881 Argentina/Chile Treaty.

The Convention itself is of limited scope. It confines its application to treaties between states. The Convention acknowledges and does not purport to affect the validity of agreements entered into by other international persons.

The International Law Commission has completed a draft Convention on the law of treaties concluded between states and international organisations or between two or more international organisations. The draft Convention is modelled upon the Vienna Convention on the Law of Treaties. As yet no diplomatic

---

[1] U.K.T.S. 58 (1980) Cmnd. 7964; 8 I.L.M. 679 (1969); 63 A.J.I.L. 875 (1969).
[2] I.C.J. Rep. 1971, p. 16 at p. 47.
[3] 17 I.L.M. 623 at 645 (1978).

Conference has been called to consider and to adopt the draft as a Convention.

DEFINITION OF A TREATY

Treaty is the generic term used to embrace convention, agreement, arrangement, protocol, and exchange of notes. International law does not distinguish between agreements identified as treaties and other agreements. The name accorded to an agreement is not in itself important and is of no legal effect.[4]

For the purposes of the Convention " 'treaty' means an international agreement concluded between States in written form and governed by international law . . . "[5]

The Convention concerns itself only with written agreements. But can states enter into oral agreements?

Treaties invariably are in written form. It cannot be stated unequivocably, however, that an oral agreement has no legal significance. Oral statements have been held to be binding.

In 1919 the Danish Government informed the Norwegian Government through their representative in Norway that they would not raise any objection at the Paris Peace Conference to the Norwegian claim over Spitzbergen, if Norway would not challenge Danish claims of sovereignty over all Greenland. The then Norwegian Foreign Minister, M. Ihlen, subsequently reported to his Danish counterpart that "the Norwegian Government would not make any difficulty." Denmark argued before the Permanent Court of International Justice in the *Legal Status of Eastern Greenland*[6] that Norway had by the "Ihlen Declaration" recognised Danish sovereignty. The Court denied that the "Ihlen Declaration" constituted a recognition of Danish sovereignty, but did, however, maintain that Norway had incurred a legally binding obligation to refrain from contesting Danish sovereignty over Greenland. The Permanent Court did not, however, characterise the "Ihlen Declaration" as an oral agreement nor did it define the circumstances, if any, when a unilateral statement could be binding. The Court rather emphasised the contemporaneous acceptance by Denmark of the Norwegian claims over Spitzbergen.

The International Court of Justice was confronted with the legal nature of unilateral declarations in the *Nuclear Tests Cases*[7] in

---

[4] Within a municipal system "treaty" may have specialised meaning as, *e.g.* in the United States.
[5] Article 2(1)(a).
[6] P.C.I.J. Rep., ser A/B, No. 53 (1933).
[7] I.C.J. Rep. 1974, pp. 253, 457.

which Australia and New Zealand sought a decision from the Court against France that the latter's testing of nuclear weapons in the atmosphere was contrary to international law. The Court found that the series of public statements made by France announcing that she would refrain from further testing were sufficient to commit her and negate Australian and New Zealand objections.

Not all written agreements necessarily establish binding relations. The parties may not intend the agreement to establish legal relations between them, *e.g.* the Final Act adopted at the Conference of Security and Co-operation in Europe clearly states that the agreement is "not eligible for registration under Article 102 of the Charter."[8] Article 102 of the United Nations Charter provides for the registration with the Secretariat of the United Nations every treaty and international agreement entered into by any Member State and unless a treaty or international agreement is registered it cannot be invoked before any organ of the United Nations. Registration provides tangible evidence that the agreement is to be regarded as a treaty and that that is the intention of the parties concerned.

For the Vienna Convention to apply to an international agreement the latter must be in written form, must reflect the intention of the parties to be bound and must be governed by international law.

TREATY-MAKING COMPETENCE

Municipal Law

Arrangements for the exercise of a state's treaty-making powers are left to each state and the constitutional requirements with respect to the ratification of treaties vary widely. A state may not plead a breach of its constitutional provisions relating to treaty-making so as to invalidate an agreement unless such a breach was manifest and "objectively evident to any State conducting itself in the matter in accordance with normal practice and in good faith."[9]

International Law

A state representative may conclude a treaty on behalf of a state if (a) he possesses full powers, or (b) if, from the practice of the states concerned or from other circumstances, it can be deduced that he enjoys full powers.

"Full powers" refers to the document:

[8] 14 I.L.M. 1292 at 1325 (1975).
[9] Article 46.

"emanating from the competent authority of a State designating a person or persons to represent the State for negotiating, adopting or authenticating the text of a treaty, for expressing the consent of the State to be bound by a treaty, or for accomplishing any other act with respect to a treaty."[10]

Heads of State, governments and foreign affairs ministers are regarded as possessing by virtue of their office "full powers."

An act relating to the conclusion of a treaty performed by a person who cannot be considered as enjoying "full powers" and thereby authorised to represent a state for that purpose, is without legal effect unless afterwards confirmed by that state.[11]

Adoption and Confirmation of the Text of a Treaty

The text of a treaty may be adopted by the consent of all states participating in the drafting or alternatively by the majority vote of two-thirds of states present and voting, or by a different procedure if the two-thirds majority so agree.[12]

Article 10 provides that the same procedures should be adopted for declaring the text as authentic and definitive.

Expression of Consent

A state may indicate its consent to be bound by a treaty in a variety of ways: *e.g.* signature, signature *ad referendum*, ratification and accession.

Simple signature may be sufficient to bind parties, but frequently signature *ad referendum* is employed, *i.e.* signature subject to later ratification. Although lacking legal effect *ad referendum* implies political approval and a moral obligation to seek ratification. Ratification in international law refers to the subsequent formal confirmation (subsequent to signature) by a state that it is bound by a treaty. Ratification is employed most frequently by those states (*e.g.* the United States) which are required to initiate some parliamentary process to gain approval to their being bound by the international agreement in question. Between signature and ratification a state is under an obligation to refrain from acts which would defeat the object and purpose of the treaty.[13]

---

[10] Article 2(1)(c).
[11] Article 8.
[12] Article 9.
[13] Article 18(a).

Accession

A state may, in acceding to a treaty, express its consent to be bound by the terms of the treaty, *i.e.* a non-signatory state may subsequently become a party under a procedure provided for in the treaty concerned. The term "adhesion" may also be encountered. Adhesion is distinct from accession in that it refers to a state's acceptance of either only certain aspects of the treaty or certain principles contained in it.

Reservations

Treaties may be likened to legislation, but unlike municipal law, where legislative measures apply uniformly to all, international law allows a state to become a party to a treaty while nevertheless opting out from the application of certain provisions.

Article 2(1)(d) of the Vienna Convention defines a reservation as a "unilateral statement, however phrased or named, made by a State, when signing, ratifying, accepting, approving or acceding to a treaty, whereby it purports to exclude or to modify the legal effect of certain provisions of the treaty in their application to that State."

Reservations only apply in respect of multilateral treaties. They cannot apply with regard to bilateral treaties, where the rejection of a proposed provision constitutes the refusal of an offer made and therefore demands a renegotiation of the proposed terms.

Traditionally, it was maintained that a reservation could only be inserted if all contracting parties to the treaty consented. In the absence of unanimous agreement, the reservation was null and void. However, with the increase in the number of states and the simultaneous growth in the complexity of treaty subject-matter, achieving the concurrence of all the states involved became a problem. What was required if states were not to reject completely treaties which contained a particular provision to which they took exception was a more flexible approach to reservations. The Advisory Opinion requested in respect of *Reservations to the Convention on Genocide Case*[14] heralded the necessary change in approach.

The Court was of the view that a state, making a reservation to which one or more, but not all, parties to the Convention had raised an objection, could be regarded as a party to the Convention *provided* (emphasis added) the reservation was compatible with the object and purpose of the Convention. As to the effect of a reservation between the reserving states and (i) those objecting and (ii) those accepting the reservation, the Court's response was:

[14] I.C.J. Rep. 1951, p. 15.

"(a) that if a party to the Convention objects to a reservation which it considers to be incompatible with the object and purpose of the Convention, it can in fact consider that the reserving State is not a party to the Convention;

(b) that if, on the other hand, a party accepts the reservation as being compatible with the object and purpose of the Convention, it can in fact consider that the reserving State is a party to the Convention."[15]

The Court's opinion introduced the test of compatibility. A test which is applied by states themselves, as compatibility in the light of the Court's opinion, became a matter of subjective interpretation. The Court's opinion marked a sharp contrast to the previous approach, *viz.* one of unity and a minimising of deviance from treaty provisions. The Court's opinion opened up the possibility of different legal relationships existing between different parties to the same agreement.

The Vienna Convention allows reservations unless:

"(a) the reservation is prohibited by treaty; *e.g.* Article 64 of the European Convention on Human Rights prohibits 'reservations of a general character'

(b) the treaty provides that only specified reservations, which do not include the reservation in question, may be made; or

(c) in cases not falling under sub-paragraphs (a) and (b), the reservation is incompatible with the object and purpose of the treaty."[16]

Incompatibility with the object and purpose of the treaty can relate either to substantive provisions of the treaty, or to the nature and spirit of the treaty. A Convention may provide a mechanism for deciding whether a provision is compatible or not, *e.g.* the Convention on Racial Discrimination deems a reservation to be incompatible if at least two-thirds of Contracting Parties object to it.

Acceptance of and Objection to Reservations

A reservation which is expressly authorised by a treaty does not demand the subsequent approval of other contracting parties unless required by the treaty.

If, however, it is apparent from the limited number of states

---

[15] *Ibid.* pp. 29, 30.
[16] Article 19.

concerned and from the object and purpose of the treaty "that the application of the treaty in its entirety between all the parties is an essential condition of the consent of each one to be bound by the treaty," then any reservation must be accepted by *all* the parties.

In respect of a treaty which is the constituent instrument of an international organisation a reservation, unless it is otherwise provided, must be accepted by the competent organ of the relevant organisation.

The general rules to be followed in other cases are that:

> "(a) acceptance by another contracting State of a reservation constitutes the reserving State a party to the treaty in relation to that other State if or when the treaty is in force for those States;
>
> (b) an objection by another contracting State to a reservation does not preclude the entry into force of the treaty as between the objecting and reserving States unless a contrary intention is definitely expressed by the objecting State;
>
> (c) an act expressing a State's consent to be bound by the treaty and containing a reservation is effective as soon as at least one other contracting State has accepted the reservation."[17]

If a state does not object to a reservation (a) within 12 months of having been informed of the reservation, or (b) within 12 months of having expressed consent to be bound by the treaty—depending on which is later—that state will be deemed to have expressed its consent to be bound by the treaty.[18]

Legal Effects of Reservations and of Objections to Reservations

The effect of a reservation established with regard to another party is that it:

> "(a) modifies for the reserving State in its relations with that other party the provisions of the treaty to which the reservation relates to the extent of the reservation; and
>
> (b) modifies those provisions to the same extent for that other party in its relations with the reserving State."

If a state objects to a reservation, but does not oppose the entry into

[17] Article 20(4).
[18] Article 20(5).

force of the treaty between itself and the reserving state, the provisions to which the reservation relates do not apply as between the two states to the extent of the reservation. The provisions of the treaty for the other contracting parties are not modified by the reservation.[19]

The effect in practice of a reservation is that a multilateral agreement becomes fragmented. States will be parties to the same agreement, but in effect one agreement will exist between some contracting parties while another agreement will exist between other parties. In other words, under the umbrella of one multilateral convention several, separate agreements may evolve. The overall purpose of the reservation system is to induce as many states as possible to adhere to a multilateral agreement.

A reservation and an objection to a reservation, must be expressed in writing, but may be withdrawn at any time, unless otherwise provided for in the treaty. The withdrawal of a reservation becomes operative only when the state(s) concerned receive notice of the withdrawal. Similarly, the withdrawal of an objection to a reservation only has effect when received by the reserving state. An express acceptance of a reservation must also be formulated in writing.

Entry into Force

A treaty enters into force in such a manner and upon such a date as it (the treaty) may provide, or as the negotiating states may agree.[20] A multilateral treaty normally comes into force following receipt of a stipulated number of ratifications or accessions, *e.g.* the Vienna Convention provided for its own entry into force "on the thirtieth day following the date of deposit of the thirty-fifth instrument of ratification or accession."[21] Once the required number of ratifications has been received, the treaty will normally provide how soon after receipt of consent an agreement enters into force at the international level for the states concerned.

OBSERVANCE AND APPLICATION OF TREATIES[22]

States are charged with performing and fulfilling their treaty obligations which are binding in good faith—*pacta sunt servanda* is the maxim which expresses this basic canon of treaty observance. As a rule treaties do not have retroactive effect. If they are to have

---

[19] Article 21.
[20] Article 16.
[21] Article 84(1).
[22] Article 26.

such effect this will be expressly stated. Unless otherwise provided, a treaty applies to all the territory of a contracting party. The Vienna Convention did not address itself to the question of dependencies. An agreement may spell out the dependencies to which it is to apply, *e.g.* the EEC Treaty. If silent then, *e.g.* under United States law an agreement will be deemed to apply to all dependencies of the United States. Parties to a multilateral treaty may agree to conclude a new treaty and accordingly negate any preceding agreement.

All is well if all states consent. However, there may be parties to the old treaties which do not accede to the new agreement. The relationship between two such states will be governed by the treaty to which both states are parties (*i.e.* the former).[23]

TREATY INTERPRETATION

How is a treaty to be interpreted? There are three main approaches in international law to treaty interpretation.

> *The "objective" approach*—interpretation in accordance with the ordinary use of the words of the treaty.
> *The "subjective" approach*—interpretation in accordance with the intention of the parties to the treaty.
> *The "teleological" approach*—interpretation in accordance with the treaty's aims and objectives.

Although characterised as distinct, the three approaches are, in practice, not mutually exclusive. In practice, credence may be given to the principles of the three approaches as is reflected in the international jurisprudence which has emerged.[24]

The Vienna Convention adopts an integrated approach to interpretation, but nevertheless gives emphasis to the ordinary meaning approach. Article 31 of the Convention articulates the general rule of interpretation as being that:

> "A treaty shall be interpreted in good faith in accordance with the ordinary meaning to be given to the terms of the treaty in their context and in the light of its object and purpose."

Article 31 allows the use of the teleological approach, but only to shed light on the ordinary meaning of the words of the treaty

---

[23] Article 30(4)(b).
[24] See Harris, pp. 597–604.

provisions. It is invoked as an ancillary aid in interpretation and not as an independent approach of interpretation. A special meaning may be given to a term if it is evident that that is what the relevant parties intended. "Context" includes the text of the treaty, the preamble, any annexes and also:

> "(a) any agreement relating to the treaty which was made between all the parties in connexion with the conclusion of the treaty;
> (b) any instrument which was made by one or more parties in connexion with the conclusion of the treaty and accepted by the other parties as an instrument related to the treaty."[25]

In addition account may be taken of:

> "(a) any subsequent agreement between the parties regarding the interpretation of the treaty or the application of its provisions;
> (b) any subsequent practice in the application of the treaty which establishes the agreement of the parties regarding its interpretation;
> (c) any relevant rules of international law applicable in the relations between the parties."[26]

If giving the ordinary meaning to the terms of the treaty would lead to an ambiguous or obscure meaning, or would produce a manifestly absurd and unreasonable approach, supplementary means of interpretation may be invoked. Supplementary means includes "the preparatory work of the treaty and the circumstances of its conclusion."[27]

Preparatory work—*travaux préparatoires* is not defined in the Vienna Convention, but the term, it is accepted, refers to records documenting the treaty's drafting and includes the records of negotiations between the participating drafting states.

In certain cases, the opinion of expert bodies may also be utilised. "Circumstances" of its "conclusion" refers not only to contemporary circumstances, but also the historical context against which the treaty was concluded, *e.g.* as in *Anglo-Iranian Oil Co. Case.*[28]

---

[25] Article 31(2).
[26] Article 31(3).
[27] Article 32.
[28] I.C.J. Rep. 1953, p. 3 at p. 105.

Interpretation of Treaties Authenticated in Two or More Languages

A text is equally authoritative in each language, unless the agreement provides and the parties agree that, in the case of divergence, a particular text shall prevail. One text may be designated as authoritative whilst other versions may only be recognised as having the status of "official texts" (*i.e.* a text signed by the negotiating states, but not adopted as authoritative). If there is doubt as to the meaning between texts, the more limited interpretation and the one which will restrict the least a state's sovereignty is preferred.

THIRD STATES

Pacta tertiis nec nocent nec prosunt—a treaty does not create either obligations or rights for a third state without its consent. This rule of customary international law is spelt out in Article 34 of the Vienna Convention. This does not preclude a provision contained in a treaty from becoming law for a non-party when the provision has crystallised into international law. The non-party is bound not by the treaty, but rather by customary international law.[29] Article 34 contains the general rule—there are exceptions—special territorial arrangements may produce obligations which third parties are obliged to respect (*e.g.* the Aaland Islands). Article 2(6) of the United Nations Charter provides that:

> "the organisation shall ensure that States which are not members of the United Nations act in accordance with these principles so far as may be necessary for the maintenance of international peace and security."

Article 2(6) today is regarded as a part of customary international law and any state acting contrary to Article 2(6) would be violating customary international law.

A treaty can produce obligations for a third state "if the parties to the treaty intend the provisions to be the means of establishing the obligation and the third State expressly accepts that obligation in writing."[30] A third state may derive rights from a treaty, *e.g.* such as those guaranteeing freedom of passage through the Suez and Kiel Canals, if that is the intention of the parties to the treaty and the assent of the third state has been secured. In contrast, however, to the assent of states on which an obligation is incumbent the assent

[29] Article 38.
[30] Article 35.

of a benefiting state "shall be presumed so long as the contrary is not indicated, unless the treaty otherwise provides."[31]

AMENDMENT AND MODIFICATION

Both amendment and modification relate to a revision of treaty terms by parties. Amendment is the more formal process involving at least *prima facie* all parties to the treaty, while modification is a "private arrangement" between particular parties and in respect of particular provisions.

Amendment

In a bilateral treaty amendments are straightforward, but in a multilateral treaty the agreement of all states to a proposed amendment may be difficult to secure. Article 40 lays down the procedure which, if not provided by the treaty, is to be followed. Article 40 allows for amendment by less than all contracting parties to the original treaty by permitting amendment between those parties in agreement *after* (emphasis added) all states have been given the opportunity to participate in considering amendment proposals. An amending agreement does not, of course, bind a state which, although a party to the original treaty, fails to become a party to the amending agreement.

Modification

Article 41 allows two or more parties to a multilateral treaty to conclude a modifying agreement between themselves, provided that the possibility of modification is recognised by the treaty, is not prohibited by the treaty and does not affect the rights of other parties, or does not relate to "a provision, derogation from which is incompatible with the effective execution of the object and purpose of the treaty as a whole."[32]

VALIDITY OF TREATIES

The Vienna Convention stipulates five grounds on which the validity of an agreement may be challenged. The Convention is exhaustive—states may not invoke other grounds of invalidity. The five grounds are:

Non-compliance with municipal law requirements;

[31] Article 36(1).
[32] Article 41(1)(b)(ii).

Error;
Fraud and corruption;
Coercion;
Jus cogens.

Non-Compliance with Municipal Law Requirements

See above at p. 198.

Error

Error is of limited significance. It plays a much less important role in international law than error in the municipal law of contract. Error may only be invoked by a state if "the error relates to a factor or situation which was assumed by that State to exist at the time when the treaty was concluded and formed an essential basis of its consent to be bound by the treaty."[33]

Error has been invoked almost exclusively in respect of boundary questions. A state which contributed by its behaviour to the error, or should have known of a possible error, cannot relieve itself subsequently of its treaty obligations.[34] Errors in the wording of the treaty are not a ground for invalidating the treaty. These must be corrected in accordance with Article 79 of the Convention and by a procedure which may be quite informal.

Fraud and Corruption

Like error, fraud and corruption are of little significance. Article 49 provides that a treaty may be invalidated "if a State has been induced to conclude a treaty by the fraudulent conduct of another negotiating State...." Article 50 provides that a treaty may be invalidated if a state's consent to a treaty "has been procured through the corruption of its representative directly or indirectly by another negotiating State." Neither "corrupts," "fraudulent conduct" or "corruption" are defined in the Convention or by international jurisprudence.

Coercion

A treaty will be of *no legal effect* (emphasis added) if a state's consent "has been procured by the coercion of its representative through acts or threats directed against him.... "[35] The use of coercion against a state's representative is rare especially as Article 51 is concerned with coercion of the representative's person rather than with coercion by way of a threat of action against his state.

---

[33] Article 48(1).
[34] Article 48(2); see also the *Temple Case*, I.C.J. Rep. 1962, p. 6 at p. 26.
[35] Article 51.

Acceptance of a treaty through coercion and the threat of coercion against a state "in violation of the principles of international law embodied in the Charter of the United Nations" renders a treaty void.[36] Article 52 reflects modern international law's prohibition on the use of force. The Vienna Convention refers explicitly to the use of force as contained in Article 2(4) of the United Nations Charter. Political and economic coercion was not included in spite of the efforts of the less developed countries. To have extended Article 52 would have been to open the "flood gates" and would have undermined the basic tenet, *pacta sunt servanda*.

Jus Cogens

Jus cogens refers to peremptory norms of international law. A peremptory norm is defined, for the purposes of the Convention, as one which is "accepted and recognised by the international community of States as a whole" and from which "no derogation is permitted and which can be modified only by a subsequent norm of general international law having the same character."[37] Any treaty which conflicts at the time of its conclusion with such a norm will be deemed void. Should a new peremptory norm of general international law develop any existing treaty which is contrary to that norm becomes void and terminates.[38] The Vienna Convention establishes that there are certain rules of international law which are of a superior status and which, as such, cannot be affected by treaty. What these peremptory norms are remains unidentified and uncertain. What is certain is that the norm must not only be accepted by the international community, but is must also be accepted as being of peremptory force. Rules which might be categorised as *jus cogens* are those prohibiting genocide, slavery and the use of force.

TERMINATION OF A TREATY

A treaty may be terminated as provided for by the treaty or by the consent of the parties. Material breach by one of the parties may also terminate or suspend a treaty as may a supervening impossibility or a substantial change in circumstances.

Termination by Treaty Provision or Consent

A treaty may provide for termination. A treaty which is silent

[36] Article 52.
[37] Article 53.
[38] Article 64.

regarding termination may not be denounced unless it is apparent that the parties intended to admit the possibility of denunciation or withdrawal or where such a right may be implied by the nature of the treaty. Two or three parties to a multilateral treaty may at any time conclude an agreement suspending the operation of certain provisions temporarily between them, provided that the treaty allows it, it does not restrict the rights of other parties and it is not incompatible with the object and purpose of the treaty.[39] It is common today for a treaty either to be for a fixed term, *e.g.* the treaty establishing the European Coal and Steel Community has a term of 50 years, or to provide that a party may withdraw after giving a certain period of notice. If all parties to a treaty conclude a later treaty relating to the same subject-matter the original treaty will be considered terminated. Similarly where it appears that the matter should be governed by the later treaty, or where the provisions of the later treaty "are so far incompatible with those of the earlier one that the two treaties are not capable of being applied at the same time."[40]

Material Breach

A mere breach of a treaty provision is not sufficient to terminate a treaty. Article 60 of the Vienna Convention defines a material breach as one constituting either:

"(a) a repudiation of the treaty not sanctioned by the present Convention; or

(b) the violation of a provision essential to the accomplishment of the object or purpose of the treaty."

In a bilateral treaty, material breach may be invoked by the innocent party to terminate the treaty or suspend its operation in whole or in part. Material breach of a multilateral treaty allows the "innocent" parties to suspend by unanimous agreement the operation of the treaty in whole or in part or to terminate it either "(i) in the relations between themselves and the defaulting State, or (ii) as between all the parties."

The party particularly affected by the breach may invoke the breach as reason for suspending the operation of the treaty in whole or in part in the relations between itself and the defaulting state, while any other party other than the defaulting state may invoke the breach so as to suspend the operation of the treaty in whole or in part with respect to itself, if the treaty is of such a character that a

[39] Article 58(1).
[40] Article 59(1).

material breach of its provisions by one party radically changes the position of every party with respect to the further performance of its obligations under the treaty. Neither the definition of material breach nor the consequences of such a breach apply to:

> "provisions relating to the protection of the human person contained in treaties of a humanitarian character, in particular to provisions prohibiting any form of reprisals against persons protected by such treaties."[41]

The breach by one party of its obligation under a humanitarian or human rights convention does not entitle other parties to either terminate or suspend their own obligations arising from the convention. As to whether there has been a breach? Each party may decide for itself except where the treaty provides a procedure for doing so.

Supervening Impossibility of Performance

Article 61 of the Vienna Convention which provides for termination of a treaty on the grounds of a supervening impossibility of performance, was designed to cover such relatively rare happenings as the "submergence of an island, the drying up of a river or the destruction of a dam or hydro-electric installation indispensible for the execution of a treaty."[42] Performance may become impossible because a party ceases to exist as a state (for the position when this occurs see below "State Succession.") If the impossibility is temporary, it may be invoked only as a ground for suspending the operation of the treaty. Impossibility of performance may not be invoked by a party if that party has been responsible for making performance impossible.

Fundamental Change of Circumstances

The doctrine of *rebus sic stantibus* may be invoked to terminate a treaty. The operation of this doctrine which literally means "things remaining as they are" rests on the assumption that a treaty may be denounced if circumstances change profoundly from the ones prevailing at the time of the treaty's conclusion. In the *Fisheries Jurisdiction Case*[43] Iceland challenged the Court's jurisdiction to hear the dispute between herself and Britain and Germany on the grounds that there had been a fundamental change of circumstances since the conclusion of the 1961 Exchange of Notes which

---

[41] Article 60(5).
[42] Y.B.I.L.C., 1966, II, p. 256.
[43] *Fisheries Jurisdiction Case (Jurisdiction)*, I.C.J. Rep. 1973, p. 3.

contained *inter alia* a compromissory clause providing for reference
to the International Court of Justice. Iceland alleged that there had
been a fundamental change of circumstances as a consequence of
changes in fishing techniques. The Court identified the changes of
circumstances which would be recognised as fundamental or vital as
those "which imperil the existence or vital development of one of
the parties."[44]

The Court held, however, that:

> "apprehended dangers for the vital interests of Iceland,
> resulting from changes in fishing techniques, cannot constitute
> a fundamental change with respect to the lapse or subsistence
> of the compromissory clause establishing the Court's jurisdic-
> tion,"[45]

and that for a change of circumstances to justify termination of a
treaty there would have to be:

> "a radical transformation of the extent of the obligations still to
> be performed. The change must have increased the burden of
> the obligations to be executed to the extent of rendering the
> performance something essentially different from that origi-
> nally undertaken."[46]

The changed circumstances doctrine will only be successfully
invoked when it applies to circumstances which were not contem-
plated by the parties when the treaty was concluded. In the *Fisheries
Jurisdiction Case* the Court maintained that not only had the
jurisdictional obligation not been radically transformed, it had
remained precisely as it was in 1961. The compromissory clause
indeed anticipated a dispute such as the one that had arisen. *Rebus
sic stantibus* may not be invoked in respect of a boundary settlement
or by a state which has caused the fundamental change.

Severance of Diplomatic or Consular Relations

The severance of diplomatic or consular relations between parties to
a treaty does not affect legal relations between the parties, except in
so far as the existence of diplomatic or consular relations is vital for
the treaty's application.[47]

Termination of an agreement normally applies to the whole

---

[44] *Ibid.* p. 19.
[45] *Ibid.* p. 20.
[46] *Ibid.* p. 21.
[47] Article 63.

treaty unless the treaty provides otherwise. This is the norm reflected in Article 44. Exception is admitted if the ground for termination relates to particular clauses which can be separated from the rest of the treaty. These clauses may be terminated if their acceptance was not an essential basis of the consent of the other parties to be bound and if continued performance of the remainder of the treaty would not be unjust. A party, a victim of fraud or corruption, has the option of invalidating the agreement as a whole or in part. Such an option is not available in respect of the use or threat of force or violation of *jus cogens*.

A state loses its right to initiate a claim for invalidating, terminating, withdrawing from or suspending the operation of a treaty if subsequent to becoming aware of the facts it has expressly agreed that the treaty is valid, or by its conduct it can be said to have acquiesced in the validity of the treaty.[48]

CONSEQUENCES OF INVALIDITY, TERMINATION OR SUSPENSION

A treaty which is established as invalid is void. The provisions of a void treaty have no legal force. If, however, acts have been performed in reliance upon such a treaty:

"(a) each party may require any other party to establish as far as possible in their mutual relations the position that would have existed if the acts had not been performed;

(b) acts performed in good faith before the invalidity was invoked are not rendered unlawful by reason only of the invalidity of the treaty."[49]

The above does not apply "with respect to the party to which the fraud, the act of corruption or the coercion is imputable."[50]

Termination of a treaty, unless otherwise provided, releases the parties concerned from any future obligations, but does not affect any right, obligation or legal situation of the parties created through the execution of the treaty prior to its termination. If a treaty is declared void under Article 53 (conflict with a peremptory norm) the parties are charged with eliminating as far as possible the consequences of any act performed in reliance on the offending provision and with bringing their mutual relations into conformity with the peremptory norm of general international law. If Article 64 is invoked to terminate a treaty, the parties are released from any

[48] Article 45.
[49] Article 69(2).
[50] Article 69(3).

further obligation to perform the treaty, but the rights, obligations and legal situation of the parties created prior to the treaty's termination are not affected, provided that "those rights, obligations or situations may thereafter be maintained only to the extent that their maintenance is not itself in conflict with the new peremptory norm of general international law."[51]

Suspension has for the period of suspension a similar affect as termination. During the period of suspension parties are to refrain from acts which would be likely to obstruct the resumption of the treaty's operation.

Parties to the Vienna Convention are called to seek a peaceful solution to disputes relating to the validity of treaties. This general rule is reinforced by Article 66 which provides that if a solution is not achieved on the lapse of 12 months, the parties shall submit to the International Court of Justice, to arbitration or to the consultation procedure provided for in the Convention's Annex.[52]

STATE SUCCESSION

What happens to a state's treaty obligations when it is replaced by another state on the international plane? In 1978 the International Law Commission produced a Convention which sheds some light on current international thinking on the subject.[53] The Convention reflects predominantly the views of the "newer" states and as such represents progressive development rather than a codification of existing law. Essentially, the "clean slate" view is favoured with respect to successor states—*i.e.* a state is not to be tied by its predecessor. The obligations maintained by a state's predecessor by way of multilateral or bilateral agreements are not automatically incumbent on a state. A state has the option of assuming the multilateral treaties of its predecessor. It is not required to do so. The continuance of a bilateral treaty depends upon agreement, either express or implied, between the parties, *i.e.* the succeeding state and the other contracting state.

There is, however, an exception to this general rule. It does not apply in respect of treaties establishing boundaries, territorial regimes and to those imposing restrictions on a territory for the benefit of another state. To apply the clean slate principle in such instances would prove too disruptive. Accordingly, a successor state is bound by such treaties to which its predecessor has been a party. In the event of states uniting or separating, the Convention

---

[51] Article 71(2).
[52] See Harris, pp. 631–632.
[53] Misc. No. 1 (1980) Cmnd. 7760; 72 A.J.I.L. 971 (1978); Harris, pp. 634–636.

stipulates that treaties continue in force for the territory concerned unless the parties have agreed otherwise, or the result would be inconsistent with the object and purpose of the treaty and would radically change the conditions for its operation.[54]

---

[54] State succession raises issues other than those raised by succession to treaties, but these are outwith the subject-matter of this text.

FURTHER READING

Cases and Materials

D.J. Harris, *Cases and Materials on International Law* (1983), Chapter 10.

L. Henkin, R. Pugh, O. Schachter and H. Smit, *International Law: Cases and Materials* (1980), Chapter 10.

J. Sweeny, C. Oliver and N. Leech, *The International Legal System: Cases and Materials* (1981), Chapters 15 and 16.

Specialised Texts

Lord McNair, *The Law of Treaties* (1961).

I. Sinclair, *The Vienna Convention on the Law of Treaties* (1985).

General Texts

M. Akehurst, *A Modern Introduction to International Law* (1982), Chapter 10.

I. Brownlie, *Principles of Public International Law* (1979), Chapter XXV.

L. Green, *International Law: A Canadian Perspective* (1984), Part V, §1.

D.W. Greig, *International Law* (1976), Chapter 9.

J.G. Starke, *An Introduction to International Law* (1979), Chapter 16.

Chapter Eleven

THE USE OF FORCE

The use of force is prohibited by international law. The United Nations Charter requires Member States to settle disputes amongst themselves by peaceful means and to refrain in their international relations with each other from either the threat or the use of force.[1] Contemporary international law may prohibit the use of force, but international law cannot prevent the use of force any more than municipal criminal law can prevent murder. International law consequently aims to *control* the use of force, and so there is accordingly a widely accepted distinction between the legitimate and illegitimate use of force. Nevertheless, prohibition on the use of force remains the general rule with the exceptions admitted by international law clearly defined. This, however, has not always been the case.

THE LAW BEFORE 1945

In earliest history a just war was regarded as a legitimate use of force. St. Augustine (354–430) articulated the just war as one designed to avenge injuries which had been sustained and which:

> "the nation or city against which war like action is to be directed has neglected either to punish wrongs committed by its own citizens or to restore what has been unjustly taken by it."

The just war was founded in theological doctrine. However, the breakdown of the Church's authority was followed by the emergence of the sovereign nation state. The right to use force was recognised as an inherent right of every independent sovereign state. International law placed no restraints on the use of force—factors other than legal considerations obviously would affect a state's resort to force and the use of force was a legitimate action for any state to adopt.

The unprecedented devastation of the First World War prompted states to establish an international forum in which states could

---

[1] United Nations Charter, Articles 2(3) and 2(4).

discuss their problems. It was hoped thereby to reduce the possibility of a resort to force. Consequently, the League of Nations was founded. The Covenant of the League of Nations signed in 1919 did not abolish war, but rather placed limitations upon the use of force. In the event of a dispute which was potentially disruptive, Member States agreed under the Covenant to submit the dispute to arbitration or judicial settlement or to inquiry by the Council of the League. War was not to be resorted to until three months after the award by the arbitrator, the judicial decision or the Council's report had been made. In this way the Covenant provided a cooling-off period for protagonists. Members also agreed not to go to war with fellow Members of the League who complied with either an arbitral award, judicial decision or with a unanimous report of the Council.

The Covenant required Member States "to respect and preserve as against external agression the territorial integrity and political independence of all Members of the League."[2] In 1928 the international community was successful in agreeing on a comprehensive ban on war as an instrument of national policy. Sixty-three states signed the General Treaty for the Renunciation of War (also known as the Kellogg-Briand Pact or the Pact of Paris),[3] in which parties agreed to seek a peaceful solution to all disputes arising between them. Nevertheless, the right of self-defence still existed. This Treaty, although it has never been terminated, has been superseded by Article 2(4) of the United Nations Charter.

Treaties, however, cannot prevent wars and the Second World War broke out in 1939 only 11 years after the signing of the Renunciation Treaty.

THE LAW AS OF 1945

Article 2(3) of the United Nations Charter requires all Member States to "settle their international disputes by peaceful means in such a manner that international peace and security, and justice are not endangered," while Article 2(4) demands that all Member States:

> "refrain in their international relations from the threat or use of force against the territorial integrity and political independence of any State, or in any manner inconsistent with the purposes of the United Nations."

---

[2] Article 10 of the Covenant. U.K.T.S. 4 (1919) Cmd. 153.
[3] U.K.T.S. 29 (1929) Cmd. 3410; 94 L.N.T.S. 57; 22 A.J.I.L. Supp. 171; Harris, p. 639.

Article 2(4), as a provision of the United Nations Charter, is addressed to all Members of the United Nations; however the prohibition on the use of force is now regarded as a principle of customary international law, and, as such, is addressed to all members of the international community.

Extent of the Prohibition Contained in Article 2(4)

Article 2(4) prohibits the use of force. It is not concerned only with the outlawing of war: Article 2(4) does not distinguish between war and the use of force falling short of war, *e.g.* reprisals.[4] Article 2(4) thus embraces all threats of and acts of violence without distinction.

Article 2(4) specifically refers to the threat or use of force used "against the territorial integrity or political independence of any State...." Can force be used to enforce a right when force is not employed against territorial integrity or political independence? Can force be used to protect human rights?

Article 2(4) should be read as a whole within the context of the United Nations Charter. Force contrary to "the purposes of the United Nations" is also prohibited. The purposes of the United Nations are spelt out in Article 1 of the Charter. The purposes include respect for the principle of equal rights and self-determination and respect for human rights, but nevertheless the overriding purpose of the United Nations remains:

> "[T]o maintain international peace and security, and to that end: to take effective collective measures for the prevention and removal of threats to the peace, and for the suppression of acts of aggression or other breaches of the peace, and to bring about by peaceful means, and in conformity with the principles of justice and international law, adjustment or settlement of international disputes or situations which might lead to a breach of the peace."[5]

The emphasis is on the maintenance of peace and security and on solving both potential and actual conflicts by peaceful means.

Article 2(4) has been supplemented by the 1970 General Assembly Declaration on Principles of International Law Concerning Friendly Relations and Co-operation Among States in

---

[4] A declaration of war is seldom made by states parties to hostilities. War is a technical term. Acknowledgment of war produces consequences under international law, *e.g.* role of neutral states, and municipal law, *e.g.* the status of aliens.
[5] United Nations Charter, Article 1(1).

Accordance with the Charter of the United Nations.[6] The Resolution is only a resolution and therefore is not legally binding on Members. Nevertheless it is regarded as representing the consensus view of the international community on the legal interpretation to be given to the principles enunciated in the United Nations Charter. This Declaration adds flesh to the prohibition on the use of force. It provides, *inter alia*, that:

A war of aggression constitutes a crime against the peace for which there is responsibility under international law.

Every state has the duty to refrain from the threat or use of force to violate the existing international boundaries of another state or as a means of solving international disputes, including territorial disputes and problems concerning frontiers of states. States have a duty to refrain from acts of reprisal involving the use of force.

Every state has the duty to refrain from any forcible action which deprives peoples of realising equal rights and self-determination.

Every state has the duty to refrain from organising or encouraging the organisation of irregular forces or armed bands, including mercenaries, for incursion into the territory of another state.

Every state has the duty to refrain from organising, instigating, assisting or participating in acts of civil strife or terrorist acts in another state or acquiescing in organised activities within its territory directed towards the commission of such acts when the acts involve a threat or use of force.

The territory of a state shall not be the object of military occupation resulting from the use of force. The territory of a state shall not be the object of acquisition by another state resulting from the threat or use of force. No territorial acquisition resulting from the threat or use of force shall be recognised as legal.

To put it simply, any threat or use of force by a state, other than in accordance with the exceptions provided for under the United Nations Charter, is contrary to and prohibited by contemporary international law.

---

[6] G.A. Resolution 2625 (XXV), October 24, 1970—Harris, Appendix III, p. 783. See also Resolution on the Definition of Aggression 1974, G.A. Resolution 3314 (XXIX); 69 A.J.I.L. 480 (1975); Harris, p. 677.

Does Article 2(4) Prohibit Only the Use of Armed Force?

Force does not necessarily have to refer to armed force. Force can be economic and/or political. Does Article 2(4) confine itself to prohibiting only the use of armed force or are other categories of force similarly prohibited?

The Preamble of the United Nations Charter and Article 51 (on a state's inherent right to self-defence—considered below) specifically mention "armed force." The 1970 Declaration, on the other hand, is inconclusive. It recalls the duty of states to refrain in their international relations from military, political, economic or any other form of coercion, but in the section on the use of force, force is not qualified. The imprecision of definition reflects the dichotomy which existed essentially between developed and developing states. The latter would have interpreted force to encompass economic and political force,[7] whilst the former maintained that it was only armed force which was outlawed. However, the former group of states did concede that economic and political pressure could constitute illegal intervention, but although economic coercion is prohibited in the 1970 Declaration's section on non-intervention it remains undefined.

As far as Article 2(4) and the legal regime envisaged by the United Nations Charter is concerned, the prohibition is one aimed at outlawing armed force and "gunboat diplomacy" in relations between states.

Exceptions to the Prohibition on the Threat or Use of Force

The use of force only remains legitimate under international law in particularly well-defined circumstances:

　　—in self-defence—either individual or collective—in accordance with Article 51 of the United Nations Charter;
　　—collective measures taken under the auspices of the United Nations; and
　　—if authorised by a competent organ of the United Nations.

Self-defence

Customary international law recognised a state's right of self-defence, but the extent of that right was ill-defined. It was only as restrictions were imposed on the employment of force by states that

---

[7] See also Para. 4(e) of the 1974 Declaration on the Establishment of a New International Economic Order, 13 I.L.M. 715 (1974).

the need to articulate the concept of self-defence in international law became more acute.

Under customary international law, the use of force had to be justified if states were at peace. The use of force by one state against another with which it was not at war was *prima facie* unlawful. The circumstances which allowed the exercise of self-defence were articulated in the now famous communication of the United States Secretary of State Webster to the British Government following the *Caroline* incident.[8]

The *Caroline* was a vessel which operated from United States territory supplying rebel insurrectionaries in Canada. A British force destroyed the *Caroline* and two United States citizens were killed. A British subject, McLeod, was charged with murder and arson.

In his letter Secretary Webster emphasised that for the success of the British Government's defence, that their action was justified on grounds of "the necessity of self-defence and preservation," it must be demonstrated that the need for self-defence was "instant, overwhelming and leaving no choice of means, and no moment for deliberation." It was also necessary for Britain to show that the Canadian authorities had done nothing "unreasonable, or excessive; since the act justified by the necessity of self-defence, must be limited by that necessity, and kept clearly within it."

To summarise, the exercise of force in self-defence was justified under customary international law provided that the need for it was:

> instant;
> overwhelming;
> immediate;
> there was no viable alternative action which could be taken.

The extent of force used in self-defence had to be commensurate to the violation it was being utilised to repel.

The above criteria still apply today.

Article 51, United Nations Charter. Article 51 of the United Nations Charter acknowledges the right of self-defence as an inherent right of every state:

> "Nothing in the present Charter shall impair the inherent right of individual or collective self-defence if an armed attack occurs against a Member of the United Nations, until the Security Council has taken measures necessary to maintain international peace and security. Measures taken by Members

[8] 29 B.F.S.P. 1137–1138; 30 B.F.S.P. 195–196; Harris, p. 655.

in the exercise of this right of self-defence shall be immediately reported to the Security Council and shall not in any way affect the authority and responsibility of the Security Council under the present Charter to take at any time such action as it deems necessary in order to maintain or restore international peace and security."

Self-defence is permissible if an armed attack has taken place and Article 51 confines itself to self-defence only in this situation. When does such an attack occur? The launching of a missile undoubtedly constitutes an attack. What of the training of guerillas for use against another Member State? Can a state resort to force in anticipation of an armed attack?

Anticipatory self-defence is excluded from Article 51. Does that mean it is prohibited? The right of self-defence which Article 51 acknowledges as "inherent" exists under customary international law—*i.e.* independently of Article 51. Does, therefore, the right of anticipatory self-defence exist under customary international law?

States do employ force in anticipation of an alleged armed attack, *e.g.* Israel's strike on the United Arab Republic in June 1967. The justification for anticipatory self-defence can be reconciled with the obligation on United Nations Member States to refrain from either "the threat or use of force." States which are threatened with the use of force may take appropriate anticipatory measures to repel such a threat, but such measures can only be justified if:

a state is the target of hostile activities of another state;
the threatened state has exhausted all alternative means of protection;
the danger is imminent;
the defensive measures are proportionate to the pending danger.

States enjoy the right of self-defence in the event of an armed attack under Article 51 of the United Nations Charter. They also enjoy under customary international law the right to use force in circumstances falling short of an armed attack. However states, although they enjoy such rights, are at all times required by the United Nations Charter and customary international law to settle their disputes by peaceful means.

Use of force to Protect Nationals Abroad. What if a state's nationals or property are harmed abroad? Does that state have a right to intervene to defend its nationals when its territory has not been the object of an armed attack?

The Anglo–French invasion of Suez, the Israeli raid on Entebbe Airport 1976,[9] the abortive United States rescue mission of the hostages in Iran and United States intervention in Grenada in 1983 are instances of force being used by the intervening state to protect its nationals. The legitimacy of intervention to afford such protection is not firmly established in international law. Such intervention can be reconciled with the doctrine of self-defence if the basic concept underlying diplomatic protection is stretched, so that an imminent threat of danger to nationals abroad may be regarded as an imminent threat to the national state itself. In other words, by invoking a legal fiction, intervention on behalf of one's nationals can be reconciled with self-defence.

Non-fulfilment by the host state of its international duty to safeguard, to at least a minimum international standard, the interests of aliens may lend support to intervention by the host state. Thus, in the Security Council debate held in July 1976 on the Entebbe incident an Israeli representative maintained that Uganda had "violated a basic tenet of international law in failing to protect foreign nationals on its territory".[10]

Intervention to protect nationals is open to obvious abuse, particularly as it involves a subjective interpretation by a state of when its nationals are in danger. Even if protective intervention is accepted, it must be recognised as the exception rather than the norm, not least because it involves violations of another state's territorial integrity and ssovereignty. Protective intervention is more likely to be accepted by the international community if the danger to the rescuing state's nationals can be shown to be overwhelming. A successful mission, although it may not be legally condoned, is more likely to be accepted as expedient than is one which fails—*e.g.* compare the Entebbe raid with the United States abortive mission to rescue the American hostages in Iran. As with self-defence, the force used in such circumstances must be proportionate to the danger.

Humanitarian Intervention. Humanitarian intervention is distinct from protective intervention in that it involves intervention to protect another state's nationals (or a group of nationals) and possibly those of the territorial state. The intervening state is, in other words, not protecting its own right. Although it may be contended that, at least superficially, the intervening state is playing

---

[9] Harris, pp. 667–672.
[10] See 15 I.L.M. 1224 (1976); Harris, p. 669.

a more objective role than when intervening to protect its own nationals, humanitarian intervention is equally open to abuse. The intervening state may ostensibly intervene to promote an altruistic interest, but in reality intervention may be prompted by political motives and an anxiety to secure for itself some long-term benefit. For example, was the United States intervention in the Dominican Republic in 1965 designed to secure a right-wing regime rather than a left-wing one, or was it indeed to preserve law and order and safeguard for inhabitants the exercise of their democratic rights?

The legitimacy of humanitarian intervention remains disputed in international law. Protagonists of humanitarian intervention support its use for the prevention of serious violations of basic human rights, normally the right to life.

Collective Self-defence. The right of collective self-defence is recognised by Article 51. Collective self-defence is something of a misnomer, as it refers to the right of each state to use force in defence of another state. The force is therefore employed on behalf of another state.

Collective self-defence refers, strictly speaking, to collective defence rather than self-defence. Article 51 is the legal basis of such collective agreements as the NATO Alliance and the Warsaw Pact in which an attack on one Member is treated as an attack on all. Under Article 5 of the North Atlantic Treaty[11] the Contracting Parties:

"agree that an armed attack against one or more of them in Europe or North America shall be considered an attack against them all; and consequently they agree that, if such an armed attack occurs, each of them, in exercise of the right of individual or collective self-defence recognized by Article 51 of the Charter of the United Nations, will assist the Party or Parties so attacked by taking forthwith, individually, and in concert with the other Parties, such action as it deems necessary, including the use of armed force, to restore and maintain the security of the North Atlantic area."

The Warsaw Pact's counterpart to Article 5 is Article 4.[12]

All measures adopted by Member States in self-defence must be reported to the Security Council and the use of force in individual or collective self-defence may only be employed until the Security

---

[11] U.K.T.S. 56 (1949) Cmd. 7789; 34 U.N.T.S. 243; Harris, p. 672.
[12] 219 U.N.T.S. 3; 49 A.J.I.L. Supp. 194 (1955); Harris, p. 674.

Council has taken appropriate measures to maintain international peace and security.

Reprisals. Reprisals are acts which in themselves are illegal under international law and are adopted by a state in response to its having been the victim of an unlawful act by another state. They seek to impose on the offending state reparation for the offence, a return to legality and an avoidance of new offences.[13] Reprisals involving armed force have now to comply with the contemporary international law on the use of force if they are not to be contrary to international law. Reprisals falling short of the use of force may still be taken legitimately.

Retorsions. Retorsions are generally acts not involving the use of force, such as the severance of diplomatic relations or foreign aid, taken in response to an unfriendly act, whether illegal or not. An act of retorsion is a lawful means of expressing displeasure at the conduct of another state.

Regional Arrangements. The right of states to make regional arrangements to deal with matters of international peace and security is protected by the United Nations Charter and in particular by Article 52.

Article 52(1) provides:

> "Nothing in the present Charter precludes the existence of regional arrangements or agencies for dealing with such matters relating to the maintenance of international peace and security as are appropriate for regional action, provided that such arrangements or agencies and their activities are consistent with the Purposes and Principles of the United Nations."

Article 52(2), however, charges members of regional organisations with making "every effort to achieve pacific settlement of local disputes through such regional arrangements or by such regional agencies before referring them to the Security Council." Action taken via regional organisations will only be legitimate if it is consistent with the purposes and principles of the United Nations Charter and does not amount to "enforcement action" unless this has been authorised by the Security Council. The Security Council must, under Article 54, be kept fully informed at all times "of activities undertaken or in contemplation under regional arrangements or by regional agencies for the maintenance of international peace and security."

[13] See *The Naulilaa Case*, 2 R.I.A.A. 1012 (1928); Harris, p. 9.

The Organisation of Eastern Caribbean States' peace-keeping mission which, with the support of Barbados, Jamaica and the United States, landed in Grenada on October 25, 1983 is an instance of action being taken under the auspices of a regional organisation. Arguments supporting the legality of the invasion are founded *inter alia* on its legitimacy as a regional peace-keeping mission under Article 52 of the United Nations Charter, especially as it was prompted by the breakdown of government authority and in response to a request by the Governor-General Sir Paul Scoon.[14]

The legitimacy of the 1962 United States quarantine imposed in respect of vessels destined for Cuba, purported to be based on Article 52, namely through the authorisation of the Organisation of American States.[15]

Collective Measures Through the United Nations

Under the United Nations Charter the primary responsibility for peace-keeping lies with the Security Council.[16] Member States agree under Article 25 to accept and carry out the decisions of the Security Council. The Security Council can act either under Chapter VI or Chapter VII of the Charter.

Under Chapter VI the Security Council can make recommendations with the objective of achieving a peaceful settlement to disputes.

Chapter VII deals with the enforcement measures which the Security Council can adopt. Under Article 39, the Security Council is empowered to determine "the existence of any threat to the peace, breach of the peace, or act of aggression...."

What Constitutes Aggression? A General Assembly Resolution adopted in 1974[17] defined aggression as "the use of force by a State against the sovereignty, territorial integrity or political independence of another State, or in any other manner inconsistent with the Charter of the United Nations...." Examples of acts that would be identified as aggression include the invasion or armed attack by one state against the territory of another state, the blockade of the ports or coasts of a state by the armed forces of another state, the sending by or on behalf of a state of armed bands, groups, irregulars or mercenaries, to employ armed force against another state.[18]

[14] For some of the arguments for and against the lawfulness of the Grenada Invasion, see 78 A.J.I.L. 131–175 (1984); also W.C. Gilmore, *The Grenada Intervention* (Mansell, 1984).

[15] See Harris, pp. 659–660.

[16] Article 24.

[17] G.A. Resolution 3314 (XXIX), *supra,* n. 6.

[18] *Ibid.* Article 3.

Following an affirmative decision under Article 39, the Security Council can make recommendations or decide what measures are to be taken in accordance with the Charter to maintain peace and security. In practice, the Security Council seldom discusses the issue of whether it enjoys jurisdiction under Article 39 and, consequently, which aspect (*i.e.* "threat to the peace" or "breach of the peace") it is basing its action on is not identified. "Threat to the peace," which should be read as international peace, has become of minimal significance in light of the Security Council's characterisation of the situation in Southern Rhodesia and South Africa (essentially an internal matter) as threatening international peace and security. A "breach of the peace" has only been specifically identified in two cases, the *Korean* and the *Falkland/Malvinas Islands* cases. Article 40 provides that the Security Council may call upon the parties concerned to comply with such provisional measures as it deems necessary or desirable, *e.g.* the Security Council could call for a cease fire. The enforcement action which the Security Council may consider necessary may be either:

(i)   measures not involving the use of force (Article 41); or
(ii)   armed force (Article 42).

(i) Acting under Article 41, the Security Council may call upon Members of the United Nations to employ economic sanctions or diplomatic sanctions against a "defaulting" state. The Resolutions calling for sanctions against South Africa[19] have been based on Article 41 as were those imposing sanctions against Southern Rhodesia[20] following the unilateral declaration of independence in 1965.

(ii) If the Security Council considers that Article 41 measures would be or have proved inadequate, it may take such action by air, sea or land forces as may be necessary to maintain or restore international peace and security. Such action may include demonstrations, blockades and other operations by air, sea or land forces of Members of the United Nations.

Article 42 is supplemented by Article 43, according to which states undertake to provide, under special agreements with the Security Council, armed forces, assistance, and facilities, including rights of passage, to the extent necessary for maintaining peace and

---

[19] S.C. Resolution 181 (1963), S.C.O.R., 18th year, *Resolutions and Decisions*, p. 9; S.C. Resolution 418 (1977), S.C.O.R., 32nd year, *Resolutions and Decisions*, p. 5; see Harris, pp. 690–691.
[20] S.C. Resolution 232 (1966), S.C.O.R., 21st year, *Resolutions and Decisions*, p. 5; S.C. Resolution 253 (1968), S.C.O.R., 23rd year, *Resolutions and Decisions;* 7 I.L.M. 897 (1968).

security. No such agreements have been concluded. No Member State is therefore obliged to participate in military operations nor can the Security Council order a Member State to participate.

The *raison d'être* of Article 43 was to provide the Security Council with a procedure by which it could act. The absence of agreements has not prevented the Security Council from adopting alternative means, and forces, made up of contingents from Member States, have been formed when required (see *Expenses Case* below). There is, however, no permanent force and forces are established *ad hoc*.

The force which operated in Korea in 1950 was designated a United Nations force, but whether it was one in the true sense remains doubtful. The Security Council Resolutions calling upon Members to assist the United Nations in securing the withdrawal of the North Korean forces,[21] to furnish "such assistance to the Republic of Korea as may be necessary to repel the armed attack and to restore international peace and security in the area"[22] and authorising the use of the United Nations flag,[23] were adopted through the fortuitous absence of the Soviet Union representative in the Security Council.[24] Control over the forces, provided by 16 states, was maintained throughout by the United States and, indeed, the troops were provided pursuant to agreements made by the United States and the countries involved.[25]

Under the Charter, the General Assembly may discuss any questions relating to the maintenance of international peace and security, provided the matter is not before the Security Council.[26] Whilst the Security Council can make decisions, the General Assembly can only make recommendations. Under the Charter, the role envisaged for the General Assembly was a less active one than that envisaged for the Security Council, but in practice the Security Council has been rendered impotent by the use of the veto and this, to some extent, has resulted in a more active role than that originally anticipated being assumed by the General Assembly.

---

[21] S.C. Resolution of June 25, 1950, S.C.O.R., 5th year, *Resolutions and Decisions*, pp. 4–5; Harris, p. 682.
[22] S.C. Resolution of June 27, 1950, S.C.O.R., 5th year, *Resolutions and Decisions*, p. 5; Harris, p. 683.
[23] S.C. Resolution of July 7, 1950, *ibid;* Harris, *ibid.*
[24] The Soviet Union representative was absent in protest at the Seating of the Nationalist Chinese delegation.
[25] For treatment of the *Korean Question* and analysis of, *inter alia*, the constitutionality of the Security Council Resolutions, see Harris, pp. 682–687.
[26] Articles 11 and 12.

The Veto. Every Member of the Security Council has one vote.[27] Procedural issues in order to be adopted must receive the affirmative vote of nine Members, while non-procedural matters require nine votes including the concurring vote of the Five Permanent Members (*i.e.* China, France, the United Kingdom, the United States and the Soviet Union). Absence and abstention is taken as concurrence. The decision as to whether a matter is or is not procedural is itself a non-procedural issue, *i.e.* the concurring vote of the Five Permanent Members is required.

The possibility of exercising a double veto is therefore open to a Permanent Member. If, because of the veto, the Security Council is unable to make any decisions, the General Assembly, with residual authority for the maintenance of peace, can assume the responsibility which the Security Council is unable to discharge. The inability of the Security Council to take further action for the management of the Korean campaign (because of the return to his seat of the Soviet Union representative and his consequent use of the veto) led to the Uniting for Peace Resolution in November 1950.[28]

The Uniting for Peace Resolution provided that in the event of the Security Council being unable because of a lack of unanimity of the Permanent Members, to discharge its primary responsibility for the maintenance of international peace and security, the General Assembly could, where there appears to be a threat to the peace, breach of the peace or act of aggression:

> "consider the matter immediately with a view to making appropriate recommendations to Members for collective measures, including in the case of a breach of the peace or act of aggression the use of armed force when necessary, to maintain or restore international peace and security."

If the General Assembly is not in session at the time an emergency session may be called. An emergency session may be requested by the Security Council on the vote of any nine Members, or by a majority of the Members of the United Nations. The General Assembly has invoked the Uniting for Peace Resolution on a number of occasions, *e.g.* the Suez Question (1956), the Congo Question (1960), the Pakistan Civil War (Bangladesh) (1972), Afghanistan (1980), Namibia (1981) and the Question of Occupied Arab Territories (1982). The Uniting for Peace Resolution has been

---

[27] Article 27.
[28] Resolution 377 (V), November 3, 1950; G.A.O.R., 5th Session, Supp. 20, p. 10. Harris, p. 691.

effective in allowing issues to be discussed in the General Assembly rather than as a means of preventing crises and preserving international peace and security.

Peace-keeping Forces. The United Nations Charter does not provide for those peace-keeping forces—*i.e.* forces which are designed to maintain peace rather than take enforcement action—which have made an important contribution in major crises areas. Peace-keeping forces, which consist of troops given voluntarily by United Nations Member States, must remain at all times impartial. They have been responsible for supervising a cease fire, as was the United Nations Emergency Force (UNEF) in the Middle East in 1956, in assisting a return to peace, as did the United Nations Force in the Congo (ONUC) in 1960, and in patrolling a buffer zone, as does the United Nations Disengagement Observation Force (UNDOF) between Israel and Syria and the United Nations Interim Force in the Lebanon (UNFIL) along the Israeli and Lebanese border. United Nations peace-keeping forces in practice only operate in a territory as long as the host state consents.

The constitutionality of peace-keeping forces was affirmed in the *Certain Expenses of the United Nations Case.*[29] The International Court of Justice was requested by the General Assembly to give an advisory opinion on the legality of expenses levied on Members for the purpose of financing the United Nations forces in the Middle East (UNEF) and the Congo (ONUC) following the refusal of a number of states, including the Soviet Union and France, to make their contributions. The International Court held that the expenses were legitimate as they were made for the fulfilment of a purpose of the United Nations.[30]

Regarding the respective roles of the Security Council and General Assembly in the maintenance of international peace and security, the Court emphasised that while the Security Council enjoyed a primary responsibility its responsibility was not exclusive. The Court did, however, acknowledge that only the Security Council could "require enforcement by coercive action against an aggressor."[31] In other words, the authorisation of enforcement measures involving the use of force is the prerogative of the Security Council. The General Assembly's competence is, in the light of the Court's opinion, limited to action which falls short of enforcement action *per se.* The General Assembly may not be competent to authorise enforcement measures which involve the use of force, but

[29] I.C.J. Rep. 1962, p. 151.
[30] *Ibid.* at p. 172.
[31] *Ibid.* at p. 163.

it can nevertheless recommend action when that does not involve "enforcement action" but rather, the establishment of a peacekeeping force designed to maintain the peace.

Under the United Nations, regime although the Security Council is the organ exclusively competent to authorise the use of force, the General Assembly enjoys residual competence to recommend action falling short of coercive or enforcement action.

Domestic Jurisdiction Limitation. Article 2(7) of the United Nations Charter prohibits the United Nations from intervening in matters which are essentially within the jurisdiction of any state. This limitation does not apply in respect of Chapter VII enforcement action. Domestic jurisdiction has been interpreted restrictively and Article 2(7) has not impeded the work of the United Nations.

Force Authorised by a Competent Organ of the United Nations

A state may be authorised by the Security Council to use force even in circumstances when the use of force would otherwise be illegal. This is the conclusion to be drawn from Security Council Resolution 221 (1966) which called upon the United Kingdom:

> "to prevent by the use of force if necessary . . . vessels reasonably believed to be carrying oil destined for Rhodesia, and . . . to arrest and detain tanker known as the Joanna V upon her departure from Beira in the event her oil cargo is discharged there."[32]

Apparently, as Article 42 authorises the Security Council to use force in circumstances where force would normally be illegal, the Security Council can authorise states to do likewise.

Intervention in Civil Wars. Civil wars are not prohibited by international law. Article 2(4) prohibits the use of force in respect of international relations only. International law does, however, have something to say on participation by other states.

The general rule is one of non-intervention. The General Assembly's Declaration on the Inadmissibility of Intervention in the Domestic Affairs of States and the Protection of their Independence and Sovereignty prohibits any state from intervening:

> "directly or indirectly, for any reason whatever, in the internal or external affairs of any other State. . . . no State shall

---

[32] S.C.O.R., 21st year, *Resolutions and Decisions*, p. 5. 5 I.L.M. 534 (1966).

organize, assist, foment, finance, incite or tolerate subversive, terrorist or armed activities directed towards the violent overthrow of the regime of another State, or interfere in civil strife in another State."

The prohibitions enunciated in the 1965 Declaration were reaffirmed in the 1970 Declaration on Principles of International Law.

States may, for a variety of political reasons, intervene to support either the rebels or alternatively to support the established authorities. Policy rather than law will determine a state's decision to intervene. Non-intervention is undoubtedly the best policy. The danger of intervention by a state in support of one party is that it will attract counter-intervention by another state in support of the other party and consequently an internal matter can escalate into an international war.[33]

NUCLEAR WEAPONS

Nuclear weapons have added a new dimension to the use of force. International relations, especially between the United States and the Soviet Union have throughout the last 20 years been dominated, albeit with varying emphasis, by arms limitation talks.

Nuclear weapons are an important issue in international relations and although developing and Communist countries would like them to be declared illegal under international law, this is untenable to Western states in view of the relative weakness of their conventional forces.

Major Agreements on Nuclear Weapons

Multilateral

Limited Test Ban Treaty (LBTB) 1963.[34] This treaty, to which there are now some 111 parties, prohibits nuclear tests in the atmosphere, in outer space and under water.

Treaty on the Non Proliferation of Nuclear Weapons (Non Proliferation Treaty) 1968.[35] Under this treaty, to which there are some 119 parties, the "nuclear weapons parties" undertake not to transfer to any recipient nuclear weapons or devices, or to assist any "non-nuclear weapon State" to manufacture, acquire or control

---

[33] See Harris, pp. 648–655 for more extensive coverage of this subject.
[34] 480 U.N.T.S. 43; U.K.T.S. 3 (1964) Cmnd. 2245; 14 U.S.T. 1313.
[35] 729 U.N.T.S. 161; U.K.T.S. 88 (1970) Cmnd. 4474; 21 U.S.T. 483; 7 I.L.M. 809 (1968).

such weapons or devices. "Non-nuclear weapon parties" undertake corollary obligations.

Treaty for the Prohibition of Nuclear Weapons in Latin America 1967 [36] *and Additional Protocols I* [37] *and II.* [38] The treaty establishes Latin America as a deneutralised region. Protocol I requires states from outside the region to apply the treaty to territories within the region for whose international rules they are responsible and Protocol II requires states with nuclear weapons to respect the deneutralised states of the region.

Strategic Arms Limitation Talks (SALT I). The Strategic Arms Limitation Talks held between 1969–1972 produced a number of agreements, namely, the 1971 Agreement on Measures to Reduce the Risk of Outbreak of Nuclear War (the Accidents Agreement),[39] the 1971 Agreement on Measures to Improve the Direct Communications Link (the Hot-Line Upgrade Agreement),[40] and the 1972 Treaty on the Limitation of Anti-Ballistic Missile Systems (ABM).[41] The SALT II negotiations did not prove so fruitful. Only one treaty was produced, namely the 1979 Treaty on the Limitation of Strategic Offensive Arms and this has never been ratified by the United States Senate.

The 1980s have witnessed the initiation of new talks—Strategic Arms Reduction Talks (START) and Reduction of Intermediate-Range Nuclear Forces (INF) and the Geneva meeting of President Reagan and Gorbachov in November 1985. The emphasis is now, it will be noted, on reduction rather than elimination.

Talks have also been held on anti-satellite weapons and the United Kingdom has also participated in negotiations designed to achieve a comprehensive test ban treaty. These have proved inconclusive.[42]

By-products of the negotiations have been an acceptance by

---

[36] 634 U.N.T.S. 326; U.K.T.S. 54 (1970) Cmnd. 4409; 22 U.S.T. 762; 6 I.L.M. 521 (1967).

[37] U.K.T.S. 54 (1970) Cmnd. 4409; T.I.A.S. 10147; 6 I.L.M. 533 (1967).

[38] 634 U.N.T.S. 364; U.K.T.S. 54 (1970) Cmnd. 4409; 22 U.S.T. 754; 6 I.L.M. 534 (1967).

[39] 10 I.L.M. 1172 (1971).

[40] 22 U.S.T. 1598; 806 U.N.T.S. 402; 10 I.L.M. 1174 (1971).

[41] 23 U.S.T.S. 3435; 11 I.L.M. 784 (1972). A fourth agreement, *viz.* an interim agreement of May 1972 on certain measures with respect to the Limitation of Strategic Offensive Arms is no longer in force.

[42] For the negotiation process and the role of the lawyer, see J.H. McNeill, "U.S.-U.S.S.R. Nuclear Arms Negotiations: The Process and the Lawyer" 79 A.J.I.L. 52 (1985).

states of the use of reconnaisance satellites for monitoring treaty compliance by the other party.

Conclusion

Force, save in the accepted exceptions acknowledged by international law, is prohibited by contemporary international law. A resort to force in other circumstances is, especially in the nuclear age, to turn from law to an alternative which, if states are to co-exist and to continue to meet, is untenable.

FURTHER READING

Cases and Materials

D.J. Harris, *Cases and Materials on International Law* (1983), Chapter 11.

L. Henkin, R. Pugh, O. Schachter and H. Smit, *International Law: Cases and Materials* (1980), Chapters 14 and 15.

J. Sweeny, C. Oliver and N. Leech, *The International Legal System: Cases and Materials* (1981), Chapters 19 and 20.

Specialised Texts

D.W. Bowett, *United Nations Forces* (1964).

I. Brownlie, *International Law and the Use of Force by States* (1963).

R.A. Falk (ed.) *The International Law of Civil War* (1971).

General Texts

M. Akehurst, *A Modern Introduction to International Law* (1982), Chapter 13, pp. 180–215, Chapters 15 and 16.

L. Green, *International Law: A Canadian Perspective* (1984), Part VI.

D.W. Greig, *International Law* (1976), Chapter 16.

J.G. Starke, *An Introduction to International Law* (1984), Chapters 17, 18 and 19.

Chapter Twelve

ARBITRATION AND THE JUDICIAL SETTLEMENT OF DISPUTES

States, always reticent to submit disputes to independent impartial adjudication have been particularly reluctant to agree *in advance* to the compulsory jurisdiction of an independent judicial body. The majority of inter-states disputes are settled by direct negotiation. Negotiation is the primary vehicle for attaining settlement on the international scene, as peaceful co-existence and conciliation are seen as being more important than the characterisation of one state as "guilty" and another as "innocent." Hence, in the *North Sea Continental Shelf Case* the International Court of Justice declared "the parties are under an obligation to enter into negotiations with a view to arriving at an agreement, . . . "[1] Negotiation may be required by international agreements before other settlement procedures may be attempted. Other methods involving the participation of a third party, *e.g.* a state, a group of states or an individual, may be utilised if the states in dispute consent. Such methods include good offices, conciliation, mediation and commissions of inquiry.[2]

Good Offices

A third party may bring the disputing states to the negotiating table and may suggest the general framework for producing a settlement.

Mediation

The mediator may be active in attempting to reconcile the positions and claims of the respective interested parties. Suggestions of the third party do not have binding effect.

Conciliation

The task of a conciliation Commission is to examine the claims of the parties and make proposals to them for a friendly solution. If agreement is not reached the Commission produces a report containing observations, conclusions and recommendations. The

[1] I.C.J. Rep. 1969, p. 3 at p. 47.
[2] All such methods are identified in Article 33, United Nations Charter.

Commission's findings or proposals are not binding upon the parties.

Commission of Inquiry

The primary function of a Commission of Inquiry is to establish the facts pertaining to the dispute, for example, by the hearing of witnesses or visiting the area where the alleged breach of international law is said to have occurred. Dispute settlement may also be initiated either in or by international organisations, *e.g.* specialised agencies of the United Nations such as GATT (General Agreement on Tariff and Trade) have offered assistance in arranging for and providing good offices, mediation or commission of inquiry or conciliation.

The success of these methods cannot be denied, but it is only with arbitration and judicial settlement that adjudication is done in accordance with legal principles and an award made which is accepted as binding on the contesting parties.

ARBITRATION

The International Law Commission defined arbitration as "a procedure for the settlement of disputes between States by a binding award on the basis of law and as a result of an undertaking voluntarily accepted."[3]

The essential difference between arbitration and judicial settlement is that in arbitration parties are more active in deciding, for instance, the law to be applied and the composition of the tribunal, whereas parties submitting to judicial settlement must accept an already constituted tribunal with its jurisdictional competency and procedure laid down in statute. Arbitration allows parties a degree of flexibility which is denied to them in judicial settlement.

The idea of entrusting an impartial authority with finding a legally based solution to international disputes is an old one and examples of arbitration settlement were evident in ancient Greece, China and amongst Arabian tribes. However, the modern history of arbitration and the revitalisation of an interest in arbitration as a mode of settlement is traced from the 1794 Jay Treaty between the United States and Great Britain. That Treaty provided for the establishment of three mixed Commissions to which both states nominated an equal number of members presided over by an umpire. Although, strictly speaking, the Commissions were not organs of third party adjudication they were intended to function to

[3] Y.B.I.L.C., 1953, II, p. 202.

some extent as tribunals, *e.g.* the Commissions were to decide for themselves whether a claim fell within their jurisdictional competence. Throughout the nineteenth century arbitration was frequently utilised with each party to the dispute nominating two representatives to serve on the tribunal. In 1871 under the Treaty of Washington, whereby the United States and Britain agreed to submit to arbitration alleged breaches of neutrality by Britain during the American Civil War, it was provided that while the United States and Britain were to nominate a member of the tribunal of five so also were Brazil, Italy and Switzerland. The nomination and involvement of three independent states was an innovation and the *Alabama Claims Arbitration*[4] heralded an increasing utilisation of arbitration as many treaties provided for recourse to arbitration in the event of a dispute.

The 1899 Convention on the Pacific Settlement of Internatiional Disputes[5] adopted by the First Hague Peace Conference, marked a new era in arbitration settlement with the Convention providing for the creation of a Permanent Court of Arbitration. In 1907 following a Second Hague Conference, a further Convention was adopted revising its predecessor, but maintaining the Court.[6]

The Permanent Court of Arbitration established in 1900 began functioning in 1902. It is still in existence, but is neither a court nor a permanent institution. It is rather a panel of some 300 persons (four nominated by each Contracting Party to the 1899 and 1907 Conventions) from whom states may select one or more arbitrators to constitute a tribunal for the settlement of a particular dispute. Only the Bureau of the Court which acts as a registry is permanent. What was established in 1899 was essentially a machinery to call tribunals into being. Since its inception the Court has heard 25 cases including some of considerable importance, *e.g.* the *Island of Palmas Case.*[7]

Arbitration presupposes and depends upon the willingness of the states involved to submit to adjudication and their desire to reach a settlement. A state is not required to submit a dispute to arbitration. Consent is prerequisite. The identity of the arbitrators, the formulation of the question to be submitted to the tribunal, the rules of law to be applied and the time limit within which an award must be made must also be mutually agreed upon by the states concerned. Such issues are spelt out in a special agreement between the parties known as the *Compromis.* The functioning of the

---

[4] Moore, 1 Int.Arb. 495 (1872).
[5] U.K.T.S. 9 (1901) Cd. 798.
[6] U.K.T.S. 6 (1971) Cmnd. 4575.
[7] 2 R.I.A.A. 829 (1928).

Permanent Court therefore presupposes that the states not only have a desire to reach a settlement, but that they reach agreement on the issues which are the content of the *Compromis*.

Model rules on arbitration procedure which were adopted by the 1899 Convention were considerably revised in 1907. Arbitration agreements may refer to these while others may refer to the General Act on the Pacific Settlement of International Disputes adopted under the auspices of the League of Nations in 1928 and revised by the United Nations in 1949.[8] "Model Rules on Arbitral Procedures" were submitted by the International Law Commission to the General Assembly and adopted in 1958. Normally awards of arbitration tribunals are binding and the *Compromis* will expressly provide for this.[9]

Compliance with arbitration awards has been high. Rejection of an award has only occurred when the tribunal has allegedly exceeded its jurisdiction or has been guilty of a manifest procedural error.

The use of arbitration as a medium of dispute settlement declined, especially as disputes between states and the treatment of aliens were increasingly solved by a "lump sum settlement agreement."[10] Arbitration has in recent years, however, been re-employed, *e.g.* the Convention on the Settlement of Investment Disputes between States and Nationals of Other States 1965[11] makes available conciliation and arbitration procedures for the settlement of cases between contracting parties and companies of the nationality of a contracting party when both sides consent, and the Iran/United States Claims Tribunal established in 1981[12] is currently considering the respective claims of both parties against each other.

Only with the establishment of a judicial organ by and through the League of Nations[13] was there created a permanent international judicial institution, *i.e.* a court in the real sense of the term, ready to function at any time. There was established an international tribunal of a corporate character before which a state could, by unilateral application, bring a dispute against another state calling upon it to appear before the Court, without the need for prior

[8] 71 U.N.T.S. 101.
[9] A dispute may be referred to arbitration for an advisory report. In which case the parties to the dispute will normally be charged with putting that report into effect.
[10] Discussed in Chapter 7: State Responsibility.
[11] U.K.T.S. 25 (1967) Cmnd. 3255; 575 U.N.T.S. 159; 4 I.L.M. 532 (1965).
[12] 20 I.L.M. 223 (1981).
[13] The Court was never an integral part of the League of Nations. There was close association between the two bodies, *e.g.* the League Council and Assembly elected the members of the Court and both the Council and the Assembly were competent to request an advisory opinion from the Court.

agreement to be reached on the composition of a tribunal and the questions to be submitted to it, provided, that is, the other state had accepted the jurisdiction of the Court.

The Permanent Court of International Justice was the forerunner of the International Court of Justice.[14] The Permanent Court of International Justice (P.C.I.J.) sat for the first time at the Peace Palace in The Hague on February 15, 1922. The Court's activities were interrupted by the outbreak of the Second World War and the Court was dissolved in 1946 on the dissolution of the League of Nations.

THE INTERNATIONAL COURT OF JUSTICE

The International Court of Justice is the principal judicial organ of the United Nations and as such is an integral part of the organisation,[15] with its Statute annexed to the United Nations Charter. Although favouring the creation of a new Court, the delegates at the San Francisco Conference wished to maintain continuity with the Permanent Court of International Justice and the Statute of the International Court is essentially that of its predecessor. The International Court adopted without any substantial amendment the Rules of Court of its predecessor.[16] At the last meeting of the Permanent Court it was decided to take the necessary steps to ensure the transfer of the archives and effects to the then new International Court of Justice. The judges of the Permanent Court resigned on January 31, 1946, and at the first meeting of the United Nations General Assembly the judges to the International Court were elected. The Permanent Court was formally dissolved in April 1946.

Composition of the International Court

The Court is composed of 15 judges. The judges, of whom no two may be nationals of the same state, are elected by an absolute majority at separately and in theory, simultaneously held meetings of the Security Council and the General Assembly. In practice, the frequent disagreement and political bargaining over the appointment of judges means the Security Council is aware of what the General Assembly is doing and *vice-versa*. Candidates for election are nominated by the national groups in the Permanent Court of Arbitration or by specially constituted groups for those United

[14] Both Courts are frequently referred to as the World Court.
[15] Article 92, United Nations Charter.
[16] The Rules of Court have since been substantially amended and new rules entered into force in September 1972 and July 1978.

Nations members who are not represented in the Permanent Court of Arbitration. Persons eligible for election are those "of high moral character, who possess the qualifications required in their respective countries for appointment to the highest judicial offices, or are jurisconsults of recognised competence in international law."[17] Under the Court's Statute judges are to be elected without regard to nationality and there is no entitlement on the part of any one state to membership. In practice an equitable geographical distribution is sought and the five permanent members of the Security Council, save China, have always been represented.[18] Judges are appointed for a nine year term and may be re-elected. To ensure continuity elections are staggered with five judges being elected every three years. A judge who is elected to fill a sudden vacancy holds office only for the remainder of his predecessor's term. The judges elect from amongst their number a President and Vice-President for three years and both may be re-elected.

A judge may only be dismissed from office when he is considered no longer fit to discharge his function and only then on the unanimous vote of the other judges. This has never happened. During his term in office, a judge may not perform any political or administrative function, nor may he act as counsel, agent or advocate in any suit or participate in the decision of a case in which he has represented one of the parties involved. Nevertheless, a judge is not barred from sitting on the bench even if he has previously participated in an international forum when what is essentially the subject-matter of the case was being discussed, *e.g. Legal Consequences for States of the Continued Presence of South Africa in Namibia (South West Africa)* (1971) *Notwithstanding Security Council Resolution 276)*[19]—members of the bench including the President had been members of the Security Council when it had condemned South Africa's continued presence in Namibia. In spite of South African representations, the Court refused to withdraw those concerned.

A judge is not prohibited from sitting in a case in which the state of his nationality is a party. The Rules of Court do specify that if the President is a national of one of the parties to a case before the Court, then he will refrain from exercising his functions as President for that particular case. If a state to a dispute does not have a representing judge an *ad hoc* (for that purpose only) judge may be appointed. If the bench includes no judge of the nationality of the parties involved, each of the parties may select an *ad hoc* judge. An

---

[17] Article 2, I.C.J. Statute.
[18] China was not represented from 1967 to 1984 when no candidate was put forward. On November 7, 1984 Judge Ni Zhangyu was elected.
[19] I.C.J. Rep. 1971, p. 16.

ad hoc judge need not be of the same nationality as the nominating state. Cases which are conducted in either of the Court's two official languages, English and French,[20] are decided by a majority of the judges present. In the event of a tie, the President has the casting vote, which may be different from his initial vote. Dissenting judgments and separate opinions are published in full. Cases may be heard by either a full Court (a quorum of nine being sufficient) or by a Chamber of three or more judges constituted for handling a particular case or a particular category of case. The Court's Statute makes provision for the establishment of Chambers.[21] In January 1982 the Court approved, for the first time, the creation of a Chamber to deal specifically with the dispute between Canada and the United States over the Gulf of Maine area.

Jurisdiction of the Court

The Court can hear contentious cases and deliver advisory opinions.

Contentious Cases

Ratione personae. (Locus standi before the Court). Only states have *locus standi* and may be party to a contentious case before the Court.[22]

All members of the United Nations are *ipso facto* parties to the Court's Statute. A non-United Nations member may become a party to the Court's Statute on conditions determined by the United Nations General Assembly pursuant to a Security Council recommendation. These conditions are (i) an acceptance of the provisions of the Court's Statute; (ii) an agreement to accept and enforce the Court's judgments (*i.e.* an acceptance of Article 94, United Nations Charter); and (iii) an undertaking to contribute to the Court's expenses as may be assessed by the General Assembly. Switzerland, Liechtenstein and San Marino are three states which have lodged such instruments of acceptance.

Access to the Court may also be available to a state which is neither a member of the United Nations nor a party to the Court's Statute, if that state lodges a special declaration with the Court's registry accepting the obligations of the Court's Statute and Article 94 of the United Nations Charter. A declaration may be either particular or general. A particular declaration accepts the Court's jurisdiction in respect of a particular dispute or disputes which have already arisen. A general declaration accepts the Court's jurisdic-

---

[20] A Party may be authorised by the Court to use another language.
[21] Article 26.
[22] Article 34, I.C.J. Statute.

tion in respect of all disputes, or of a particular class or classes of dispute(s) which have already arisen or which may arise in the future.

A state may be entitled to appear before the International Court of Justice, but no state, unless it has expressed its consent, is required to appear in proceedings before the Court. The Security Council can recommend, but only recommend, that disputing states refer to the Court.[23] Such a recommendation does not confer jurisdiction on the Court independently of the wishes of the parties to the dispute. A state must have agreed that the dispute or the class of dispute should be dealt with by the Court.

Acceptance of the Court's jurisdiction may be expressed in different ways.

Article 36(1). Article 36(1) of the Court's Statute provides that the Court has jurisdiction in all cases "which States in a dispute may agree to refer to it and all matters specially provided for in the Charter of the United Nations or in treaties and conventions in force." States may agree by special agreement ("compromis") to submit an already existing dispute to the Court and thereby recognise the Court's jurisdiction over that particular case. The Court may entertain the case once the special agreement has been lodged with the Court. Examples of cases which have come before the Court via a special agreement are the *Asylum Case*,[24] *Minquiers and Ecrehos Case*,[25] *Continental Shelf (Tunisia* v. *Libya) Case*.[26]

Forum Prorogatum. Occasionally the Court has prorogated jurisdiction. This arises when at the initiation of proceedings only one state has expressly consented to the Court's jurisdiction for that particular dispute. The absence of express consent by one party has not acted as an obstacle to the Court being seised of the case as consent can be implied. A letter from the Albanian Deputy Minister for Foreign Affairs was taken by the Court in the *Corfu Channel (Preliminary Objection) Case*[27] as expressing Albania's consent, whilst consent to submit to the Court has been inferred through the acts of a state.[28] *Prorogatum* jurisdiction is rare as states not wishing to submit to the Court's jurisdiction will refrain from behaviour from which consent could be deduced.

---

[23] Article 36, United Nations Charter.

[24] I.C.J. Rep. 1950, p. 266.

[25] I.C.J. Rep. 1953, p. 47.

[26] I.C.J. Rep. 1982, p. 18.

[27] I.C.J. Rep. 1948, p. 15.

[28] See, *e.g.* the *Rights of Minorities in Polish Upper Silesia*, P.C.I.J. Rep., ser. A, No. 15 (1928); the *Monetary Gold Case*, I.C.J. Rep. 1954, p. 19.

Attempts by one state to bring by unilateral application proceedings against another state when the former acknowledges that the latter has not recognised the Court's jurisdiction have proved unsuccessful. The applicant state relying on the doctrine of *forum prorogatum* invites a positive reaction from the respondent state, that is, a subsequent acceptance of the Court's jurisdiction.[29]

Jurisdiction is also conferred on the Court by treaties which states have negotiated. Many bilateral and multilateral treaties contain compromissory clauses providing for recourse to the Court in the event of a dispute. Compromissory clauses are found in treaties which are one of two types: (i) those designed specifically to promote the pacific settlement of disputes between two or more states and which frequently provide not only for judicial settlement, but for the employment of conciliation and arbitration, *e.g.* Revised 1928 General Act for the Pacific Settlement of International Disputes 1949[30] and the European Convention for the Pacific Settlement of Disputes 1957[31]; and (ii) those on a particular subject which contain a provision for recourse to the Court in the event of a dispute arising over the interpretation or application of the treaty, *e.g.* Convention for the Suppression of Unlawful Seizure of Aircraft 1970,[32] United Nations Convention on the Law of the Sea 1982.[33] Treaties with such compromissory clauses are registered with the United Nations Secretariat while the Yearbook of the International Court publishes the text of the compromissory clauses.[34]

Article 36(2)—The Optional Clause. States may accept the Court's jurisdiction by way of a declaration under Article 36(2):

> "The States Parties to the present Statute may at any time declare that they recognize as compulsory *ipso facto* and without special agreement, in relation to any other State accepting the same obligation, the jurisdiction of the Court in all legal disputes concerning:
> (a) the interpretation of a treaty;
> (b) any question of international law;

---

[29] *e.g. Treatment in Hungary of Aircraft of the U.S.A. Cases,* I.C.J. Rep. 1954, pp. 99, 103 and the *Antarctica Cases,* I.C.J. Rep. 1956, pp. 12, 15. See also Harris, pp. 716–717.

[30] 71 U.N.T.S. 101.

[31] 320 U.N.T.S. 243; U.K.T.S. 10 (1961) Cmnd. 1298.

[32] 860 U.N.T.S. 105; U.K.T.S. 39 (1972) Cmnd. 4956.

[33] 21 I.L.M. 1261 (1982).

[34] Article 37 of the I.C.J.'s Statute stipulates that in respect of compromissory clauses which conferred jurisdiction on the P.C.I.J., the I.C.J. is to be substituted thus preventing such clauses from losing their effectiveness.

(c)　the existence of any fact which, if established, would constitute a breach of an international obligation;

(d)　the nature or extent of the reparation to be made for the breach of an international obligation."

States are not required to make a declaration under Article 36(2). Declarations under Article 36(2) are optional, but once the Court's jurisdiction has been accepted reference to the Court is compulsory. Such declarations, being unilateral acts, obviate the need for agreement. The effectiveness of Article 36(2) depends on the participation of many states. States have been reluctant to make declarations (46 states have currently made a declaration under Article 36(2)).[35] Declarations must be lodged with the United Nations Secretary-General and copies transmitted to parties to the Statute and the Registrar of the Court. States which have made a declaration accepting the Court's jurisdiction, in principle, possess the right to bring before the Court another state accepting the same obligation, whilst conversely it has by its declaration undertaken to appear before the Court should proceedings be initiated against it. The subject-matter of the dispute must fall within the terms of the acceptance lodged by both parties as the Court only has jurisdiction to the extent that the declarations coincide. Common ground is not always easy to find as Article 36(3) provides that declarations may be made "unconditionally or on condition of reciprocity on the part of several or certain states or for a certain time." Reservations are found in most declarations and the Court's jurisdiction over a case is restricted to those disputes that states have not excluded from its jurisdiction. If, for example, State A has accepted the compulsory jurisdiction of the Court as of April 2 and State B accepts the Court's jurisdiction but excludes all disputes relating to incidents arising before May 14, the Court will only have jurisdiction to hear a case arising after May 14. This would be the case regardless of which state was the applicant—*i.e.* if State B in spite of its reservation attempted to bring before the Court a dispute relating to an incident on April 30, State A could rely on State B's reservation to prevent the Court being seised of the case. A reservation of this type is a reservation *ratione temporis.* In the case of *Military and Paramilitary Activities in and against Nicaragua,*[36] the Court held that Nicaragua (whose declaration contains no reservation) was entitled to invoke against the United States the six-month time proviso, contained in the latter's 1946 declaration, stating that

---

[35] As the number of states, parties to the Court's Statute increases this represents a decrease in percentage terms.

[36] I.C.J. Rep. 1984, p. 392.

the declaration could be terminated, but that termination would only be effective six months after notice of such intention had been intimated. The undertaking to give six months' notice formed an integral part of the declaration and accordingly the 1984 notification providing for immediate effect could not override "the obligation of the United States to submit to the jurisdiction of the Court *vis-à-vis* Nicaragua."[37] A state may, in other words, invoke a reservation to an acceptance which it has not expressed in its own declaration, but which the other party has expressed in its own declaration.[38]

Reservations most frequently exclude disputes for which another means of peaceful settlement is provided; which arose before a specific date or which relate to a situation prior to that date, normally the date of the state's initial declaration; which arose during or because of hostilities; which arise between certain states, *e.g.* as between Commonwealth countries[39]; or which relate to matters falling within the domestic jurisdiction of the declaratory state, as determined by international law[40] or by the declaratory state itself as, for example, is expressed in the 1946 United States declaration.[41] Such automatic or self-judging reservations particularly undermine the idea of compulsory jurisdiction. It is possible for a government, relying upon such a reservation, to declare that a question in relation to the subject-matter of the proceedings initiated against it falls within its domestic jurisdiction and thereby seek to deprive the International Court of jurisdiction. Such a reservation was successfully invoked in the *Certain Norwegian Loans Case*[42] when the International Court of Justice discussed the French claim and allowed Norway to invoke, on the basis of reciprocity, the automatic/self-judging reservation contained in the French declaration.[43] Although the Court itself has not pronounced on the validity of such reservations, judges in both the *Norwegian Loans Case* (Judges Lauterpacht and Guerrero) and the *Interhandel Case* (Judges Lauterpacht, Spender and Klaestad) have questioned their validity, the principal objection being that they are contrary to

---

[37] *Ibid.*

[38] See decision in *Norwegian Loans Case*, I.C.J. Rep. 1957, p. 9; and judgment in *Interhandel Case*, I.C.J. Rep. 1959, p. 6.

[39] As in the current United Kingdom Declaration 1969—Misc. No. 4 (1969) Cmnd. 3872; Harris, p. 718.

[40] *e.g.* as in Canadian Declaration 1985.

[41] United States Declaration, August 26, 1946, 61 Stat. 1218; 1 U.N.T.S. 9.

[42] *Supra* n. 38.

[43] It was also invoked in the *Interhandel Case*, but was not dealt with by the Court as the case was dismissed on grounds of the non-exhaustion of local remedies; see also *Aerial Incident of July 27, 1955 Case*, I.C.J. Rep. 1960, p. 146.

Article 36(6) of the Court's Statute, which provides that "in the event of a dispute as to whether the Court has jurisdiction, the matter shall be settled by the decision of the Court." The Court is also prohibited as an organ of the United Nations from intervening in matters "which are essentially within the domestic jurisdiction of any State. . . . "[44]

Declarations are generally made for a specific period, normally five years, with tacit renewal. Declarations can generally be terminated on notice, taking effect after a specified time or immediately. Ideally, at least from the Court's standpoint, declarations should be for a definite period as a declaration which can be unilaterally terminated at any time provides a state, anticipating a dispute, with the opportunity of denying the Court jurisdiction. Thus, in 1954 Australia withdrew its existing declaration and issued a new one excluding from the Court's jurisdiction any disputes relating to pearl fishing off the Australian coast, the possibility of Japan raising a dispute on such a matter under Article 36(2) having prompted this move. A temporal reservation relating to the termination of acceptance cannot operate retroactively so as to disseise the Court of a case already submitted to it. States may attempt to deny the Court's jurisdiction by reserving to themselves the right to remove on notice certain classes of disputes from the Court's competence, *e.g.* on April 6, 1984 the United States withdrew from the Court's jurisdiction "disputes with any Central American State or any dispute arising out of or related to events in Central America over a period of two years." The International Court, as already mentioned, found it had jurisdiction as, *inter alia*, the United States could not validly derogate from the time-limit proviso included in its 1946 declaration, namely, "this declaration shall remain in force for a period of five years and thereafter until the expiration of six months after notice may be given to terminate this declaration." The United Kingdom Government in its acceptance reserves:

> "the right at any time, by means of notification addressed to the Secretary-General of the United Nations, and with effect as from the moment of such notification, either to add to, amend or withdraw any of the foregoing reservations, or any that may hereafter be added . . . "

Declarations must be valid at the time of application for proceedings to be initiated. However, should a declaration lapse during the case, the Court will not become disseised.

---

[44] Article 2(7), United Nations Charter.

Reservations apply only to the Court's jurisdiction under Article 36(2). The Court may have jurisdiction over the subject-matter in question by some other means, *e.g.* a treaty. The majority of cases come before the Court by means other than Article 36(2). During the last 24 years only in two cases has the Court based its jurisdiction on Article 36(2)—the *Temple Case* 1962[45] and *Military and Paramilitary Activities in and against Nicaragua.*[46] Nevertheless, Article 36(2) must be examined as it is the only provision which seeks to establish universal compulsory jurisdiction by an international legal body over disputes which arise between states.

Incidental Jurisdiction. The Court may be called upon to exercise an incidental jurisdiction, *i.e.* independently of the main proceedings, of preliminary objections; an application to intervene; and interim measures.

Preliminary Objections. A party may challenge the Court's jurisdiction. The most common instance is that of preliminary objections raised by the respondent state in an attempt to prevent the Court from delivering a judgment on the merits. The filing of objections suspends the proceedings on the merits (and obviously delays any decision on the merits) and gives rise to independent proceedings pursuant to which the Court will either uphold or reject each objection.

Intervention. A state which is a party to a convention, the construction of which is before the Court but is not a party to the main proceedings has the right to intervene.[47] Under Article 62 of the Court's Statute a state which considers it has an interest of a legal nature which may be affected by the decision in the case may submit a request to the Court for permission to intervene. It is for the Court to decide upon a request to intervene, *e.g.* in 1981 Malta's request to intervene in the case between *Tunisia* v. *Libyan Arab Jamahiriya* was rejected by the Court. The Court considered that the interest invoked by Malta would not be affected by the decision in the case.[48]

Interim Measures. Article 41 of the Court's Statute provides that

---

[45] I.C.J. Rep. 1961, p. 17—Judgment on Preliminary Objections.
[46] *Supra* n. 36. The Court found it had jurisdiction to hear the case on the basis of Article 36, paras. 2 and 5. Article 36(5) provides that declarations which refer to the Permanent Court of International Justice shall be regarded as applying to the International Court of Justice.
[47] Article 63, I.C.J. Statute.
[48] I.C.J. Rep. 1981, p. 3.

the Court "has the power to indicate, if it considers that circumstances so require, any provisional measures which ought to be taken to preserve the respective rights of either party." The Court can, on the basis of Article 41, indicate interim measures of protection. If appropriate, the Court then may call upon the parties to refrain from any acts that might jeopardise the effectiveness of any decision which the Court may make on the request. A request for interim protection is given priority and a decision is reached quickly. Interim orders may request parties not to take any action that may aggravate the tension between the parties or increase the difficulty of resolving the dispute, *e.g. Case Concerning United States Diplomatic and Consular Staff in Tehran.*[49] Interim measures may be indicated to prevent "irreparable prejudice" to the rights which are in dispute as, for example, in the *Nuclear Tests Cases*[50] where the possible effect on Australian and New Zealand territory of radioactive fall-out as a consequence of the French tests was considered irreparable. The principal difficulty confronting the Court in respect of interim measures has been that of identifying the conditions in which measures should be indicated before the Court's jurisdiction has been established. Accordingly, the Court will be satisfied that there is at least *prima facie* a good basis for jurisdiction. Interim measures will only be indicated if the Court is of the opinion that it does not manifestly lack jurisdiction, but they are "indicated" only and are not required or ordered. Requests for interim measures have to date come only from an applicant state, though they may be requested by the respondent state or by a motion of the Court itself.

The Law Applied by the Court. The function of the International Court of Justice is "to decide in accordance with international law such disputes as are submitted to it"[51] and in furtherance of its task the Court applies:

"(a) international conventions, whether general or particular, establishing rules expressly recognized by the contesting States;

(b) international custom, as evidence of a general practice accepted as law;

(c) the general principles of law recognized by civilized nations;

(d) subject to the provisions of Article 59, judicial decisions

[49] I.C.J. Rep. 1979, p. 21.
[50] I.C.J. Rep. 1973, pp. 99, 135.
[51] Article 38(1), I.C.J. Statute.

and the teachings of the most highly qualified publicists of the various nations, as subsidiary means for the determination of rules of law."[52]

The Court may also decide a case *ex aequo et bono*—according to the principles of equity—should the parties agree thereto.[53]

The Decision. A case may be brought to a conclusion in one of three ways:

(i) At any stage in the proceedings the parties concerned may inform the Court that they have reached a settlement. On receipt of this information, the Court will issue an Order for the removal of the case from its list. This has not occurred during the lifetime of the International Court of Justice.

(ii) The applicant state may decide to withdraw and not proceed any further with the case. An Order for the case to be removed from the Court's list will then be made. If the Court is not sitting, the President will issue the Order.

(iii) The Court delivers a judgment.

Effect of judgment. "The decision of the Court has no binding force except between the parties and in respect of that particular case."[54] In spite of the absence of *stare decisis* the Court does in fact have regard to previous decisions and cites previous decisions to substantiate its reasoning for arriving at a judgment. There would have to be good reason, *e.g.* the subsequent development of international law, for the Court to depart from an earlier decision if confronted with a similar case.

The Court's decision is binding, final and without appeal.[55] The Court will, however, interpret at the request of either party a judgment where there is uncertainty or disagreement as to the meaning and ambit of the Court's judgment. A revision of the Court's judgment may be requested if there should come to light material of a decisive nature previously unknown to both the Court and the party requesting a revised judgment.[56] A revision of the judgment must be requested within six months of the new fact emerging and within 10 years of the delivery of the judgment.

In 1985 the Tunisian Government requested a revision and interpretation of the judgment of February 24, 1982 in the

[52] See Chapter 2 in which Article 38 is fully discussed.
[53] This provision has never been applied.
[54] Article 69, I.C.J. Statute.
[55] A number of treaties provide that appeal may be made to the Court following a decision, for example, from an organ of an international organisation.
[56] Article 61, I.C.J. Statute.

Continental Shelf (Tunisia v. Libya) Case. This was the first time that the International Court had received a request to revise one of its judgments and only the second time it had been requested to interpret a judgment.[57] The Tunisian request was also the first combined request for a revision and an interpretation.

Compliance with the Court's Decision. The majority of the Court's judgments have been complied with by the parties. There have been exceptions, *e.g.* Albania did not adhere to the Court's order to pay compensation to the United Kingdom for the damage inflicted on the latter's warships whilst passing through the Corfu Channel in 1946,[58] and Iran failed to comply with the Court's decision in the *Case Concerning United States Diplomatic and Consular Staff in Tehran.*[59]

Non-appearance, however, presents a problem. There have been a number of cases particularly recently in which the respondent state has failed to appear, absenting itself from either certain parts of the proceedings or from the entire case. The Court will proceed with the case if it is satisfied that it has jurisdiction and will eventually issue judgment, though it is likely to be disregarded by the respondent state, as in the *Fisheries Jurisdiction Case.*[60]

Advisory Opinions

In addition to its jurisdiction in contentious cases, the International Court of Justice is also competent to give an advisory opinion[61] on any legal question at the request of the General Assembly of the United Nations, the Security Council[62] and other bodies so authorised. States are excluded from seeking an advisory opinion, but they may participate in proceedings before the Court.[63] Advisory opinions are not legally binding on the requesting body, though an international organisation may undertake to recognise such an opinion as binding. As such an advisory opinion is in theory a weaker statement of law than a judgment. In practice, however, advisory opinions have been accepted by the requesting body and

---

[57] The first application for an interpretation was in respect of the Judgment given by the Court in the *Asylum Case*, November 1950. The Court ruled unanimously on December 10, 1985 that the request for a revision of the 1982 judgment was inadmissible and that although the request for an interpretation was admissible the 1982 judgment should be implemented.

[58] *Corfu Channel Case (Assessment of Compensation)*, I.C.J. Rep. 1949, p. 244.

[59] I.C.J. Rep. 1980, p. 3.

[60] I.C.J. Rep. 1974, p. 3.

[61] Article 65, I.C.J. Statute.

[62] Article 96, U.N. Charter.

[63] Article 66, I.C.J. Statute.

any other party so affected, and certain advisory opinions have undoubtedly contributed to the development of international law, e.g. *Advisory Opinion on Reparation for Injuries Suffered in the Service of the United Nations 1949* (legal personality of United Nations),[64] *Advisory Opinion on Certain Expenses of the United Nations* (legitimate expenses of the organisation),[65] and *Advisory Opinion on Western Sahara* (decolonisation).[66] The system of advisory opinions has been comparatively seldom employed with the International Court of Justice delivering fewer opinions than the Permanent Court of International Justice. The P.C.I.J. delivered 27 opinions, whereas the I.C.J. has delivered only 18, of which 11 were delivered between 1948 and 1956.[67]

Role and Future of the Court

The Court may be a permanent institution, but it does not have a high work load, especially when compared with, for example, the European Court of Human Rights whose judges are part-time. The Court has given judgments and advisory opinions which have contributed to the development of international law. That development may be somewhat *ad hoc* as the Court has to wait until it is seised of a case or requested to give an opinion. The Court remains the only judicial organ with the potential to deal with at least the legal aspect of the problems which may arise between states. The Court's jurisdiction is restricted to legal disputes, but the Court has never rejected a case on the grounds that it has involved non-legal issues and has maintained that to dismiss a case because the legal aspect is only one element of a political dispute would be to impose a "far-reaching and unwarranted restriction upon the role of the Court in the peaceful settlement of international disputes."[68] In international relations political and legal issues are intertwined and the decision to seek judicial settlement is itself often a political one. Only once has an advisory opinion been refused. The delivering of an opinion in the *Eastern Carelia Case*[69] the Permanent Court felt would be tantamount to giving a decision in a dispute.[70]

As a permanent institution, the Court is a constant reminder to

---

[64] I.C.J. Rep. 1949, p. 174.

[65] I.C.J. Rep. 1962, p. 151.

[66] I.C.J. Rep. 1975, p. 12.

[67] This can be explained at least in part by the fact that fewer opinions were requested of the I.C.J. on issues relating to World War II than were sought from the P.C.I.J. on matters relating to World War I.

[68] *Case Concerning United States Diplomatic and Consular Staff in Tehran*, I.C.J. Rep. 1980, p. 3 at p. 20.

[69] P.C.I.J. Rep., ser. B, No. 5 (1923).

[70] See Harris, pp. 737–742 for further discussion on legal questions.

states that there does exist judicial channels through which the peaceful settlement of international disputes may be sought. Again because it is permanent, the Court's procedures and jurisdiction are known to the international community. In the final analysis the future role of the Court does not lie with the Court but with states. The Court's Statute provides for recourse to its jurisdiction by states. States however must be willing to submit their disputes to independent ajudication.

FURTHER READING

Cases and Materials

D.J. Harris, *Cases and Materials on International Law* (1983), Chapter 12.
L. Henkin, R. Pugh, O. Schachter and H. Smit, *International Law: Cases and Materials* (1980), Chapter 13.

Specialised Texts

J. G. Merrills, *International Dispute Settlement* (1984).

General Texts

M. Akehurst, *A Modern Introduction To International Law* (1982), Chapter 14.
I. Brownlie, *Principles of Public International Law* (1979), Chapter XXXI.
L. Green, *International Law: A Canadian Perspective* (1984), Part VII, §1.
D.W. Greig, *International Law* (1976), Chapter 11.
J.G. Starke, *An Introduction to International Law* (1984), Chapter 17, pp. 463–469.

Chapter Thirteen

CONCLUSION

Students are often disconcerted when confronted with international law. Why? Its character is intrinsically different from municipal law yet the law student and the trained lawyer are guilty of approaching international law with the prejudices of the lawyer trained to deal with a mature municipal legal system.

Law is most commonly associated with authoritative institutions possessing the competence to lay down the necessary legal rights and duties for the community. International law does not fit into such a mould. Consequently, to the legally trained, international law may in character be confusing and in effect be disappointing.

The sources of international law are not as readily indentifiable and established as those of the municipal legal system. Article 38 of the Statute of the International Court of Justice is only a direction to the Court on how disputes confronting the Court should be tackled. It is not an exhaustive statement on the sources of international law. Furthermore, with respect to one established source, international agreements (international law's nearest equivalent to legislation) the student is confronted with the provision for states to opt out by way of "reservations." The student finds himself dealing with a legal system which is essentially voluntary in character rather than mandatory. International law is not imposed on states, but has evolved through the concerns of states and is adhered to because of the need for states to co-exist.

In examining international personality, students find that the concept of personality is not static and that any definition must be sufficiently flexible and open ended to accommodate new entities which may be required to participate on the international plane. In looking at the recognition of states, the student is brought face to face with politics in inter-state relations. The role of politics is something which lawyers must appreciate. Lawyers, howwever, are guilty of over-emphasising the role of law in inter-state relations and consequently fail to appreciate that states are primarily motivated by politics and that in international relations there is, as a norm, more than one acceptable course of action. Lawyers, therefore, must not be blinkered in their approach to international law but rather must attempt to perceive problems from a standpoint

256

other than that of the lawyer and try to see, for example, how international law is interpreted by the politician. International law may be utilised by politicians to identify and accomplish goals and is accordingly their "box of tools"[1] which may be used to further a state's national interests. If law will not further a state's interests, then law may be denied any influence. It will not be flouted blatantly, but the state may articulate the issue as exclusively political and thus incapable of settlement by the application of legal principles. In withdrawing from the proceedings of the case brought by Nicaragua, the United States maintained that the International Court's decision of November 26, 1985 (finding that it had jurisdiction) represented "an over-reaching of the Court's limits, a departure from its tradition of judicial restraint, and a risky venture into treacherous political waters."[2] Lawyers must therefore recognise that a decision to initiate legal procedures or legal principles for the settlement of a dispute will be a political decision.

The absence of mandatory sanctions distinguishes international law from municipal law. This should not be seen as a fault or weakness in the international legal system, but rather as a consequence of the intrinsically different character of international law. The overriding aim of international law is to achieve international peace and security not through the characterisation of an alleged offending state as "guilty," but through the promotion of conciliation. Hence, low key negotiations are the principal channels initially utilised in efforts to settle a dispute between states.

Lawyers must appreciate that although all states on the international scene are in theory equally sovereign, such states do not today share common interests. The international community has grown some three-fold in the last 40 years and the impact of this growth has been a questioning and challenging of some of the older established rules of international law. International law is not confined to regulating the relations of a homogeneous grouping of states, but rather is attempting to bring within its ambit a hetrogeneous grouping of states which differ politically, economically, ideologically and socially from each other.

The subject-matter of international law is not exhaustively defined and its boundaries are not firmly established. International law is still a young and developing system which is constantly embracing subject-matter which once was considered exclusively domestic.

Why is it that the expectations of international law are higher

---

[1] R. Fisher, "International Law: A Toolbox for the Statesman" (1979) 9 C.W.I.C.J. 3.
[2] Dept. of State File No. P85 0009–2151 reproduced in 79 A.J.I.L. 441 (1985).

than the expectations of the municipal law? Why should it be anticipated that international law can prevent all violations of international law when it is accepted, for example, that the domestic criminal law does not prevent all crimes and that the existence of contract law does not prevent contracts from being broken? Lawyers and laymen seem to forget that the municipal law is disregarded daily and base their criticism and scepticism of international law on the fact that international law is broken. They forget that international law itself cannot exert influence independently, but only primarily through the organ of states. It is also forgotten by its critics that international law functions very efficiently over a wide range of subject-matter every day and that when violations of international law occur it is in politically sensitive issues which, consequently, are newsworthy and receive extensive media coverage. Critics of the international legal system must see violations of international law in perspective.

To obtain the optimum advantage from a study of international law, students must rid themselves of their preconceived notions about "law." They must refrain from attempting to fit international law into the character of municipal law. If they do not, international law will most definitely be seen to be deficient. Students must also guard against having too high an expectation of international law. International law can only be utilised to the extent that states will allow it to be used: it is dependent upon and not independent of states. International law must be approached with an open mind as to the nature of law and with an appreciation that law is not the only influence on inter-state relations. Only then will the role, present and potential, of law on the international scene be fully appreciated and articulated. A belief that international law has a positive role to play is essential if states are to continue to co-exist and to meet each other again in international fora, rather than destroying each other in armed conflict.

INDEX

Aaland Islands, 19, 206
Abduction,
  infringement of state jurisdiction, 107
Accession to a treaty, 200
Accretion, 87
Act of State (American doctrine of),
  48–50
Adhesion to a treaty, 200
Adoption of a treaty, 199
Ad referendum, 199
Advisory Opinions, 252–253
  competence to seek, 252
  effect of, 252
Aerial Incident, 93
Afghanistan. *See* Uniting for Peace
  Resolution.
African Charter on Human and Peoples'
  Rights, 186
Aggression. *See* Force, use of.
  definition of, 220, 227
Agreement on Measures to Improve the
  Direct Communications Link (Hot-
  Line Upgrade Agreement), 234
Agreement on Measures to Reduce the
  Risk of Outbreak of Nuclear War
  (Accidents Agreement) 1971, 234
Agreement on the Rescue of
  Astronauts, the Return of
  Astronauts and the Return of
  Objects Launched into Outer
  Space 1968, 95
Agreement Relating to the
  International Communications
  Satellite Organisation
  (INTELSAT), 96
Agrément, 111
Aircraft, 93–94
  hijacking of, 105
  right of transit, 129–130
Airspace,
  aerial incident, 93
  Bermuda type bilateral agreements,
    93
  boundary of, 91
  civil aircraft in distress, 93–94

Airspace—*cont.*
  customary international law of, 91
  Five Freedoms Agreement, 93
  hijacking, 105
    conventions on, 105
  International Civil Aviation
    Organisation, 94
  Korean aircraft, shooting down, 94
  Libyan aircraft, shooting down, 93
  Paris Convention, 91
  sovereignty over, 81, 91–94
    Chicago Convention, 91–93
  state aircraft, 92
  Two Freedoms Agreement, 92–93
Alaska, purchase of, 87
Aliens. *See also* State responsibility.
  arbitrary, unjustified expulsion of
    prohibition on, 163
  expropriation of property of. *See*
    Expropriation.
  treatment of,
    international minimum standard,
      162
    national treatment standard, 161,
      162
    state responsibility for, 160 *et seq.*
Amendment, treaty of, 207
American Convention on Human
  Rights, 186
American law,
  Act of State, 48–50
  executive agreements, 45, 46
  executive congressional agreements,
    46
  international law, as part of
    customary international law,
      41–42
    treaties, 42–48
      self-executing, non self-
        executing, 43–45
  non-recognition of governments, 78
  recognition of governments, 71
  sovereign immunity, law of, 109
  State Department "Suggestion", 48
Antarctic, 1959 Convention on, 91

259

Antarctica, 88–91
  Byrd Claim, 88
  peaceful use of, 91
  U.K. claim to, 91
Anti-trust laws, 103
Apartheid,
  Convention on the Suppression and
    Punishment of the Crime of, 193
  international crime as, 156
Arab territories. *See* Uniting for Peace
  Resolution.
Arbitration,
  Compromis, 23, 239–240
  Convention on the Pacific Settlement
    of International Disputes, 239
  definition of, 238
  evolution of, 238–239
  investment disputes,
    Iran/United States Claims
      Tribunal, 240
    use in, 240
  judicial settlement distinguished, 238
  Model Rules on Arbitral Procedures,
    240
  Permanent Court of Arbitration, 239
Archipelagic states. *See* Sea, law of the.
Arctic, 88
Argentina,
  Eichmann, abduction from, 107
  exclusive sovereignty claims over
    coastal waters, 143
Arrest, illegal, 107
Australia,
  attitude to nuclear tests in Pacific,
    132, 250
  Article 36 (2) 1954, declaration
    withdrawal of, 248
Avulsion, 87

Bangladesh,
  Indian intervention in, 57
Baselines. *See* Sea, law of the.
Bays. *See* Sea, law of the.
Boundary,
  rivers, 87
Bricker Amendment, 45

Calvo Clause,
  definition of, 168
  validity of, 168
Canada,
  Arctic claim to, 88–89
  declaration under Optional Clause to
    I.C.J., 247

Canada—*cont.*
  international law/municipal law,
    problem of federal state, 46–48
  recognition of Israel, 73
Case Act 1972, 46
Cession, 87
Charter of Economic Rights and Duties
  of States 1974, 166
Chicago Convention on International
  Civil Aviation 1944, 91
Chile,
  Antarctica, claim to, 88, 91
  continental shelf claim, 143
Civil war,
  intervention in, 232–233
Claims,
  nationality of, 169–172
Commission of Inquiry, 238
Committee on the Elimination of All
  Forms of Racial Discrimination,
  192
Common Market. *See* European
  Communities.
Companies. *See* Shareholders.
  espousal of claim on behalf of,
    171
  nationality of, 171
  state responsibility for, 171
Compromis (the), 23, 239, 240
Compromissory clauses,
  in treaties, 245
Conciliation, 237
Conflict of laws, 1
Congo. *See* Uniting for Peace
  Resolution.
Conquest,
  territorial acquisition of, 57, 87
Consular agents,
  immunities of, 116–117
Consular relations,
  severence of,
    effect on treaties, 212
Contiguity principle, 88
Contiguous zone. *See* Sea, law of the.
Continental margin. *See* Sea, law of the.
Continental shelf. *See* Sea, law of the.
Contract,
  breach of,
    state responsibility for, 168
    Calvo clause, 168
    "internationalised", 168
Contract regarding an Interim
  Supplement to Tanker Liability for
  Oil Pollution 1971, 137

Conventions,
Barcelona Convention for the
Protection of the Mediterranean
against Pollution 1976, 138
Brussels Convention for the
Unification of Certain Rules
relating to the Immunity of State
Owned Vessels, 109
Civil Liability for Oil Pollution
Damage, Convention on, 137
Continental Shelf, Convention on
the, 119 *et seq.*
Creation of an International Criminal
Court, Convention for the, 193
Distribution of Programme-Carrying
Signals Transmitted by Satellite,
Convention Relating to the, 96
Elimination of All Forms of
Discrimination against Women,
Convention on the, 193
Establishment of an International
Fund for Compensation for Oil
Pollution Damage, Convention
on the, 137
Fishing and Conservation of Living
Resources of the High Seas,
Convention on, 135
High Seas, Convention on the, 119 *et
seq.*
International Liability for Damages
Caused by Outer Space Objects,
1972 Convention on, 95
Law of the Sea 1982, Convention on
the, 119 *et seq. See* Sea, law of
the.
London Convention on the
Prevention of Marine Pollution
by Dumping of Wastes and Other
Material 1972, 137
Long-Range Transboundary Air
Pollution 1979, Convention on,
98
Oslo Convention for the Prevention
of Marine Pollution by Dumping
from Ships and Aircraft 1972, 137
Pacific Settlement of International
Disputes 1899, Convention on
the, 239
Pacific Settlement of International
Disputes 1907, Convention on
the, 239
Paris Convention for the Prevention
of Marine Pollution from Land-
Based Sources 1974, 137–138

Conventions—*cont.*
Prevention and Punishment of Crimes
against Internationally Protected
Persons including Diplomatic
Agents, Convention on the, 105
Prevention and Punishment of the
Crime of Genocide, Convention
on the, 105
Prevention and Punishment of
Terrorism 1937, Convention for
the, 193
Prevention of Pollution from Ships
(MARPOL), Convention for
the, 136
Prevention of the Pollution of the Sea
by Oil (OILPOL), Convention
for the, 136
Registration of Objects Launched
into Outer Space 1975,
Convention on, 96
Settlement of Investment Disputes
between States and Nationals of
Other States 1965, Convention
on the, 167, 240
Status of Refugees 1951, Convention
Relating to the, 163
Suppression and Punishment of the
Crime of Apartheid, Convention
on the, 193
Territorial Sea and Contiguous Zone
1958, Convention on the, 119 *et
seq.*
Convenant on Civil and Political Rights,
187–190
optional protocol, 190–192
Covenant on Economic, Social and
Cultural Rights, 187, 188, 189
Cuba,
U.S. quarantine, 227
Customary international law,
acquiescence in, 12
amendment of, 13
before municipal courts,
U.K. practice, 34–37
rules inconsistent with British
domestic law, 36–37
U.S. practice, 41–42
characteristics of, 9–16
creation of new custom, 12, 13
definition, 9
dissent, effect of, 12
instant custom, 15, 16
local/regional/general distinguished,
12

Customary international law—*cont.*
    opinio juris sive necessitatis, 14–16
    source of international law, as, 8–16
    state practice,
        duration, 9
        evidence of, 14
        extent of, 10
        status of states involved, 11
Customs,
    regulations,
        enforcement of, 130

Deep sea bed. *See* Sea, law of the.
Deep Sea Bed Hard Mineral Resources
    Act 1980 (U.S.A.), 152
Deep Sea Mining (Temporary
    Provisions) Act 1981, 152
de facto recognition, 72
    effect of, 73–76
de jure recognition, 72
    effect of, 73–76
Diplomatic agents,
    Convention on the Prevention and
        Punishment of Crimes against,
        105
Diplomatic Privileges Act 1964 (U.K.),
    116
Diplomatic privileges and immunity,
    110–118
    customary international law of,
        111
    diplomatic agents,
        immunity from jurisdiction,
            civil, 114
            criminal, 114
        inviolability of person, 114
    diplomatic mission,
        exemption from taxation, 115
    diplomatic premises,
        functions of, 112
        inviolability of, 112–113
    immunity from jurisdiction,
        diplomatic agents/administrative
            and technical staff,
            distinguished, 115
        diplomatic agents/service staff
            distinguished, 115
        waiver of, 115
    obligations of diplomatic personnel,
        115
    persona non grata, 111, 115
Diplomatic relations,
    severence of,
        effect on treaties, 212

Domestic jurisdiction,
    limitation on U.N. intervention, 248
Dominican Republic,
    U.S. intervention in, 225
Double jeopardy, 107–108
Draft Declaration on Rights and Duties
    of States 1949, 86
Drug trafficking,
    jurisdiction over, 103
Drugs,
    narcotic,
        suppression of illicit traffic in, 134
Dualistic school of thought (dualism),
    32–33

El Salvador,
    exclusive claims over coastal waters,
        143
Entebbe,
    raid on, 224
Environment,
    international protection of the, 97–99
    Convention on Long-Range
        Transboundary Air Pollution,
        98
    customary international law on, 97
    European Communities
        programme, 98–99
    international crime as,
        pollution of atmosphere and
            seas, 156
    liability for extra-territorial
        damage, 98
    liability to victims of pollution, 98
    Principle 22, 98
    Treaty Banning Nuclear Weapons
        Tests in Outer Space and
        Under Water, 99
Equity,
    source of international law, as, 21–22
Estonia, 86
European Commission on Human
    Rights. *See* Human rights.
European Communities,
    environmental programme, 98–99
    European Atomic Energy Authority
        (EURATOM),
        international legal capacity of, 63
    European Coal and Steel Community
        (ECSC),
        international legal capacity of, 63
    international legal capacity of, 63–65
European Convention for the Pacific
    Settlement of Disputes 1957, 245

European Convention for the
  Protection of Human Rights and
  Fundamental Rights, 177 *et seq.*
European Convention on State
  Immunity 1972, 110
European Court of Human Rights. *See*
  Human rights.
European Court of Justice,
  fundamental freedoms,
  recognition of, 185
Exclusive Economic Zone (E.E.Z.).
  See Sea, law of the.
Executive Agreements (U.S.), 8,
  45–46
Executive Certificate, 40
Executive Congressional Agreements
  (U.S.), 46
Expropriation,
  challenge to traditional international
    law, 166
  Charter of Economic Rights and
    Duties of States, 166
  compensation for, adequate
    definition of, 166
  "creeping", 167
  definition, 164
  disputes, settlement of,
    Convention on, 167
    lump sum, 167
  General Assembly Resolution 1803,
    164, 166
  non-discrimination, 165
  property of aliens, 164
  public purpose, 165
Extradition, 106–107
  obligation under Hijacking
    Convention, 105
Extra-territorial jurisdiction. *See* State
  jurisdiction.

Falkland Islands,
  British claim, basis of, 86
  dispute, 228
Federal states,
  problems in relation of international
    and municipal law, 46–48
Final Act,
  Conference of Security and Co-
    Operation in Europe,
    status of, 198
Finland,
  statehood of, 55
Fisheries. *See* Sea, law of the.
"Fitzmaurice Compromise", 32

Five Freedoms Agreement, 93
Force, use of, 217–236. *See also*
  Aggression.
  collective measures of U.N., 227
  contemporary law on, 218–235
  economic, 221
  intervention, limitation on, 224–225
  law before 1945, 217–218
  League of Nations Covenant, 218
  legitimate use of, 221–226
    collective self-defence, 225–226
    self-defence, 221–223
  nuclear weapons, 233–235
  political, 221
  protection of nationals abroad, 223
  regional arrangements, 226
  reprisals, 226
  retorsions, 226
  self-defence, anticipatory, 223
  Strategic Arms Limitation Talks
    (SALT I and II), 234
  threat of, 219, 223, 227, 228
  UN Charter, 217, 218, 219, 220, 221
  UN role of,
    General Assembly, 229, 230, 231,
      232
    Security Council, 227, 228, 229,
      231, 232
Foreign Claims Settlement Commission
  of the United States, 167
Foreign Compensation Commission
  (U.K.), 167
Foreign Sovereign Immunities Act
  (U.S.A.), 109
Foreign states,
  immunity of. *See* Sovereign
    immunity.
forum prorogatum, 244
France,
  optional clause,
    domestic limitation in, 151
    pioneer investor, as, 151

General Act on the Pacific Settlement of
  International Disputes 1928, 240
General Assembly,
  recommendations relating to
    maintenance of peace and
    security, 229
General Assembly Declaration of
  Principles Concerning the Sea Bed
  and the Ocean Floor and the
  Subsoil thereof, Beyond the Limits
  of National Jurisdiction 1970, 150

General Assembly Declaration on
Principles of International Law
concerning Friendly Relations and
Co-operation Among States in
Accordance with the Charter of
the United Nations 1970, 57, 58, 86,
220, 227
General Assembly Declaration on the
Granting of Independence to
Colonial Territories and Peoples
(Resolution 1514), 26, 58
General Assembly Declaration on the
Inadmissibility of Intervention in
the Domestic Affairs of States
1965, 232–233
General Assembly Resolution 1803 on
Permanent Sovereignty over
Natural Resources 1962, 164
General Assembly Resolutions,
possible source of international law,
as, 26–27
General Assembly Uniting for Peace
Resolution, 230
sessions initiated under, 230
General Principles of law . . .
source of international law, as,
19–21
Genocide,
Convention on Prevention of, 105
international crime as, 105, 156
Good Offices, 237
Grenada,
intervention in, 224, 227
Grotius, Hugo, 131
Gulf of Foncesca, 124

Hague Convention on the Suppression
of Unlawful Seizure of Aircraft
1970, 105
Heligoland,
exchange of, 87
Helsinki Conference on Security and
Co-operation in Europe,
Final Act of, 176
Hickenlooper Amendment, 49
High seas. *See* Sea, law of the.
Hijacking,
Achille Lauro, of, 134
Convention on, 105
crime of, 105
Holy See,
international personality of,
67–68
Hudson Bay, 124

Human Rights, 175–195. *See also*
Individuals; Nationals, treatment
of; State responsibility for aliens
Council of Europe,
aim of, 177–178
Social Charter, 185
Covenant on Civil and Political
Rights, 187, 188, 190
Optional Protocol, 190–192
Covenant on Economic, Social and
Cultural Rights, 187–190
European Commission,
composition of, 179
enforcement measures of, 182
report of, 181
work of, 180–182
European Convention, 176–185
Committee of Ministers,
composition of, 179
role of, 181–182
Court of Human Rights, 179
access to, 182
effect of judgment, 183
"just satisfaction", 183–184
procedure before, 183
enforcement machinery,
179–184
impact of, 184–185
individual petition, 180
Protocol 4, 178
Protocol 6, 178
Protocol 8, 179
relation to domestic law of Member
states, 184–185
right of individual petition,
U.K. acceptance of, 180
European Court of Justice,
recognition of fundamental rights,
185
individual petition,
Convention on the Elimination of
All Forms of Racial
Discrimination, 192
international criminal law, 193
interpretation of, 175
minority treaties, 175
protection of,
before 1945, 175–176
post-1945, 176
regional protection of,
African Charter, 186
American Convention on Human
Rights, 186
terrorism, 193

Human Rights—*cont.*
  United Nations,
    apartheid, Convention on, 193
    Charter under, 176, 186, 187
    Committee on, 186
    Human Rights Committee, 189,
      190, 191
    implementation machinery,
      individual communication to
        Committee of Human
        Rights, 189
      inter-state complaint, 188–190
      reporting system, 188–189
    protection of, 186–194
    Resolution 1503, 192
    role of ECOSOC, 189–190
  Universal Declaration of Human
    Rights, 186

"Ihlen Declaration", 197
Illegal arrest, 107
Immunity from jurisdiction. *See*
  Sovereign Immunity; Diplomatic
  privileges and immunity.
India,
  Bangladesh, intervention in, 57
  pioneer investor as, 151
Individuals. *See also* Aliens; Human
  rights and State responsibility.
  international procedural capacity of,
    66–67
  rights recognised by international
    law, 175–176
Indonesia,
  archipelagic state as, 125
International Civil Aviation
  Organisation (ICAO), 94
International Convention Relating to
  Intervention on the High Seas in
  Cases of Oil Pollution Casualties
  1969 and 1973 Protocol, 136–137
International Court of Justice. *See*
  World Court.
International criminal law,
  human rights, 193–194
  international crime,
    apartheid, 156
    definition of, 156
    genocide, 105, 156
    piracy, 104
    pollution of atmosphere and seas,
      98
    slavery, 156
    torture, 106

International criminal law—*cont.*
  International Law Commission,
    work on, 156
International dispute settlement. *See*
  also Arbitration and World Court.
  obligation on states, 237
International judicial decisions,
  subsidiary source of international law
    as, 22–24
International Labour Organisation, 28
International law,
  before municipal courts, 34–50
    U.K. practice, 34–40
      customary international law,
        34–37
      treaties, 37–40
    U.S. practice, 40–50
      customary international law,
        40–42
      treaties, 42–46
  characteristics of, 3
  codification of, 27–28
  conclusions on, 255–257
  definition, 1
  development of, 4
  distinct from conflict of laws, 1
  harmonisation with municipal law, 32
  international law as law, 2
  municipal law as defence for non-
    compliance, 33–34, 198
  nature of, 2
  progressive development of, 27
  relation to municipal law, 31–50
International Law Association, 28
International Law Commission,
  work of, 27–28
  work on,
    international criminal
      responsibility, 156
    law of the sea, 119
    possible source of international law
      as, 27–28
    state responsibility, 155, 162
    treaties, 198
International Maritime Organisation,
  138
International minimum standard. *See*
  Aliens, treatment of.
International organisations. *See also*
  International personality.
  employees of, diplomatic protection,
    117
  immunity from territorial state
    jurisdiction, 117

International personality, 52–80
  conclusion on, 68
  Holy See, of, 67–68
  individuals, of, 65, 67
  international organisations, 60–65
    determination of personality,
      60–61
    EURATOM, 63
    European Coal and Steel
      Community, 63
    European Communities, 63–65
    United Nations, 61–63
  international person,
    definition of, 52
  Liechtenstein, 56
  mandated territories, 57–60
  Monaco, 56
  non-recognition,
    effect of, 76–78
  protected state, 57
  San Marino, 56
  Sovereign Order of Malta, 68
  states, 52. *See also* States,
    characteristics of; and
    Statehood.
  Transkei, 56
  unrecognised states, of, 70
International Sea Bed Authority, 150,
  152–153
International straits,
  passage through, 129
International Telecommunications
  Convention and Optional Protocol,
  96
International Telecommunications
  Union (ITU), 96
International Tribunal for the Law of
  the Sea, 153
Interpretation of treaties. *See* Treaty
  interpretation.
Intervention in civil wars, 232
Iran,
  hostages incident, 113
  U.S. abortive rescue attempt,
    224
Iran/United States Claims Tribunal
  1981, 240
Islands. *See* Sea, law of the.
Israel, 86
  Eichmann, abduction of, 107
  Entebbe raid on, 224
  Libyan aircraft, shooting down of by,
    93
  strike of June 1967, 223

Japan,
  pioneer investor as, 151
Jay Treaty 1794, 238
Judicial decisions,
  subsidiary source of international law
    as,
    international decisions, 22–24
    municipal decisions, 24–25
Judicial settlement. *See* World Court.
Jurisdiction. *See* State jurisdiction.
Juristic writings,
  source of international law as, 25–26
Jus cogens,
  definition, 28–29
  effect of, 19, 28–29
  possible source of international law
    as, 28–29

Kellogg-Briand Pact (Pact of Paris),
  218
Kiel Canal, 18, 206
Korean crisis 1950, 228, 229

Latvia, 86
Law,
  international law as law, 2
League of Nations,
  Covenant of,
    use of force under, 218
  work on terrorism, 193
Lebanon,
  U.N.F.I.L. in, 231
Legal personality. *See* International
  personality.
Liechtenstein, 56, 57
Limited Test Ban Treaty 1963, 233
Lithuania, 86
Litvinoff Agreement, 45
Lousiana,
  purchase of, 87

Malta,
  Sovereign Order of,
    international personality of, 68
Mandated territories,
  international personality of,
    57–60
Modification,
  treaty of, 107
Monaco, 56
Monistic school of thought (Monism),
  32
Montevideo Convention on Rights and
  Duties of States 1933, 53, 54

Montreal Convention for the
    Suppression of Unlawful Acts
    against the Safety of Civil Aviation
    1971, 105
Moon,
    exploration and exploitation of, 95
    Treaty 1967, 1979, 95
Municipal court decisions,
    subsidiary source of international law
      as, 24–25
Municipal law,
    international law in, 33–34
    international law in relation to, 31–50
    recognition of governments,
      effect of in U.K., 73–76

Namibia 1981, 230
    initiation of Uniting for Peace
      Resolution, 230
    mandate over, 59
    personality, 57–60
Nationality,
    absence of, 170
    acquisition of,
      jus sanguinis, 169
      jus soli, 169
    genuine link,
      ships, 132–133
    jurisdiction based on, 103
Nationality of claims, 169–172
    companies, 171–172
    individuals, 169–171
    local remedies. *See* Remedies.
    U.K. practice, 172
Nationality principle, 103
Nationals,
    obligation to accept, 163
National treatment standard. *See*
    Aliens, treatment of.
New states,
    attitude to deep sea bed, 150
    attitude to exploration, 164–165
    independence of, 87–88
Non liquet,
    principle of, 19, 20
North Atlantic Treaty Organisation
    (NATO),
    collective self-defence, 225
Norway,
    Article 36 (2), self-judging
      declaration, 247–248
    baselines, use of, 12, 23, 121–123
    claim to Antarctica, 88
    claim to Eastern Greenland, 83

Norway—*cont.*
    Spitzbergen, 88
Nuclear tests,
    prohibition on,
      atmosphere in the, 233
      high seas on the, 132
      outer space in, 233
      under water, 233
    Test Ban, 132
Nuclear weapons,
    Limited Test Ban Treaty, 233
    non-proliferation of, 233–234
    outer space in, 233
    prohibition in Latin America, 234
    Reduction of Intermediate-Range
      Nuclear Forces (INF), 234
    Strategic Arms Limitation Talks, 234
    Strategic Arms Reduction Talks, 234
Nuremberg Military Tribunal,
    Charter of, 105
    judgment of, 66, 193

Objective approach to treaty
    interpretation, 204
Occupation,
    acquisition of territory by, 81–85
    critical date, 84–85
    effective, 82–85
    intention, 83
    prescription distinguished, 85
ONUC, 231
Opinio juris sive necessitatis. See
    Customary international law.
Optional clause. *See* World Court.
Organisation of American States (OAS)
    human rights, 186
    authorisation of quarantine for
      Cuba, 227
Outer space,
    Agreement Relating to the
      International Communications
      Satellite Organisation, 96
    airspace, boundary between, 94
    astronauts, assistance to, 95, 96
    Convention on Registration of
      Objects launched into, 1975, 96
    Convention Relating to the
      Distribution of Programme-
      Carrying Signals Transmitted by
      Satellite, 96
    exploration of, 94–96
    International Telecommunications
      Convention and Optional
      Protocol 1982, 96

Outer space—*cont.*
  International Telecommunications
    Union (ITU), 96
  Moon,
    exploitation of resources of, 95
    exploration of, 95
  Moon Treaty, 95
  nuclear weapons, prohibition of use
    in, 95
  rules on,
    as instant custom, 16
  space objects,
    jurisdiction over, 95
    liability for, 95, 96
    registration of, 95, 96
  "Star Wars", 95
  Treaty on, 94–95

Pact of Paris (Kellogg-Briand Pact), 218
Pacta tertiis nec nocent nec prosunt, 206
Pakistan,
  Iraqi Embassy raid on, 113
Paris Convention on the Regulation of
  Aerial Navigation 1919, 91
Passive personality principle, 106
Peacekeeping forces,
  constitutionality of, 231
  United Nations, 231
Peremptory norms. *See Jus cogens.*
Permanent Court of International
  Justice. *See* World Court.
Peru,
  continental shelf claims, 143
Philippines,
  archipelagic state, as, 125
Pioneer investors,
  deep sea bed, 151
Piracy,
  definition, 104
  international crime, 104
  jurisdiction over, 104
Poland,
  British recognition of Government in
    Exile,
  Provisional Government, effect of,
    75–76
Polar territories, 88–91
Pollution. *See also* Environment,
  international protection of.
  compensation for, 98
  high seas of, 136–138
    1982 Convention regime, 138
    noxious harmful substances,
      136–137

Pollution—*cont.*
  high seas of—*cont.*
    oil by, 136
      Torrey Canyon incident, 136
    international crime as, 156
    liability for, 98
    Stockholm Declaration,
      Principle 21, 97
      Principle 22, 98
Ponsonby rule, 38
Possible sources of international law,
  International Law Commission,
    27–28
Prescription,
  acquisition of territory by, 81
Protected state, 57
Protective (Security) principle, 103
Pueblo incident, 70

Question of Occupied Arab Territories,
  initiation of Uniting for Peace
    Resolution, 230

Recognition, 68–80
  constitutive school, 69
  declaratory school, 70
  definition of, 69
  duty to recognise, 70
  effect in municipal law (U.K.), 73–76
  governments of, 71–72
    British practice, 71–72
    de facto and *de jure*, 72–73
    United States practice, 71–72
  granting of,
    modes of according, 79
  non-recognition,
    international law, effect of, 76
    municipal law, effect of,
      U.K. practice, 76–78
      U.S. practice, 78
    territory acquired by conquest, 86
  retroactivity of, 74–76
  states of, 57, 71
  states and governments of, 68–69
Refugees,
  status, Convention on, 163
Remedies,
  local,
    definition, effective only,
      exhaustion of, 172–173
Reparation,
  forms of,
    apology, monetary compensation,
      restitution, 159–160

Reparation—*cont.*
  object of, 159
  rules governing, 159
Reprisals, 226
Reservations to treaties. *See* Treaties.
Resolutions, General Assembly. *See*
  General Assembly Resolutions.
Retorsions, 226
Revised 1928 General Act for the Pacific
  Settlement of International
  Disputes 1949, 245
Rights and Duties of States, 1949 Draft
  Declaration on, 86
Rivers,
  boundary, 87

SALT (Strategic Arms Limitation
  Talks) I and II, 234
  Agreement on Measures to Improve
    the Direct Communications Link
    (Hot-Line Upgrade Agreement)
    1971, 230
  Agreement on Measures to Reduce
    the Risk of Outbreak of Nuclear
    War (Accidents Agreement),
    234
  Treaty on the Limitation of Anti-
    Ballistic Missile Systems (ABM),
    234
San Marino, 56
Satellites,
  reconnaisance, 234–235
Sea, law of the, 119–154
  Bays,
    definition of, 123–124
      historic definition of, 124
      non-application of 1958 and
        1982 Conventions to, 124
      twenty-four mile rule,
        application of, 124
  Contiguous Zone, 130
  Continental margin,
    definition, 145
  Continental shelf, 143–149
    artificial installations, 147
    coastal state's rights over,
      145–147
    Commission of, 149
    definition, 143–145
    delimitation of,
      application of equitable
        principles, 148
      between states with opposite or
        adjacent coasts, 147–149

Sea, law of the—*cont.*
  Continental shelf—*cont.*
    developing states as net importers
      of resources from, 147
    equidistance principle, 148–149
    equitable sharing of, 147
    exploration and exploitation of, 145
    Truman Proclamation on, 143
  Convention (UNCLOS III) 1982, 119
    et seq.
  Deep Sea Bed, 149–153
    General Assembly Declaration on,
      150
    interim arrangements, 152
    International Sea Bed Authority,
      150, 152–153
    mineral resources of, 149
    municipal legislation on,
      U.K., U.S., 152
    parallel access, 150
    pioneer investor, 151
    preparatory investment protection,
      150
    resources of, 149–152
    U.K. attitude to, 150
    U.S. attitude to, 150
  Exclusive Economic Zone, 138–143
    coastal state rights in, 140–142
    definition of, 138
    delimitation of between states with
      opposite or adjacent coasts,
      142–143
    fisheries in, 141–142
    rights and duties of states other
      than coastal state, 141–143
  Fisheries Zone,
    independent/territorial sea, 140
    Iceland's fifty mile claim, 140
    twelve mile rule as customary
      international law, 140
  Geneva Conventions on, 119 *et seq.*
  High Seas,
    definition, 131
    fishing activities on, 135
    freedom of, 131
      exceptions to, 133–138
        piracy, 133–134
    jurisdiction on, 133
    pirate broadcasting, 135
    pollution of, 136–138
      International Maritime
        Organisation, 138
      liability for, 137
      regional arrangements for, 138

Sea, law of the—*cont.*
  High Seas—*cont.*
    prohibition on nuclear testing, 131,
      132
  Hot Pursuit, 135–136
  International Law Commission,
    work on, 119
  International Straits, 129–130
    innocent passage through, 129
    transit, right of, 129–130
  Islands,
    definition of, 124
  Territorial Sea,
    archipelagic states,
      definition of, 125–126
      territorial sea of, 125–126
    civil jurisdiction of coastal state,
      128
    coastal state's sovereignty over, 121
    criminal jurisdiction of coastal
      state, 128
    determination of between opposite
      or adjacent states, 125
    economic interests, consideration
      of, 122–123
    indented coastlines, states with,
      121–122
    innocent passage, definition of,
      126–127
      regulation by coastal state,
        127–128
    innocent passage through, 126–129
    islands capable of human
      habitation, 124
      definition of, 124
    low-tide elevations, use of, 122
    low water mark, 122
    measurement of, 121–123
    straight baselines, use of, 122–123
    warships in, 128–129
Sector principle,
  polar region, 88
Security Council,
  absence and abstention of Member,
    230
  decisions,
    involving use of armed force,
      228–229, 232
  economic sanctions, 228
  enforcement action,
    not involving armed force, 228
  membership of, 230
  recommendation to refer to World
    Court, 244

Security Council—*cont.*
  resolution on Korean crisis, 228
  veto, 230
  voting in, 230
    non procedural issues, 230
    procedural issues, 230
Self-defence. *See* Force, use of.
Self determination,
  territorial acquisition, 87, 88
Settlement of international disputes,
  raison d'être of, 237. *See also*
    Arbitration and World Court.
  under Law of the Sea Convention, 153
Shareholders,
  protection of, 172
Slavery,
  Conventions on, 175
  customary international law on, 175
Social Charter of the Council of Europe,
  185
Sources of international law, 7–29
  custom, international law as, 8–16.
    See also Customary international
    law.
  equity, 21–22
  formal and material distinguished, 8
  general principles of law as recognised
    by civilised nations, 19–21
  possible sources, 26–29
    jus cogens, 28–29
    regional organisations, 27
  subsidiary,
    judicial decisions, 22–25
    writers, 25–26
  treaties,
    bilateral/"bi-partite" and
      multilateral/"multi-partite",
    legislative effect of, 17
    relationship with customary
      international law, 17, 18, 19
South Africa,
  sanctions against, 228
South West Africa. *See* Namibia.
Southern Rhodesia,
  non-recognition of, 56
  Security Council resolution, 43, 228
Sovereign immunity, 108–110
  absolute, doctrine of, 108–109
  Commonwealth countries, practice
    of, 110
  foreign states, 108–110
  jus imperii, jus gestionis, 108–109
  modified, doctrine of, 109–110
  U.K. practice, 110

Sovereign immunity—*cont.*
　U.S. practice, 109
Soviet Union,
　Arctic claim to, 88–89
　outer space,
　　role in law of, 11, 12
　pioneer investor as, 151
　U.K. recognition of, 70
　　effect of, 74
Spain,
　British recognition of,
　Nationalist Government,
　Republican Government,
　　effect of, 73–74
State Immunity Act 1978 (U.K.), 110
State jurisdiction, 101–118
　coastal states rights in EEZ, 140–142
　concurrent, 102
　high seas, 133
　hijacking, 105
　hot pursuit, 135
　immunity from, 108–117. *See also*
　　Sovereign Immunity and
　　Diplomatic immunity and
　　Diplomatic privileges.
　consular immunities, 116–117
　international organisations, 117
　special missions, 117
　international straits,
　　coastal state's jurisdiction in, 129
　nationality principle, 103
　passive personality principle, 106
　piracy, 104
　propriety of exercise of, 101
　protective (security) principle, 103
　ships, over, 132–133
　space objects, 95–96
　territorial principle, 101–102
　　objective, 102
　　subjective, 102
　territorial sea,
　　civil, 128–129
　　criminal, 128
　universality principle, 104–105
State responsibility,
　Calvo Clause and, 168–169
　companies, 171–172. *See also*
　　Companies.
　defence pleas, recognised, 155
　direct injury, 155
　duty to protect, 158
　human rights for. *See* Human rights.
　imputability, 157
　indirect injury, 155

State responsibility—*cont.*
　individuals, acts of, 158
　insurrectionaries for, 158
　international crimes for, 104–106
　International Law Commission,
　　work of, 155–156, 193–194
　international organisations for, 158
　internationally protected persons,
　　163
　investment disputes, nationals of
　　other states, Convention on, 240
　liability nature of, 156, 157
　　customary international law, 157
　nationality of claims rule. *See*
　　Nationality of claims.
　nationals, for, 163
　officials, acts of, 158
　pollution, 97–99
　　high seas on, 136–138
　separation for breach of, 159–160
　shareholders, protection of, 172
　space objects, 95–96
　state, definition of for, 157
　theory of, 156–158
　ultra vires, acts of officials, 158
State succession,
　treaty obligations to, 214–215
Statehood. *See also* States and
　International personality,
　capacity to enter into international
　　relations, 55–60
　defined territory, 54–55
　government, 55
　permanent population, 54
　recognition. *See* Recognition.
　self-determination, 57–60
　state-like entities, 56–57
States,
　characteristics of, 53–60
　international persons, as, 52
Stockholm Declaration,
　Principle 21, 97
　Principle 22, 98
Straits,
　international, 129–130
Subjective approach to treaty
　interpretation, 204
Subsidiary sources of international law,
　judicial decisions, 22–25
　writers, 25–26
Suez, 206, 230
　Anglo-French invasion of, 224
　initiation of Uniting for Peace
　　Resolution, 230

"Suggestion",
  Department of State, 48

Taiwan,
  liability of unrecognised government,
    70
Tanker Owners' Voluntary Agreement
  Concerning Liability for Oil
  Pollution 1969, 137
Teleological approach to treaty
  interpretation, 204
Terra nullius, 81–82
Territorial jurisdiction. *See* State
  jurisdiction.
Territorial principle, 102–103
Territorial sea. *See* Sea, law of the.
Territorial sovereignty. *See also*
  Territory, limitations on, 96–99
  modes of acquiring, 81–88
Territory, 81–100. *See also* State
  jurisdiction; Territorial
  sovereignty.
  acquisition of, 81–88
    accretion and avulsion, 87
    cession, 87
    conquest, 85–86
    critical date, 84, 85
    discovery, 81–82
      inchoate title, 82
    independence, 87, 88
    occupation, 81–84
      effective, 82–84
    prescription, 85
  airspace. *See* Airspace.
  Antarctica, 88–91
  Arctic, 88
  sector principle, 88
  terra nullius, 81, 82
Terrorism, 193
Thalweg, 87
Torrey Canyon incident, 136
Torture,
  international crime as, 106
Transit,
  right of, 129–130
Transkei,
  international status in, 56
Travaux préparatoires, 205
Treaties, 196–216
  accession, 200
  adoption, 199
  amendment, 207
  breach of,
    material, 210–211

Treaties—*cont.*
  breach of—*cont.*
    state responsibility for, 155
  competence to make, 198
  compromissory clauses in, 245
  confirmation of, 199
  consent to, forms of, 199
  constitutive, 19
  definition of, 197
  effects for non-signatories, 19
  entry into force, 203
  "full powers", 198–199
  interpretation,
    aids to, 205
    "objective," "subjective" and
      "teleological" approaches,
      204
    Vienna Convention under, 204
  invalidity,
    consequences of, 213
  jus cogens, 19
    effect of on, 28–29
  law of, 196–215
  modification, 207
  municipal law,
    justification for non-performance,
      198
    presumption of interpretation,
      U.K., 39–40
      U.S., 43
  observance of, 203–204
  oral, 197
  pacta sunt servanda, 209
  registration of, 198
  relationship to municipal law,
    U.K., 37–40
    U.S., 42–48
  reservations to, 200–203
    definition of, 200
    legal effects of, 202–203
  source of international law as, 17–19.
    See also Sources.
  state succession to, 214–215
  suspension, consequences of, 213
  termination of, 209–214
    consequences of, 213–214
    diplomatic and consular relations,
      affect on, 212
    material breach, 210
    provision or consent by, 209
    rebus sic stantibus, 211–212
    supervening impossibility of
      performance, 211
  third states, effect on, 19, 206

Treaties—*cont.*
"traité-lois" and "traité contracts"
distinguished, 17
unilateral declarations, 197
validity of, 207–212
coercion, 208
corruption, 208
error, 208
fraud, 208
jus cogens, 28, 209
Treaty Banning Nuclear Weapons Tests
in Outer Space and Under Water,
99
Treaty for the Prohibition of Nuclear
Weapons in Latin America 1967
and Additional Protocols I and II,
234
Treaty interpretation, 204–206
context, 205
objective approach, 204
subjective approach, 204
supplementary means, 205
teleological approach, 204
travaux préparatoires, 205
use of two or more languages in, 206
Treaty on the Limitation of Anti-
Ballistic Missile Systems (ABM)
1972, 234
Treaty on the Limitation of Strategic
Offensive Arms 1979, 234
Treaty on the Non Proliferation of
Nuclear Weapons 1968, 233
Truman Proclamation on the
Continental Shelf, 16, 143
Trusteeship,
South West Africa,
I.C.J. opinions on, 59–60
system, 59
Two Freedoms Agreement, 92–93

UNCLOS III Third United Nations
Conference on the Law of the Sea,
119 *et seq.*
UNDOF United Nations
Disengagement Observation
Force, 231
UNEF United Nations Emergency
Force, 231
United Kingdom,
Antarctica, claim to, 88, 90, 91
deep sea bed,
legislation on, 152
Deep Sea Mining Temporary
Provisions Act, 152

United Kingdom—*cont.*
Diplomatic Privileges Act 1964, 116
EEC membership,
effect of, 40
Foreign Compensation Commission,
167
nationality of claims,
practice on, 170, 172
non-recognition,
effect of, in, 76–78
optional clause Article 36 (2),
acceptance of, 247
recognition of states and
governments. *See* Recognition.
recognition by, effect of in. *See*
Recognition.
relation of international law to law of,
34–40
customary international law, 34–37
treaties, 37–40
sovereign immunity, law of, 110
State Immunity Act 1978, 110
territorial sea (three mile), 121
United Nations,
domestic jurisdiction limitation, 232
environment programme, 138
force, use of and, 218 *et seq.*
Article 2 (4) and, 219–221
collective self-defence, 225–229
peacekeeping forces,
constitutionality of, 231
self-defence, 222–223
Uniting for Peace Resolution,
230–231
General Assembly. *See* General
Assembly.
human rights,
implementation machinery,
188–193
women, discrimination against, 193
immunity of, 117
personnel of, 117
international personality of, 61–63.
See also 19, 23.
measures of,
legal status of, 26, 27
Security Council. *See* Security
Council.
United Nations Commission on
International Trade Law, 28
United Nations Committee on the
Peaceful Uses of Outer Space,
94–96
United States. *See also* American law.

United States—*cont.*
Antarctica claim to, 88–90, 91
anti-trust laws, 103
Bricker Amendment, 45
Case Act, 46
Cuba, quarantine of, 227
Declaration accepting jurisdiction of
World Court 1946, 247
deep sea legislation,
Deep Sea Bed Hard Mineral
Resources Act 1980, 152
Diplomatic Relations Act 1978,
116
Dominican Republic, intervention in,
225
executive agreements, 45–46
Executive Congressional
Agreements, 46
Foreign Claims Settlement
Commission of the United
States, 167
Foreign Sovereign Immunities Act,
109
Grenada intervention in, 227
Iranian hostages, rescue attempt of,
224
outer space, role in development of
law on, 11, 12
recognition of states and
governments. *See* Recognition.
"Suggestion", 25
territorial sea (three mile), 121
United States/Iranian claims Tribunal,
167
Uniting for Peace Resolution, 230
Universality principle, 104
U.S.S.R. *See* Soviet Union.

Vatican City of, 67
Veto, Security Council in, 230
Vienna Convention on Consular
Relations 1963, 116
Vienna Convention on Diplomatic
Relations, 111
Vienna Convention on the Law of
Treaties. *See* Treaties, law of, 196 *et
seq.*

War,
civil, intervention in, 232
just, 217
War crimes, 104, 105
Warsaw Pact, collective self-defence,
225

Warships,
foreign, rights of, 128–129
seizure by on high seas, 134
Western Sahara, decolonisation of, 58
World Court,
access to, 243–244
non-U.N. members, 243
U.N. members, 243
advisory opinion, refusal to give, 253
composition of, 241
creation of, 241
decision of, 251
compliance with, 252
non-compliance with, 252
ex aequo et bono, 251
incidental jurisdiction,
preliminary objections, interim
measures and intervention,
249–250
judges of, 241–243
ad hoc, 242–243
dismissal of, 242
election of, 241–242
interest in proceedings, 242
judgment,
dissenting, 243
effect of, 251
interpretation and revision of,
251–252
separate opinion, 243
jurisdiction of, 243–251
advisory opinions, 252–253
compromissory clauses in treaties,
245
legal disputes, 245–246
optional, 245–249
prorogated, 244
special agreement, 244
justiciability issue of, 253
language of, 243
law applied, 250. *See also* 7–26.
optional jurisdiction,
acceptance of,
Canada by, 247
France by, 247
specific period for, 248
U.K. by, 247
U.S. by, 247
declarations under 246–249
reciprocity, need for, 246
reservations,
domestic jurisdiction, 247
ratione temporis, 246–247
temporal, 248

World Court—*cont.*
  optional jurisdiction—*cont.*
    termination of, 248
      Australia by, 248
    U.S. derogation from, 247, 248
  parties, non-appearance of, 252
  Permanent Court of International
    Justice, 240–241
  reference to by special agreement,
    245
  reference to by treaty compromissory
    clauses, 245

World Court—*cont.*
  role and future of, 253
  Security Council, recommendation to
    refer to, 244
  subject-matter, common ground
    between parties, 246
Writers,
  subsidiary source of international law
    as, 25–26

Zanzibar, exchange of, 87